MW00911316

# SOCIAL SECURITY MANUAL

## 1992 EDITION

Edited by:  William W. Thomas III, J.D., CLU
    Associate Editor, The National Underwriter Company
Reviewed by: Robert J. Myers
    Consultant on Social Security, National Association of
        Life Underwriters
    Chief Actuary, Social Security Administration, 1947-70
    Deputy Commissioner, Social Security Administration,
        1981-82
    Executive Director, National Commission on Social
        Security Reform, 1982-83

Published by

**THE NATIONAL UNDERWRITER COMPANY**
**Cincinnati, Ohio**

ISBN 0-87218-492-7

The National Underwriter Company publishes the following Social Security/Medicare publications:

Social Security Manual
All About Medicare
Social Security In A Nutshell
Social Security Slide-O-Scope
Social Security Planner
Medicare Slide-O-Scope
Social Security Earnings and Benefit Estimate Statement

# TABLE OF CONTENTS

# INDEX

# GENERAL INFORMATION

### A-1. What is the Social Security Act?

The Social Security Act has established numerous programs which provide for the material needs of individuals and families, protect aged and disabled persons against the expenses of illnesses that could otherwise exhaust their savings, and keep families together.

Congress passed the Social Security Act in 1935 and the retirement benefits program went into effect on January 1, 1937. The law has been amended many times since its original enactment.

### A-2. What programs are covered by the Social Security Act?

The following programs, grouped under two general heads, are covered by the Act:

Social Insurance

- Retirement, survivors and disability insurance (OASDI).
- Hospital and medical insurance for the aged, the disabled, and those with end-stage renal disease.
- Unemployment insurance.
- Black lung benefits.
- Supplemental security income (SSI).
- Totalization benefits.

Public Assistance and Welfare Services

- Medical assistance.
- Aid to needy families with children.
- Maternal and child-health services.
- Services for crippled children.
- Child welfare services.
- Energy assistance.
- Food stamps.

This manual deals only with the first two programs: OASDI and hospital and medical insurance for the aged and disabled. OASDI is administered by the Social Security Administration and provides what are commonly called "social security benefits." The second program, commonly called "Medicare," provides hospital and medical insurance for the aged and disabled and is administered by the Health Care Financing Administration.

The federal government operates the black lung benefit and the supplemental security income programs. The remaining programs, for the most part, are operated by the states with the federal government cooperating and contributing funds.

The original Social Security Act provided only retirement benefits for wage and salary earners. In 1939, benefits were added for family members after the worker's death or retirement. Most amendments have expanded the scope of the social security program—by extension of coverage to more groups of persons, by increasing benefits, by creating new benefits (such as disability), by liberalizing requirements for benefits, or by increasing the wage base for taxes and benefits.

**A-3. In general, what benefits are provided under the Retirement, Survivors, and Disability Program?**

- Monthly benefits for workers who are retired, or partially retired, and are at least 62 years old, and monthly benefits for their spouses and dependents.

- Monthly benefits for disabled workers and their dependents.

- Monthly benefits for the survivors of deceased workers.

- A lump-sum death benefit payment for certain insured workers.

For explanation of these benefits and eligibility requirements, see BENEFITS, SECTION E.

**A-4. In general, what benefits are provided under the Hospital Insurance Program for the aged and disabled?**

The program provides the following benefits for persons age 65 or older and persons receiving social security disability benefits for 24 months or more:

- The cost of inpatient hospital services for up to 90 days in each benefit period (for 1992, the patient pays a deductible amount of $652 for the first 60 days plus $163 a day for each day in excess of 60). There are also 60 non-renewable lifetime reserve days with coinsurance of $326 a day.

- The cost of posthospital skilled nursing facility care for up to 100 days in each benefit period (the patient pays $81.50 a day after the first 20 days).

- The cost of an unlimited number of home health service visits made under a plan of treatment established by a physician, except that there is 20% cost-sharing payable by the patient for durable medical equipment (other than the purchase of certain used items).
- Hospice care for terminally ill patients.

For detailed explanation of these benefits, see SECTION I.

### A-5. In general, what benefits are provided under the Supplementary Medical Insurance Program?

The program is offered to almost all persons age 65 and over on a voluntary basis. In addition, the program is offered to all disabled social security and railroad retirement beneficiaries who have received disability benefits for at least 24 months. There is an annual deductible of $100, paid by the patient. Then the plan pays 80% of the approved charges above the deductible for the following services:

- Physicians' and surgeons' services, whether furnished in a hospital, clinic, office, home, or elsewhere.
- Home health care visits, if not covered under hospital insurance (but with no cost-sharing except for durable medical equipment, other than the purchase of certain used items).
- Diagnostic x-ray, diagnostic laboratory tests, and other diagnostic tests (no cost-sharing).
- Outpatient physical therapy and speech pathology.
- X-ray, radium, and radioactive isotope therapy.
- Surgical dressings, rental of durable medical equipment, etc.
- Ambulance transportation.
- The cost of blood clotting factors and supplies necessary for the self-administration of the clotting factor.
- Services and supplies relating to a physician's services and hospital services rendered to outpatients; this includes drugs and biologicals which cannot be self-administered.
- Dentists' bills for jaw or facial bone surgery, whether required because of accident or disease. Also covered are hospital stays warranted by the severity of a noncovered dental procedure, and services provided by dentists which would be covered under current law when provided by a physician. Bills for ordinary dental care are not covered.

- Comprehensive outpatient rehabilitation facility services performed by a doctor or other qualified professionals in a qualified facility. Therapy and supplies are covered.

- Antigens prepared by one doctor and sent to another for administration to the patient.

- The cost of pneumococcal vaccine (no cost-sharing).

- The cost of hepatitis B vaccine for high and intermediate risk individuals when it is administered in a hospital or renal dialysis facility.

- Certified nurse-midwife services.

- Liver transplants.

- Mammography screening.

- Eyeglasses after cataract surgery.

- Self-injection of a drug to treat osteoporosis.

Maximum payment for outside-the-hospital treatment of mental, psychoneurotic, and personality disorders is limited to $1,100 a year.

For detailed explanation of these benefits, see SECTION I.


### A-6. How are the health insurance programs and the OASDI program financed?

Retirement, survivors, and disability benefits and basic hospital insurance are financed by taxes collected from employers, employees, and self-employed persons. (See SOCIAL SECURITY TAXES, SECTION J). Hospital benefits for persons not on the social security or railroad retirement rolls are paid from premiums and general revenues. (The hospital benefits premium rate is intended to meet all of the cost for persons who are covered only due to premium payment.) Effective January 1, 1983, federal employees not fully covered by Social Security began contributing to the hospital insurance program only. Effective April 1, 1986, all newly hired state and local government employees not fully covered by Social Security began contributing to the hospital insurance program only.

To finance the voluntary supplementary medical insurance program, each person who enrolls pays $31.80 a month in premiums and the government pays *at least* a matching premium per enrollee from the general funds of the Treasury. Actually, in 1992, about 75% of the cost is being paid from general funds. (See MEDICARE, SECTION I.)

## A-7. What federal agency administers the OASDI program?

The Social Security Administration. The central office is located in Baltimore, Maryland, and district offices are located in all the principal cities of the 50 states, Puerto Rico, and Virgin Islands. Regular visits to outlying areas, called contact stations, are made by the district staff.

## A-8. What federal agency administers Medicare programs for the aged and disabled?

The Health Care Financing Administration, whose central office is in Baltimore, Maryland, directs Medicare and Medicaid programs. The Social Security Administration processes Medicare applications and claims, but it does not set Medicare policy. The Health Care Financing Administration sets the standards which hospitals, skilled nursing facilities, home health agencies, and hospices must meet in order to be certified as qualified providers of services.

## A-9. How and where are Social Security records maintained?

Every individual who comes under social security (see COVERAGE, SECTION B) needs a social security number. The Office of Central Records Operations of the Social Security Administration in Baltimore, Maryland, maintains an earnings record for each individual who has a social security number.

The Social Security Administration receives reports of earnings of employees from employers and self-employed persons from the Internal Revenue Service. These amounts are then recorded in each person's earnings record.

## A-10. How does a person obtain a Social Security number?

By filling out Form SS-5 (Application for a Social Security Number Card) and submitting evidence of age, identity, and citizenship or alien status.

Parents applying for a Social Security number for their children under age 7 will need to furnish only a birth record if no other record of age or identity has been established for the child.

Applicants 18 and older must apply in person at a Social Security office.

A Social Security number is needed not only for Social Security purposes, but also for income tax purposes. The Internal Revenue Service uses this number as a taxpayer identification number for processing tax returns and controlling the interest and dividend reports of banks and other financial institutions.

All income tax returns claiming dependents (whether taxpayer's children or others) two years old or over filed before 1992 must show the dependent's Social Security number. Starting with tax returns filed in 1992, all income tax returns claiming dependents one year old or older must show the dependent's Social Security number.

Beginning after May 9, 1989, a person must have a Social Security number in order to receive Social Security benefits. Those lacking a Social Security number are required to apply for one. Beneficiaries on the rolls prior to May 10, 1989 are not required to have a Social Security number.

If a person loses his Social Security number card, he can apply for a duplicate card by filling out another Form SS-5 and showing a driver's license, voter registration card, school identification card, or other proof of identity. If the foreign born, he must also provide evidence of U.S. citizenship or current alien status. The Social Security office will check the new application against information in the applicant's record before issuing a replacement card. The new card will have the same numbers as the old.

If a person wishes to correct or update the identifying information that was given on the original application for a number, a new Form SSA-5 (Request for Change in Social Security Records) must be submitted. A change in name (for example, upon marriage) should always be reported.

Foreign-born applicants of any age must submit evidence of their United States citizenship or their alien status to show they are lawfully admitted to the United States.

Form SS-5 can be obtained from any Social Security district office.

### A-11. What is the penalty for illegal use of a social security number?

It is a misdemeanor to willfully, knowingly, and deceitfully use a social security number for any purpose.

It is unlawful to: (1) alter, (2) buy or sell, (3) counterfeit, or (4) possess a regular or counterfeit social security card with intent to sell or alter it. The maximum fine for conviction of such acts is $5,000 and the maximum prison term is five years.

Social security cards issued since October 31, 1983 are counterfeit-resistant and tamper-resistant.

### A-12. How can a person check on his Social Security earnings record and receive an estimate of future Social Security benefits?

By filling out Form SSA-7004-PC (Request for Earnings and Benefit Estimate Statement). The form can be picked up at any district office.

(Larger quantities of the Request for Earnings and Benefit Estimate Statement can be ordered from The National Underwriter Company, 420 E. Fourth Street, Cincinnati, Ohio 45202.) The Social Security Administration will mail the person a statement of total wages and self-employment income credited to his record and an estimate of current social security disability and survivor benefits and future social security retirement benefits. If a portion of earnings is not credited, the person should contact the district office and ask how to go about correcting the records. There are specific time limits for correcting an earnings record.

The Social Security Administration must provide individuals, age 25 or older, who have a social security number and have wages or net self-employment income, with a social security account statement upon the request of the individual. These statements must show (1) the individual's earnings, (2) an estimate of the individual's contributions to the social security program (including a separate estimate for Hospital Insurance), and (3) an estimate of the individual's future benefits at retirement (including spouse and other family member benefits) and a description of Medicare benefits. Starting in 1995, these statements must be automatically provided to all such individuals who attain age 60 (but are not yet receiving benefits) during that year and for whom the Social Security Administration can determine a current address. Each statement must include a notice that it is updated annually and is available upon request. Starting no later than 1999, these statements must be automatically provided on an annual basis to those under age 60 as well. (Benefit estimates will not be required for persons under age 50, although a general description of benefits will be required.)

**A-13. What events must a beneficiary report to the Social Security Administration?**

The following events, which affect the payment of benefits, must be reported immediately:

- A beneficiary (other than a disabled individual) is working and has, or expects to have, earnings in excess of the amount permitted by the annual earnings test explained in SECTION H.
- The marriage of a person who is entitled to child's, widow(er)'s, mother's, father's, parent's or divorced spouse's benefits.
- A beneficiary under age 62 entitled to spouse's, mother's or father's benefits is no longer caring for a disabled or under-age-16 child.

- A person entitled to benefits because of disability has returned to work or the condition has improved so that he or she is able to work.
- The death of a beneficiary.
- A child beneficiary who is age 18 and not disabled is no longer attending elementary or secondary school full time.
- A beneficiary works outside the U.S. for more than 45 hours in a calendar month.
- A person under age 65 who is entitled because of disability becomes entitled to workers' compensation benefits or there is a change in the public disability payment rate.
- Imprisonment following conviction of a felony.

The event should be reported to the local district office which will forward the report to the program service center. The report must show the beneficiary's claim number (social security number plus the claim symbol on the award certificate). The program service center will stop benefit payments (or start them again) as is necessitated by information coming to its attention, and will notify the beneficiary of the action.

### A-14. Which government agency issues a beneficiary's Social Security check?

Social security benefit checks are issued and mailed by the U.S. Treasury Department—not by social security program service centers. However, questions about a check should be directed to a social security district office.

### A-15. When does a Social Security beneficiary receive his monthly benefit check?

Monthly checks are usually mailed for receipt on the third day of the month following the month for which the payment is made. For example, a check for January will ordinarily be received on February 3rd. Checks usually arrive about the same day each month.

If the third day of the month falls on a weekend or legal holiday, the monthly check will be mailed earlier. Any overpayment that occurs as a direct result of the earlier delivery of checks will be waived and will not be subject to recovery. Such checks will be deemed to have been received in the succeeding calendar month.

A change of address should be reported promptly to the district social security office. Notice can be given by telephone or in writing. The social security account number and old address should be shown.

**A-16. To whom is a benefit check made payable?**

Payment is made by check to the beneficiary, by direct deposit to a financial organization, or to a representative payee if the beneficiary is incapable of managing his or her own funds.

A minor child (a child under 18 years of age) is ordinarily considered incapable of managing his own benefit payments and a representative payee (usually a parent, close relative or legal guardian) will be selected to receive payments on the child's behalf.

However, payment will be made directly to a child over 18, or to a child under 18 if there is no indication that he is immature or unstable and it appears to be in the minor's best interest to make direct payment.

**A-17. If a husband and wife are both receiving monthly benefits, do they receive one or two monthly checks?**

If they are entitled to benefits on the same social security account and are living at the same address, payments are usually combined into one check made out to them jointly. This would be the case, for example, where the husband is receiving a retirement benefit and his wife a spouse's benefit based on his account. If it is a combined check, both persons must endorse it. However, individual checks will be sent to a husband and wife if either prefers to have a separate check. If each is receiving benefits based on his own earnings record, separate checks will be issued.

**A-18. If several children are entitled to benefits, does each child receive a separate check?**

No. Benefit payments to children in one family unit are usually combined in one check. Where the children customarily reside in different households, separate checks will be issued to each family group.

**A-19. Can a power of attorney be granted for the purpose of collecting and depositing checks?**

Yes. If payments are to be deposited in an account at a United States financial organization, completion of Standard Form 1199 (Authorization for deposit of Social Security Payments) is required. This form can be obtained at the financial organization to which payments are to be directed. If payments are to be directed to a foreign financial organization, Standard Form 233 or Treasury Form 6711 (Power of Attorney by Individual to a Bank for the collection of checks drawn on the Treasury of the United States) must be completed.

## A-20. Can Social Security benefits be assigned?

No. The provision in the Social Security Act (section 207) prohibiting assignment of benefits or subjecting them to the operations of bankruptcy laws may not be superseded by another law unless the other law does so by express reference to section 207. Some bankruptcy courts have considered social security benefits listed by the debtor to be income for purposes of bankruptcy proceedings and have ordered the Social Security Administration to send all or part of a debtor's benefit check to the trustee in bankruptcy. Such orders are not appropriate.

## A-21. Can Social Security benefits be attached for the beneficary's debts?

Benefits are not subject to levy, garnishment, or attachment, except in very restricted circumstances, such as by court order for the collection of child support or alimony.

## A-22. Are Social Security benefits subject to federal taxes?

Up to one-half of the social security benefits received by taxpayers whose incomes exceed certain base amounts is subject to income taxation. The base amounts are $25,000 for a single taxpayer, $32,000 for married taxpayers filing jointly and zero for married taxpayers filing separately.

After the end of the year, Form 1099 (Social Security Benefit Statement) is sent to each beneficiary showing the amount of benefits received. A worksheet (IRS Notice 703) is enclosed for figuring whether any portion of the social security benefits received is subject to income tax.

For a detailed explanation of taxation of benefits, see SECTION G.

## A-23. What penalties are imposed for criminal fraud in connection with obtaining Social Security benefits?

The penalty for conviction of violating one of the penal provisions of the Social Security Act may be a fine, imprisonment, or both. Depending upon the provision of the law that is violated, the fines range from not more than $500 to not more than $10,000, and the imprisonment from one year to not more than 15 years.

There is also a negligence penalty for any failure to make a reasonable attempt to comply with the provisions of the Internal Revenue Code as well as any careless, reckless or intentional disregard of rules and regulations.

# COVERAGE (OASDI)

## B-1. What persons are covered by Social Security?

Generally speaking, most employees in private industry, most self-employed persons, and members of the U.S. Armed Forces are covered by Social Security. (See B-3 to B-27)

Some groups of persons are excluded from social security coverage. The main groups excluded are federal employees hired before 1984, and railroad employees, who come under the Railroad Retirement System. (See B-28 and B-29)

Some persons are subject to special coverage provisions. See: Family Employment (B-30); Employees of State and Local Governments (B-31); Ministers, Members of Religious Orders and Christian Science Practitioners (B-32); Employees of Non-Profit Organizations (B-33); Hospital Interns (B-34); Student Nurses (B-35); Domestics and Household Workers (B-36); Non-business Employment (B-37); Agricultural Laborers (B-38); Students Working for a College or College Club (B-39); Distributors and Vendors of Newspapers and Magazines (B-40, B-41); Americans Employed Outside the U.S. (B-42); Farmers (B-43); Members of Certain Religious Sects (B-44).

Actually, it is not the person, but the employment or self-employment that is covered or excluded from coverage (See WAGES AND SELF-EMPLOYMENT INCOME, SECTION C.)

## B-2. Is participation in the Social Security system compulsory?

Yes, participation is almost always compulsory unless the type of employment or self-employment is specifically excluded from coverage. This means that a person in covered employment or covered self-employment must pay social security taxes, and is entitled to benefits if he meets the insured status requirements.

However, ministers, members of religious orders and Christian Science practitioners may claim exemption on the basis of conscientious or religious objections (see B-32).

## B-3. Are employees and self-employed persons treated differently under the Social Security program?

Yes. Although benefits and insured status requirements are the same for employees and self-employed individuals, differences in the tax

11

rate, the effect of the retirement test (amount that can be earned without loss of benefits), and the computation of covered earnings make it necessary to determine whether a person is an employee or a self-employed person.

## EMPLOYEES

### B-4. Who are employees under the Social Security Act?

The Social Security Act defines three classes of workers as employees: (1) workers who are employees under the "common-law" test; (B-5); (2) officers of corporations (B-6 to B-9); and (3) persons who work in four specific occupations (B-10).

### B-5. Who are employees under the common-law test?

Under the common-law test, a worker is an employee if the person for whom he works has the right to direct and control his work not only as to what shall be done, but also as to how it shall be done. The employer need not actually exercise control; it is sufficient that he has the right to do so. In the next paragraph some factors are set forth that indicate control over details of work. These factors are to be weighed against those which point to an independent contractor status. (Independent contractors are covered as self-employed persons—unless they are included in the four occupational groups discussed in B-10 and B-11). However, no single fact, or small group of facts, is conclusive evidence of the presence or absence of control.

The following factors tend to indicate that the person is an employee: he is required to comply with instructions about when, where, and how to work; he is required to take training from a supervisor or experienced employee; his services are integrated in the general business operations; he is required to render the services personally; he is subject to discharge by the employer; the relationship between him and the person for whom he performs services is a continuing relationship; he has fixed working hours; he must devote full time to the employer's business; he must work on the employer's premises; he must perform services in a certain order set by the employer; he is required to submit regular oral or written reports to the employer; he is paid by hour, week, or month; the employer pays his business and traveling expenses; the employer furnishes tools and materials and other facilities for the work; he can end his relationship with the employer at any time without incurring liability. The guarantee of a minimum salary or the granting of a drawing account with no requirements for repayment of the excess over earnings tends to indicate the existence of an employer-employee relationship.

The following factors, on the other hand, tend to indicate that the person is an independent contractor: he is paid on a commission or job basis; he must take care of his own business and incidental expenses; he must make a significant investment in facilities used by him in performing services for another; he is in a position to realize a profit or suffer a loss as a result of his services; he has his own office (independent of the employer's offices); he works for several persons or firms at the same time; he makes his services available to the general public; he cannot be discharged as long as he fulfills his contract obligations; he cannot end his relationship with the employer at will but is legally obligated to make good for failure to complete the job.

### B-6. Is an officer of a corporation an employee for Social Security purposes?

Yes, he is considered to be an employee, even though he does not meet the definition of an employee under the common-law test (see B-5) because no one actually controls his work. He is an employee of the corporation.

A Director of a corporation is not an employee with respect to the services he performs as a director. He is self-employed with respect to these services. However, any nondirectional services which the director may perform under the control of the board of directors would be performed as an employee of the corporation. For self-employment Social Security taxes and benefit purposes, the director fees are counted in the year when paid, except that, for the retirement earnings test, they are considered on a when-earned basis.

### B-7. Is an officer of a Subchapter S corporation an employee?

Yes. Under Subchapter S of the Internal Revenue Code (IRC Secs. 1361-1379), certain small business corporations can elect not to be taxed as corporations. Corporations that make the election are called "Subchapter S corporations," or "Pseudo corporations," or "Electing corporations." Despite the election, however, officers of the Subchapter S corporation are still employees. Their salaries are considered "wages" and they are treated generally as employees for social security purposes. (But for treatment of so-called "dividends" from Subchapter S corporations, see SECTION C.)

### B-8. If an unincorporated association is taxable as a corporation, are the officers of the association treated as employees?

Yes. Under the federal income tax laws, certain unincorporated associations are taxable as corporations. Generally, an association is taxable as a corporation if it has associates engaged in business for profit, and has a majority of the following four corporate characteristics: (1) continuity of life; (2) centralization of management; (3) limited liability; and (4) free transferability of interests. If an association is taxable as a corporation, members who perform duties similar to those of a corporate officer are treated as employees. (With respect to professional corporations and associations, see B-9).

**B-9. Are the stockholders of a professional corporation employees of the corporation?**

Yes, if they perform services as employees for the corporation. Professional corporations and professional associations organized under state law are generally treated as corporations for federal tax purposes. TIR-1019; Rev. Rul. 70-101, 1970-1 C.B. 278.

**B-10. Persons in what four occupations are considered employees regardless of whether they meet the common-law test for classification as employees?**

The following persons are usually considered employees for social security purposes even though they do not qualify as employees under the common-law test, and may report their income (for income tax purposes) as independent contractors.

1. Full-time life insurance agents.

2. Agent-drivers and commission drivers who distribute food or beverages (except milk), or handle laundry or dry cleaning.

3. Full-time traveling or city salespersons soliciting orders for future delivery on behalf of another person or firm as their principal activity.

4. Homeworkers who work on material supplied by their "employer" to his specifications, who are paid at least $100 in cash wages in a calendar year, and who return the finished product to the employer or to someone whom the employer designates.

A person in one of the above occupational groups is considered an employee under social security if: (a) the contract of service contemplates that he will personally perform substantially all of the work; (b) he has no substantial investment in facilities (other than transportation facilities) used in performing the work; and (c) there is a continuing work relationship with the person for whom the services are performed.

For additional conditions with respect to classifying a life insurance agent as an employee, see B-11.

**B-11. Under what conditions is a life insurance agent classified as an employee?**

Even if he does not qualify as an employee under the common-law test (B-5), and even if he files his income tax return as an independent contractor, the life insurance agent will be considered an employee for social security purposes if he is a "full-time life insurance agent." To be a "full-time life insurance agent," he must: (1) solicit life insurance and/or annuity contracts as his *entire* or *principal* business activity; and (2) work primarily for one life insurance company. Generally the contract of employment reflects the intention of the agent and the company, or general agent, in regard to full-time activity. (The agent may be an employee of the company or of its general agent.)

Selling life insurance may be the agent's *entire* business activity even though he does not devote a normal workweek to it. In other words, an individual may work only a few hours a day, or a few days a week, and still qualify as a full-time life insurance agent if that is his only occupation. A *principal business activity* is one which takes the major part of the agent's working time and attention.

The agent's efforts must be devoted primarily to the sale of life insurance and/or annuity contracts. Occasional or incidental sales of other types of insurance for the employer or the occasional placing of surplus-line insurance will not affect this requirement. However, an agent who is primarily engaged in selling applications for insurance contracts other than life insurance and annuity contracts (for example, health, fire, automobile, etc.) is not a full-time life insurance agent.

Regardless of whether selling life insurance is his entire or principal activity, the life insurance agent will not be considered an employee unless, under his contract of employment, he is to perform substantially all the services personally. Nor will he be considered an employee if he has a substantial investment in the facilities he uses in connection with his work (other than transportation facilities).

A life insurance agent who does not qualify as an employee under the common-law test, and who is not a "full-time life insurance agent," is covered under social security as a self-employed person. For example, a general agent or broker is ordinarily treated as a self-employed individual since he is not a "full-time life insurance agent" who sells contracts primarily for one life insurance company.

**B-12. Is a manufacturer's representative an employee?**

No, a manufacturer's representative who holds himself out as an independent businessman and serves the public through his connection with a number of firms is not an employee. Likewise, a multiple-line salesperson is generally not an employee because he usually solicits orders for more than one principal. (See B-10.) However, a salesperson who solicits orders primarily for one principal can be an employee of that principal even though he carries on incidental sideline activities on behalf of other persons or firms.

### B-13. Is a farm crew worker an employee?

A farm crew worker is considered an employee of the *crew leader* if the crew leader: (1) arranges with the farm operator to furnish workers; (2) pays the workers either on his or her own behalf or on behalf of the farm operator; and (3) is not designated as the farm operator's employee in a written agreement with the farm operator.

The crew leader in this case is considered self-employed and is responsible for the payment of employment taxes and for reporting the workers for social security purposes.

### B-14. When did employees first come under Social Security?

The social security law became effective January 1, 1937. The year 1937 was the first year of coverage for employees. (Self-employed persons were first covered in 1951—see B-16).

## SELF-EMPLOYED PERSONS

### B-15. What self-employed persons are covered by Social Security?

Almost all self-employed persons are covered. In general, this includes everyone engaged in a trade, business or profession as a sole proprietor, partner, or independent contractor. Public officials, except those compensated solely on a fee basis and not covered under a state coverage agreement, are still excluded—see B-31.

### B-16. When did the various groups of self-employed persons come under Social Security?

- Most persons self-employed in a trade or business:

First year of coverage: calendar year 1951; or, for fiscal-year taxpayers, taxable years beginning after 1950.

- Architects; professional engineers; accountants (including certified, registered, or licensed and full-time public accountants); funeral directors; farmers; and (on an elective basis) ministers, members of religious orders and Christian Science practitioners:

First year of coverage: calendar year 1955; or, for fiscal-year tax-payers, taxable years ending after 1954.

- Lawyers; dentists; osteopaths; veterinarians; chiropractors; naturopaths; optometrists; and farm landlords who materially participate in the farming activities:

First year of coverage: calendar year 1956; or, for fiscal- year tax-payers, taxable years ending after 1955.

- Persons self-employed in a trade or business in Guam or American Samoa:

First year of coverage: calendar year 1961; or, for fiscal-year tax-payers, taxable years beginning after 1960.

- Physicians and Surgeons:

First year of coverage: calendar year 1965; or, for fiscal-year tax-payers, taxable years ending after 1965.

- Ministers, Christian Science practitioners, and members of religious orders:

First year of coverage: calendar year 1968; or, for fiscal year tax-payers, taxable years ending after 1967. Can opt out on grounds of religious principles or conscience.

### B-17. When did self-employed doctors of medicine come under Social Security?

The Social Security Amendments Act of 1965 extended coverage to self-employed doctors. Coverage is compulsory for every doctor regardless of whether he practices alone or as a member of a partnership.

### B-18. Is it possible to be covered by Social Security without performing personal services in a trade, business, or profession?

Yes. Income received by an owner (or part-owner) of a trade or business will count as self-employment income even though the owner performs no personal services in the trade or business. For example, absentee owners or silent partners whose businesses are carried on by employees are covered as self-employed persons.

For taxable years beginning after 1977, limited partners are excluded from social security coverage. Previously, limited partners were covered on the same basis as other partners.

### B-19. Are partners generally covered as self-employed persons?

Yes, business partners are self-employed. A partnership is generally said to be created when two or more persons join together for the purpose of carrying on a trade or business. Each partner contributes in one or more ways with money, property, labor, or skill and shares in the profits and risks of loss in accordance with the partnership agreement or understanding.

In determining whether a partnership exists, it is necessary to determine whether the parties intended to join together to carry on a trade or business and share in the profits and losses. Intention of the parties is determined not merely from their statements, but to a large degree, from their conduct in carrying on the business, not only in regard to each other, but also in regard to third parties. Further light is cast on the true intent of the parties by such matters as the abilities and contributions of each and the control which each has over the operation of the business.

A partnership is the same for social security purposes as for income tax purposes except for the exclusion from social security coverage of a limited partner in a limited partnership. (See B-18). Besides the ordinary partnership, the term "partnership" for tax purposes includes a syndicate, group, pool, joint venture, or any other unincorporated organization which carries on a business. The term does not include corporations, trusts, estates, or associations taxable as corporations.

Two or more persons, including husbands and wives, may be self-employed as partners for income tax and social security purposes, even if they do not operate under a formal partnership agreement or even if they are not considered partners under state law because they have not complied with local statutory requirements.

For tax purposes and for social security purposes, a partnership and a joint venture are essentially the same. The main distinction is that a partnership involves a continuing enterprise while a joint venture is usually for the accomplishment of a single project or transaction.

### B-20. Are real estate agents and direct sellers covered as self-employed persons?

Yes. In 1982, Congress specifically excepted qualified real estate agents and direct sellers, such as door-to-door salespeople, from the definition of an employee for social security tax purposes. The IRS has held that since these persons do not have taxes withheld as employees, they must be considered self-employed and are liable for tax on their self-employment income. Rev. Rul. 85-63, 1985-1 CB 292. (See J-6 and C-15.)

A licensed real estate agent is not an employee if he receives substantially all of his remuneration based on sales rather than hours worked and he has a written contract stating he is not an employee with the person from whom he performs his services. A direct seller must receive his remuneration from sales and have a written contract specifying he is not an employee. A direct seller is someone who sells consumer products, on a buy-sell or other basis proscribed by IRS regulations, in a home or place other than a permanent retail establishment.

**B-21. If members of the same family conduct a business enterprise as partners, is each member covered by Social Security as a self-employed person?**

Yes, if each family member is a true partner. For instance, a husband and wife or parents and children may conduct a business enterprise as a partnership. In such case, each partner is covered under social security as a self-employed person. In determining whether the legal relationship of partners exists, the same rules apply as for income tax purposes.

A family member may be a partner even though he performs no services in the business, provided he actually owns a capital interest in the partnership. In this respect, a transfer of a capital interest in a family partnership to a member of the same family generally makes him a partner if: (1) the partnership is one in which capital is a material income-producing factor; (2) there has been a bona fide gift or purchase of the capital interest; (3) the transferee actually owns the interest and is vested with dominion and control over it; and (4) a valid partnership was in existence before the transfer, or was created at the time of the transfer. Thus, even a minor child may be a partner, and his share of partnership income treated as self-employment income for tax and benefit purposes.

In deciding whether members of a family enterprise are partners in a business, the question is usually whether the parties entered into the arrangement with the intent to conduct a business as a partnership and in fact actually did so.

**B-22. Is self-employment income considered as belonging one-half to the husband and one-half to the wife in a community property state?**

No, community property laws are disregarded. If the business is a sole proprietorship, and is operated by the husband, all the income is considered his for social security purposes, and he is the only one covered (see also B-30). However, if the wife can show that she actually manages and controls the business, all the income is considered hers.

Likewise, a husband's distributive share of partnership income is treated as entirely his. But if a husband and wife carry on a business as partners, each partner's distributive share will be treated as his or her earnings from self-employment, and each will be covered.

Note, however, that the community property provision of the Social Security Act described above has been held unconstitutional on the ground that it discriminates on the basis of sex in violation of the Fifth Amendment of the constitution. *Carrasco v. Secretary of Health, Education & Welfare*, 628 F2d 624 (1980); *Hester v. Harris*, 631 F2d 53 (1980); *Becker v. Harris*, 493 F.Supp. 991 (1980). The courts found that, as a result of this provision, women responsible for a large part of the business's income were often credited with no quarters of coverage. (See D-4.) These women were either ineligible for retirement or disability benefits or entitled to a lower benefit because of the rule.

Because of the 1980 court decisions, the Internal Revenue Service determined that the rule in community property states should be the same as in noncommunity property states. That is, in the absence of a partnership, only the spouse carrying on the trade or business will be subject to self-employment tax. Rev. Rul. 82-39, 1982-1 CB 119.

### B-23. Are nonprofessional fiduciaries self-employed persons?

Generally, nonprofessional fiduciaries serve as executors or administrators only in isolated instances, and then as personal representatives for the estates of deceased friends or relatives. These individuals are not engaged in a trade or business (and their income as fiduciaries is therefore not covered by social security) unless all of the following conditions are met: (1) there is a trade or business among the assets of the estate; and (2) the executor actively participates in the operation of this trade or business; and (3) the fees of the executor are related to the operation of the trade or business.

### B-24. Is the beneficiary of a trust, the beneficiary of an estate, or the ward of a guardianship, a self-employed person?

No.

### B-25. Are fishing crews covered as self-employed persons?

Yes, services performed by a person on a boat engaged in catching fish or other forms of aquatic life constitute a trade or business if the following conditions are met:

- An arrangement exists between the person and the owner or operator of the boat whereby the person does not receive any remuneration other than a share of the catch or a share of the proceeds of the sale of the catch, and

- The amount of the share depends on the amount of the catch, and

- The operating crew of the boat is normally made up of fewer than 10 persons.

### B-26. Are writers who receive royalties engaged in a trade or business and consequently covered as self-employed persons?

Each case must be decided on the facts. A one-time venture of a short duration usually is not a trade or business, but a repetition of such ventures would constitute a trade or business. Thus, if an individual writes only one book as a sideline and never revises it, the writing activities would probably not constitute a trade or business. However, if the person prepares new editions from time to time or writes several books, the writing and editing activities would be a trade or business.

A person may engage in other related activities which, when considered together with the writing activities, may be a trade or business. For example, a college professor who writes a book on business administration and gives lectures and advice to business groups on the same subject probably would be considered in a trade or business as a self-employed person.

## MEMBERS OF THE U.S. ARMED FORCES

### B-27. Are members of the U.S. Armed Forces covered by Social Security?

Yes. Monthly retirement, disability, and survivors benefits under Social Security are payable to a veteran and dependents if he has earned enough work credits under the program. In addition, the veteran may qualify at age 65 for Medicare's hospital insurance. (A veteran can qualify for medical insurance under Medicare without work credits by applying and paying premiums.)

Active duty (or active or inactive duty for training) in the United States uniformed services has counted toward Social Security since January 1957, when contributions were first withheld from a serviceman's basic pay. Since 1957, members of the uniformed services have received non-contributory wage credits for service of up to $300 per quarter during which they received active duty pay. Starting with 1978, the credit is $100 for each $300 of covered annual military wages, up to a maximum of $1,200 per year in free credits for $3,600 or more in covered military wages. This credit is in addition to credit for basic pay and is given in consideration of allowances received, such as rations and quarters. These extra credits can result in increased benefits by increasing the average earnings on which benefits are figured. The cost of providing these wage credits comes from the general revenues.

The minimum active duty period for granting wage credits is 24 months of service or the full period called to active duty if the person served fewer than 24 months of active duty. This rule applies to: (1) persons enlisted in the Armed Forces for the first time on or after September 8, 1980; and (2) other members of the uniformed services whose active duty begins on or after October 14, 1982, provided they did not previously serve 24 months of active duty or were not discharged from prior service for the convenience of the government.

However, there are the following exceptions to these minimum service requirements: (1) discharge or release from active duty for the convenience of the government; (2) discharge or release from active duty for hardship; (3) discharge or release from active duty for disability incurred or aggravated in the line of duty; or (4) the establishment of entitlement to compensation for service-connected disability or death.

Active duty is: (1) full-time duty in the Armed Forces; (2) full-time duty (other than for training purposes) as a commissioned officer of the Regular or Reserve Corps of the Public Health Service; (3) full-time duty as a commissioned officer of the National Oceanic and Atmospheric Administration; and (4) full-time duty as a cadet or midshipman at the United States Military Academy, United States Naval Academy, United States Air Force Academy, or the United States Coast Guard Academy.

Active duty for training means: (1) full-time duty in the Armed Forces performed by Reserves for training purposes; (2) full-time duty for training purposes as a commissioned officer of the Reserve Corps of the Public Health Service; and (3) annual training duty performed for a period of 14 days or more as a member, cadet, or midshipmen of the Reserve Officers Training Corps while attending field training or practice cruises.

Individuals with active duty between September 16, 1940, and December 31, 1956, and whose discharge was other than dishonorable, can qualify for gratuitous social security earnings credits of $160 for each month of service during this period. At least 90 days of active service is required, however, unless discharged because of disability or injury incurred or aggravated in the line of duty. Persons whose military retirement pay is based on this period *are not* entitled to these social security earnings credits. The credits are not actually listed on the serviceman's social security earnings record but they will be considered when he applies for benefits. At that time proof of military service is required.

In determining their "average indexed monthly earnings," military personnel who have active service *after* 1956 may also utilize the gratuitous earnings credit of $160 for each month of military service after 1950, and before 1957, even though their armed forces retired pay is based in part on those years of service.

Social security is also a consideration of the Survivor Benefit Plan for retired military personnel. See SECTION K.

## FEDERAL GOVERNMENT EMPLOYEES

**B-28. Are civilian employees of the Federal Government who come under The Civil Service Retirement System covered by Social Security?**

The Social Security Amendments of 1983 provide for automatic coverage of the following groups: (1) all federal employees hired on or after January 1, 1984, including those with previous periods of federal service if the break in federal service lasted at least 365 days; (2) legislative branch employees on the same basis, as well as current employees of the legislative branch who are not participating in the Civil Service Retirement System as of December 31, 1983; (3) all members of Congress, the President and Vice President, effective January 1, 1984; (4) all sitting federal judges, except retired federal judges assigned to active duty, and all executive level and senior executive service political appointees, as of January 1, 1984. Federal judicial salaries will be reported as wages for social security earnings test and payroll tax purposes.

The Spending Reduction Act of 1984 addressed two problems regarding provisions of the Social Security Amendments of 1983. First, a federal employee who had been covered by Social Security (mostly the armed services which have been covered since 1956) could retire from military service, enter federal civilian service, and be exempt from social security coverage. Conversely, a person who only technically severed his federal civilian employment connection for a term of duty with an international organization could have a break-in-service upon his return and would be covered by Social Security if the break exceeded 365 days.

The Spending Reduction Act of 1984 provides that if a person returns to federal civilian employment after being transferred to an international organization, then the service performed for the organization is considered federal employment. If a person returns to federal civilian service after temporary military or reserve duty and has exercised restoration or reemployment rights, then no break-in-service is deemed to have occurred and his service in the uniformed services will count as federal employment.

The Act also provides that an individual who withdraws from the Civil Service Retirement System (CSRS) after June 14, 1984 and is refunded his contributions will not be exempt from Social Security thereafter while employed in the legislative branch. Also, an individual will not be exempt from Social Security if he is employed in the legislative branch after June 14, 1984 and his employment is not covered by the CSRS. Legislative branch employees who take a leave of absence without taking a refund of their CSRS contributions may continue their coverage under the CSRS. If they are not automatically covered again under the CSRS, they will be covered under Social Security unless they rejoin the CSRS when they resume employment.

No exemption from Social Security coverage is available to an individual who took a refund of CSRS contributions based on a separation or transfer from January 1, 1984 through June 14, 1984, or who has legislative branch employment which was not covered under the CSRS during that period. Exemption from Social Security can be reestablished, however, if the individual was covered under the CSRS on December 31, 1983, and he reentered the CSRS after his last withdrawal from it and before August 18, 1984. For an individual who is not a federal employee on July 18, 1984, the 30-day period will run from the date on which he again becomes a legislative branch employee. An individual will be treated as having reentered the CSRS if he applies to do so within the appropriate time and his coverage is subsequently made effective.

Congress has enacted the Federal Employees' Retirement System (FERS) to provide supplementary retirement protection for federal employees covered under social security as a result of the Social Security Amendments of 1983.

## RAILROAD EMPLOYEES

### B-29. Are railroad employees covered by Social Security?

No, pay for railroad work ordinarily is not counted for social security purposes. (Railroad employees have a special and separate retirement system administered by the Railroad Retirement Board.)

However, earnings from railroad employment are counted for social security purposes at the death or retirement of a worker if he does not qualify under the railroad retirement program. For example, when a railroad worker retires with less than 10 years of railroad service (120 months of credited service), no railroad retirement annuity is payable. However, his or her railroad earnings after 1936 would then be considered in determining his or her rights to social security disability or retirement benefits.

## FAMILY EMPLOYMENT

### B-30. Is employment by a member of one's own family covered by Social Security?

The following "family employment" does not come under social security:

- Employment of a child under age 18 by his father or mother.
- Employment of parent as a domestic in the home of a son or daughter. However, domestic service by a parent is covered (after 1967) if: (1) the employer (son or daughter) has a child or stepchild living in the home who is under age 18 or who has a mental or physical condition which requires the personal care and supervision of an adult for at least four continuous weeks in the calendar quarter in which the service is rendered; and (2) the employer (son or daughter) is a widow or widower or divorced person who has not remarried, or a married person whose spouse has a mental or physical condition which renders him incapable of caring for such child or stepchild.
- Employment of parent to do work not in the course of a son's or daughter's trade or business.

In applying the family employment exclusion rules, foster and step-relationships, as well as natural and adoptive relationships, are included in the terms "child," "parent," "son," "daughter," etc.

If a husband and wife work in the same business, and the business is a sole proprietorship, the spouse who is the owner of the business is covered. In addition, the spouse who is the employee is covered as an employee. This is usually true whether the couple lives in a community property state or in a common-law state—see B-22. If the husband and wife are partners, both are considered to be owners, and both are covered as self-employed persons.

If a woman works for a corporation, she will be covered as an employee of the corporation even though her husband is the sole stockholder.

Also, the rules excluding family employment do not apply to work performed as an employee of a partnership unless the relationship of minor child and parent exists between the employee and *each* of the partners. For example, if a minor is employed by a partnership composed of his father and uncle as co-partners, the minor's work is covered. But if the partnership is composed of his father and mother as sole co-partners, the minor's work is not covered. If the child is a bona fide partner, however, he is covered as a self-employed person even though his parents are the only other partners (See B-21).

A person who is an employee of a partnership composed of his spouse and one or more other partners, is covered. If he is a partner, he is covered as a self-employed person. (See B-21.)

## EMPLOYEES OF STATE AND LOCAL GOVERNMENTS

### B-31. Are employees of state and local governments covered by Social Security?

They are not covered unless the state has entered into an agreement with the Social Security Administration, or (after June 1991) unless the governmental entity does not have a retirement system (as discussed in more detail later). Such an agreement is at the election of the state. Generally, employees of publicly-owned transit systems are covered on a compulsory basis unless they are under a retirement system.

Once an agreement has been entered into, employees of a state and its political subdivisions can be brought under the agreement in groups known as "coverage groups." There are two basic types of coverage groups: (1) groups composed of employees who are not under a state or local retirement system, and (2) groups composed of employees who are under a state or local retirement system.

Federal law gives each state the right to decide which coverage groups are to be included under its agreement. However, a state may permit its political subdivisions to decide whether or not any of the subdivision's employees are to be included. A state may subsequently modify the agreement to include additional coverage groups.

Employees who are not covered by a retirement system may be divided into coverage groups composed of the following employees: (1) all state employees performing services in connection with governmental functions; (2) all state employees performing services in connection with a single nongovernmental function; (3) all employees of a political subdivision (e.g. city) performing services in connection with governmental functions; (4) all employees of a political subdivision performing services in connection with a single nongovernmental function; (5) all civilian employees of National Guard Units of the state; and (6) inspectors of agricultural products employed pursuant to an agreement between the state and the Department of Agriculture.

All, or only some, of the above groups in a specific state may be brought under social security by the state's agreement.

Beginning after June 30, 1991, state and local government workers who are not covered by a retirement system in conjunction with their employment for a state or local government are automatically covered under Social Security and must pay social security taxes. An exception is provided for students employed in public schools, colleges, and universities, for whom coverage may be provided at the option of the state government. Other exceptions are election officials or election workers if remuneration paid in a calendar year for their services is less than $100, hospital patients and "emergency" workers.

A retirement system is defined as a pension, annuity, retirement, or similar fund or system established by a state or by a political subdivision of a state. Whether an employee is a member (i.e., a participant) of a retirement system is based upon whether that individual actually participates in the program. Thus, whether an employee participates is not determined by whether he holds a position that is included in a retirement system. Instead, the worker must actually be a member of the system. For example, an employee (whose job classification is of a type that ordinarily is entitled to coverage) is not a member of a retirement system if he is ineligible because of age or service conditions contained in the plan and, therefore, is required to be covered under Social Security. Similarly, if participation in the system is elective, and the employee elects not to participate, that employee does not participate in a retirement system and is to be covered under the social security system.

Other coverage groups are composed of employees who are under a state or local retirement system. A state coverage agreement cannot bring such groups under social security initially unless a referendum is held. Generally, if a majority of eligible employees vote in favor of being included, all will be covered (but see next paragraph below with respect to splitting a retirement system group). A retirement system coverage group for referendum and coverage purposes may, at the option of the state, consist of (1) all employees under the system; (2) only state employees under the system; (3) employees of one or more political subdivisions who are under the system; (4) any combination of the foregoing groups; (5) employees of each institution of higher learning or of any hospital which is not a political subdivision in itself. This division may be made even though members of two or more of the groups are under the same state or local retirement system.

Certain states (and their political subdivisions) may split a retirement system and cover only those employees who wish to be covered. These states are: Alaska, California, Connecticut, Florida, Georgia, Hawaii, Illinois, Massachusetts, Minnesota, Nevada, New Jersey, New Mexico, New York, North Dakota, Pennsylvania, Rhode Island, Tennessee, Texas, Vermont, Washington and Wisconsin. The foregoing states may divide their retirement systems into two parts: one part consisting of members who desire coverage, and the other part consisting of members who do not desire coverage. Individuals who became members of the retirement system after the retirement system has been covered will be included in that part of the system which desires coverage.

Generally, police officers and firefighters who are under a retirement system may not be included in a coverage agreement, even with a referendum, except in the following states: Alabama, California, Florida, Georgia, Hawaii, Idaho, Kansas, Maine, Maryland, Mississippi, Montana, New York, North Carolina, North Dakota, Oregon, Puerto Rico, South Carolina, South Dakota, Tennessee, Texas, Vermont, Virginia and Washington. However, social security can be extended to firefighters in states not specifically granted that right if the Governor of the state certifies that the total benefit protection of firefighters would be improved as a result. The divided retirement system could not be used and the firefighters would have to be brought into coverage as a separate group and not as part of a group which includes persons other than firefighters.

Upon request of the Governor of Connecticut, Connecticut state police hired on or after May 8, 1984, who are members of the tier II plan of the Connecticut State Employees Retirement System, will be covered. Coverage will be for service performed after April 7, 1986.

The Social Security Amendments of 1983 prohibit states from terminating coverage of state and local government employees if the termination did not go into effect by April 20, 1983. Under prior law, a state could terminate coverage for groups of state and local employees by giving two years' advance written notice, providing the coverage had been in effect for at least five years. The Act also permits state and local groups whose coverage was terminated before April 20, 1983 to be covered again. Prior law prohibited a terminated group from being covered again.

## MINISTERS, MEMBERS OF RELIGIOUS ORDERS
## AND CHRISTIAN SCIENCE PRACTITIONERS

**B-32. Is a minister, member of a religious order, or Christian Science practitioner covered by Social Security?**

Yes, they are automatically covered for taxable years ending after 1967. This means that beginning in 1968, duly ordained, commissioned, or licensed ministers (including priests and rabbis), Christian Science practitioners, and members of religious orders who have not taken a vow of poverty, must pay social security taxes and are entitled to social security benefits under the rules applying to self-employed persons generally.

However, ministers, members and practitioners may claim exemption from social security on the ground of conscientious objection or religious principle. They must file application for an irrevocable exemption with the Internal Revenue Service together with a statement that either they are conscientiously opposed, or opposed because of religious principle, to the acceptance of public insurance benefits. As a result of legislation in 1986 (Tax Reform Act), they must also submit proof that they informed their church body that they were taking this action, and the Internal Revenue Service has the responsibility of communicating with the applicant so as to be certain that he or she is aware of the grounds for exemption and has sought exemption on such grounds.

Before a duly ordained, commissioned, or licensed minister of a church can request and be granted an exemption from social security coverage, he must be able to establish that the church qualifies as a religious organization exempt from income tax. Rev. Rul. 76-415, 1976-2 C.B. 255.

The time limit for filing an application for exemption with the Internal Revenue Service is the due date of the tax return (including extensions) for the second taxable year (whether or not consecutive) in which the minister, member or practitioner had net earnings from self-employment of $400 or more, any part of which was derived from services as a minister, member of a religious order, or Christian Science practitioner.

A valid application for exemption is effective for the first taxable year ending after 1967 for which the applicant had net earnings of $400 or more, some part of which is derived from services as a minister, member, or practitioner.

The Tax Reform Act of 1986 gave clergy members who had elected to be excluded from social security coverage a one-time opportunity to obtain coverage. Generally, the election could have been made any time up to April 15, 1988 and had to be made before the individual became entitled to benefits. Once the election was made, the individual had to pay self-employment tax.

Individuals who perform services in the exercise of their ministry are treated as self-employed persons even though their income is derived from services as an employee. Thus, the income derived from the exercise of their ministry is treated as self-employment income and the individual must pay the tax rate for self-employed persons. Coverage does not involve the church they serve.

Before the social security amendments of 1967, a minister, Christian Science practitioner, or member of a religious order was not covered by social security unless he elected coverage by filing a Waiver Certificate (Form 2031). The election to be covered was irrevocable; a person who filed a Waiver Certificate could not claim exemption from social security after the compulsory coverage resulting from the 1967 amendments was applicable.

Members of religious orders who have taken vows of poverty are not covered as self-employed individuals, but may be covered as employees if their orders elect social security coverage for their members.

## EMPLOYEES OF NON-PROFIT ORGANIZATIONS

### B-33. Are employees of non-profit religious, charitable or educational organizations covered by Social Security?

Beginning January 1, 1984, all current and future employees of non-profit organizations (charitable, religious, and educational) are covered. Non-profit organizations were not allowed to terminate coverage of employees after 1982. Non-profit employees age 55 or older on January 1, 1984 are fully insured for social security benefits after acquiring a given number of quarters of coverage, according to the following sliding scale, which is easier to meet than the regular requirements.

| If on January 1, 1984 the person is | The number of quarters needed is |
|---|---|
| Age 60 or over ........................ | 6 |
| Age 59 ..................................... | 8 |
| Age 58 ..................................... | 12 |
| Age 57 ..................................... | 16 |
| Age 55-56 ................................ | 20 |

Churches and certain church-controlled organizations opposed for religious reasons to the payment of the employer social security tax (FICA) were permitted to make a one-time irrevocable election in 1984 not to be subject to the employer-portion of the tax or any requirement to withhold social security taxes with regard to their employees.

Employees of organizations who made this election must pay the social security self-employment tax (See J-6), but they can opt out of coverage individually if they belong to certain religious sects (See B-44).

The election was available to (1) churches (including conventions or associations of churches), (2) elementary or secondary schools controlled, operated or principally supported by churches, and (3) certain church-controlled tax-exempt organizations. The election applies to services performed on or after January 1, 1984.

Employees of non-profit organizations who are covered on a mandatory basis by the Civil Service Retirement System (i.e., Legal Service Corporation employees) are considered federal employees for purposes of social security. They are covered by social security if newly hired after 1983, or if they had a break in federal service lasting more than 365 days.

Non-profit organizations cannot terminate social security coverage as they could at one time.

Participation in the social security system was optional for non-profit organizations prior to 1984. The non-profit organization had to file a certificate waiving its exemption from coverage. (In this way, the organization made itself subject to the social security tax on employers.)

## HOSPITAL INTERNS

### B-34. Are hospital interns covered by social security?

An intern is covered as an employee if he is employed by a hospital. If the hospital is a section 501(c)(3) non-profit organization, coverage became mandatory in 1984 (see B-33). If an intern is employed by a federal hospital, determinations regarding amounts of remuneration constituting covered wages are made by the head of the appropriate federal agency or instrumentality. The work is covered on the same basis as the work of other federal employees. If an intern is employed by a state or local government hospital, coverage depends on whether the position is in a group covered under the Federal-State agreement.

## STUDENT NURSES

**B-35. Are student nurses covered by Social Security?**

No. Work by a student nurse for a hospital or nurses' training school is excluded from social security coverage if the student is enrolled and regularly attending classes in a state chartered or approved nurses' training school. This work is excluded from coverage even though the work of other employees of the hospital or nurses' training school is covered.

The IRS, however, has held that a student nurse's services are not exempt from "employment" where they are performed on a full-time basis and the nurse performs the same duties and receives the same salary as the hospital's registered nurses. Rev. Rul. 85-74, 1985-1 CB 331. The IRS indicated that the services of a student nurse will be excepted from employment only where the student nurse's work at the hospital or nurse's training school is substantially less than full time, the total amount of earnings is nominal, and the services are incidental parts of the training toward a qualifying degree as a nurse or in a specialized area of nursing.

## DOMESTIC WORKERS

**B-36. Is domestic work in a private home covered by Social Security?**

Yes. If an employer pays a domestic worker $50 or more in a calendar quarter, the work comes under social security. This means that the wages must be reported and both employer and employee social security taxes must be paid. A calendar quarter is any three-month period beginning January 1st, April 1st, July 1st, or October 1st. For example, if a person is hired to clean every two weeks and is paid $40 a day, the wages come under social security.

Each calendar quarter is considered separately in determining whether the cash pay is to be counted as social security wages. If the domestic worker is paid cash wages by more than one employer, the $50-a-quarter test applies separately to the wages paid by each employer. For example, if a domestic works for five employers and in one calendar quarter receives only $45 from each employer (a total of $225), the pay does not come under social security.

Only cash payments are counted as social security wages. Room, board, and car tokens are not counted.

Domestic service means work ordinarily performed as an integral part of household duties that contributes to the maintenance of the employer's private home or administers to the personal wants and comforts of the employer, other members of the household, and guests. This includes work performed by cooks, waiters, waitresses, butlers, housekeepers, housemen, watchmen, governesses, maids, companions, nursemaids, valets, baby sitters, janitors, laundresses, furnacemen, caretakers, gardners, footmen, grooms, seamstresses, handymen, and chauffeurs of family automobiles.

A private home is the fixed place of residence of one or more persons. Any shelter used as a dwelling may, depending on the circumstances, be considered a private home. Examples include a tent, boat, trailer, or a room or suite in a hospital, hotel, sanitorium, or nursing home.

In an apartment house, each apartment together with its private stairways, halls, and porches, etc. is a private home. If a house is used mainly as a commercial rooming or boarding house, only that part of the house which is used as the operator's living quarters is considered to be a private home.

Domestic workers employed by landlords or rental agencies to do work in or about property being rented as a private home are not performing work in the private home of the employer.

Domestic work performed by a child under age 21 for his parent, by a wife for her husband, by a husband for his wife, or by a parent for a son or daughter (except under some special circumstances) is not covered by social security (see B-30).

Domestic workers in rooming-houses, hotels, etc., are covered as regular employees regardless of their earnings. Also, different rules apply for household work on a farm (see B-38).

An employer who pays a domestic worker $50 or more in any quarter must report the wages for social security even though he or she has only the one employee. Payments may be rounded to the nearest dollar. (For method of reporting, see SOCIAL SECURITY TAXES, SECTION J.)

However, a homeowner does not report payment to a worker who is employed by some type of service company and hired out for a job (such as catering help or a painter), or payment to a self-employed person such as a gardener who brings his own special equipment.

## NON-BUSINESS OR CASUAL EMPLOYMENT

**B-37. Is an employee whose work is not connected with his employer's trade or business covered by Social Security?**

Yes, but only if the "cash pay" test is met. The cash pay test is met if the employee is paid at least $100 in cash in the calendar year for the non-business work.

Where the employee performs nonbusiness work for more than one employer, the cash-pay test is applied individually to the cash pay from each employer.

Non-business employment is any type of work that does not promote or advance the employer's business, such as work performed in connection with the employer's hobby or recreational activities or work as an employee in repairing the employer's private home.

Employment for a corporation can never be considered "non-business" employment.

## AGRICULTURAL LABOR

### B-38. Under what conditions are agricultural laborers covered by Social Security?

Most types of agricultural labor were covered by social security beginning with 1951. However, only cash pay for farm work can be counted for social security purposes, and only under the following conditions:

- After 1956: The cash paid to an employee in a calendar year for agricultural labor for one employer amounts to $150 or more; or the employee performs such labor for one employer who pays out at least $2,500 in wages for agricultural labor in the year.

  However, wages paid to an employee who receives pay of less than $150 annually by an agricultural employer are not subject to social security tax even if the employer pays more than $2,500 in the year to all employees, if the employee (1) is employed as a hand harvest laborer and is paid on a piece rate basis in an operation which has been, and is customarily and generally recognized as having been, paid on a piece rate basis in the region of employment, (2) commutes daily from his permanent residence to the farm on which he is employed, and (3) has been employed in agriculture less than 13 weeks during the preceding calendar year.

- For years 1955 and 1956: The employer paid the worker cash pay of at least $100 in the calendar year.

- For years 1951 through 1954: The employee was paid cash pay of $50 or more in the calendar quarter by an employer by whom he was "regularly employed."

## STUDENTS WORKING FOR A COLLEGE OR
## FOR A COLLEGE CLUB

**B-39. Is a student working for a college or college club covered by Social Security?**

No. Work by a student for a school, college or university at which he is enrolled and regularly attending classes is excluded from social security coverage. Also excluded is domestic work by a student for a local college club, fraternity or sorority.

Work performed by a student for a private, nonprofit auxiliary organization of the school, college, or university at which the student is enrolled and regularly attending classes is also excluded from coverage if the organization: (1) is organized and operated for the benefit of, to perform the functions of, or to carry out the purposes of the school, college, or university; and (2) is operated, supervised, or controlled by or in connection with the school, college, or university.

## DISTRIBUTORS AND VENDORS OF NEWSPAPERS
## OR MAGAZINES

**B-40. Are newsboys or newsgirls under age 18 excluded from coverage?**

Yes; generally they are excluded from coverage if they are under age 18, are employees, and the newspapers, handbills, shopping guides, etc. are distributed or delivered to the ultimate consumer and not to a point from which later distribution or delivery is to be made. Delivery or distribution can be by retail sale, house-to-house delivery, or passing out handbills on the street. (The exclusion does not apply, however, to the delivery or distribution of magazines.)

If a person under age 18 performs his work as an independent contractor, his work may be covered as self-employment.

**B-41. Are newspaper vendors who are 18 or over covered by Social Security?**

Yes; but by special provision of the law, they are covered as self-employed persons even if they are employees.

## AMERICANS EMPLOYED OUTSIDE THE U.S.

**B-42. Is an American citizen who is employed by a foreign subsidiary of a U.S. Corporation covered by Social Security?**

The Social Security Amendments of 1983 permit any American employer (a corporation, sole proprietorship, or partnership) to provide coverage for U.S. citizens and U.S. residents working outside the United States for a foreign affiliate when the American employer has not less than a 10 percent direct or indirect interest in the foreign employer. The employer must enter into an agreement with the Secretary of the Treasury for the payment of social security taxes for such employees. All U.S. citizens and residents working for the subsidiary must be covered if any of such persons are to be covered. Before June 15, 1989, the agreement could have been terminated if it had been in effect for at least eight years and the employer had given two years advance notice. Currently, the employer may not terminate coverage for any workers in its foreign affiliates.

The President may enter into bilateral agreements with interested foreign countries to provide for limited coordination between the United States social security system and that of the other country. These agreements eliminate dual coverage and contributions for the same work under the social security systems of the two cooperating countries. Each agreement must be transmitted to Congress with a report on the estimated cost and number of individuals affected. The agreement goes into effect if it is not rejected by either House of Congress within 90 days after both Houses have been in session.

The U.S. has entered into bilateral agreements with Belgium, Canada, France, Italy, Netherlands, Norway, Portugal, Spain, Sweden, Switzerland, United Kingdom, and West Germany. Other agreements are pending.

## FARMERS

### B-43. Are self-employed farmers covered by Social Security?

Yes, but special rules apply for the reporting of farm income (see WAGES AND SELF-EMPLOYMENT INCOME, SECTION C).

## RELIGIOUS SECTS

### B-44. What persons can claim exclusion from Social Security because of their religious beliefs?

A person can claim exemption from the self-employment tax if he belongs to a religious sect (e.g. Old Order Amish), the teachings of which prevent him from accepting the benefits of any insurance, or social insurance, which makes payments in the event of death, disability, retirement, or for medical care. The sect must have been in existence at all times since 1950, and the exemption can be granted for all taxable years since 1950.

Prior to January 1, 1989, the exemption applied to self-employment income (e.g. farm income) only and not to earnings as an employee. Beginning on or after January 1, 1989, the exemption applies to the self-employed and their employees in cases where both the employee and the employer are members of a qualifying religious sect or division. This optional exemption applies to both the employer and employee portion of the social security tax.

Also, the exemption is available to employees of partnerships in which each partner holds a religious exemption from social security coverage. In addition, the exemption is available to workers in churches and church-controlled nonprofit organizations who are treated as self-employed because the employing church or organization exercised its option not to pay the employer portion of the social security tax.

Exemption is granted only if the individual files a waiver of all benefits under social security and only if he (or any person on his account) has never received any such benefits.

# WAGES AND SELF-EMPLOYMENT INCOME

### C-1. What earnings are subject to Social Security tax and are counted in computing Social Security benefits?

Earnings that are the *wages* of an employee or the *self-employment income* of a self-employed person. However, earnings are counted as "wages" or as "self-employment income" only if they are earned in employment or self-employment covered by the Social Security Act.

### C-2. For Social Security purposes, what is meant by the term "wages"?

"Wages" mean pay received by an employee for employment covered by the Social Security Act. The maximum amount of wages subject to the Old-Age, Survivors and Disability Insurance tax (OASDI) and credited to a worker's social security record for any calendar year cannot exceed:

| | | |
|---|---|---|
| $3,000 | received from each employer in any of the years | 1937-1939 |
| $3,000 | paid in any of the years | 1940-1950 |
| $3,600 | paid in any of the years | 1951-1954 |
| $4,200 | paid in any of the years | 1955-1958 |
| $4,800 | paid in any of the years | 1959-1965 |
| $6,600 | paid in either of the years | 1966-1967 |
| $7,800 | paid in any of the years | 1968-1971 |
| $9,000 | paid in the year | 1972 |
| $10,800 | paid in the year | 1973 |
| $13,200 | paid in the year | 1974 |
| $14,100 | paid in the year | 1975 |
| $15,300 | paid in the year | 1976 |
| $16,500 | paid in the year | 1977 |
| $17,700 | paid in the year | 1978 |
| $22,900 | paid in the year | 1979 |
| $25,900 | paid in the year | 1980 |
| $29,700 | paid in the year | 1981 |
| $32,400 | paid in the year | 1982 |
| $35,700 | paid in the year | 1983 |
| $37,800 | paid in the year | 1984 |
| $39,600 | paid in the year | 1985 |
| $42,000 | paid in the year | 1986 |
| $43,800 | paid in the year | 1987 |
| $45,000 | paid in the year | 1988 |
| $48,000 | paid in the year | 1989 |
| $51,300 | paid in the year | 1990 |
| $53,400 | paid in the year | 1991 |
| $55,500 | paid in the year | 1992 |

The employee pays the tax on wages up to the base amount from each employer, but receives a refund on his or her income tax return for the excess of total taxes paid over the tax on the base amount. Each employer pays the tax on wages up to the base amount for all of its employees.

In addition to the regular social security tax on wages, the maximum amount of wages subject to the Medicare Hospital Insurance tax (HI) is $130,200 in 1992. The maximum amount for HI was the same as for OASDI for all years before 1991 (back to 1966, when the HI tax was first applicable).

The maximum earnings base and maximum Medicare contribution base are automatically adjusted each year by the Department of Health and Human Services (i.e., the Social Security Administration) if average nationwide (covered and non-covered) total wages have increased.

Included in total wages is certain deferred compensation, including 401(k) plans. Such compensation in the aggregate has been increasing more rapidly than other wages in recent years. For purposes of determining the maximum earnings base in 1990, an estimate of deferred compensation was included in the average wage for 1988, so that the maximum earnings base ($51,300) reflected what the result would have been if deferred compensation had been included in the average-wage computations in 1984-88. (It had not been included prior to 1990.) Actual deferred compensation amounts are used beginning with 1990 wages. For purposes of benefit computations and other program amounts, actual deferred compensation amounts are included in the average nationwide total wages beginning with 1990 wages, and the effect thereof will be reflected in benefit computations and other program amounts beginning in 1993.

Benefits are automatically increased when the Consumer Price Index for All Urban Wage Earners and Clerical Workers from the third quarter of one year to the third quarter of the following year rises, and no general benefit increase has been enacted or become effective in the preceding year.

Benefits have been raised by the following percentages since 1977:

Note that the maximum amount of wages subject to the OASDI tax is also the maximum amount credited to a worker's record. For example, if an employee is paid $55,500 or less in 1992, the full amount of his wages will be subject to OASDI tax and will be credited to his social security record for benefit purposes. But if an employee is paid $75,000 in 1992, only $55,500 will be subject to OASDI tax and credited to his social security record (but he will pay HI taxes on the entire $75,000).

| Month/Year | Increase in Benefits | Month/Year | Increase in Benefits |
|---|---|---|---|
| June 1977 | 5.9% | December 1985 | 3.1% |
| June 1978 | 6.5% | December 1986 | 1.3% |
| June 1979 | 9.9% | December 1987 | 4.2% |
| June 1980 | 14.3% | December 1988 | 4.0% |
| June 1981 | 11.2% | December 1989 | 4.7% |
| June 1982 | 7.4% | December 1990 | 5.4% |
| December 1983 | 3.5% | December 1991 | 3.7% |
| December 1984 | 3.5% | | |

In other words, earnings in excess of the maximum amount for a particular calendar year are not considered wages for social security coverage purposes.

A stabilizer provision protects the system from trust-fund depletions that could occur when price increases outpace wage gains. This stabilizer provision goes into effect if reserves in the trust funds providing retirement, disability and survivor benefits fall below 20% of what is needed to meet outgo for a year. When the stabilizer takes effect, automatic cost-of-living benefit increases will be based on the lower of the annual percentage increase in the Consumer Price Index or the annual percentage rise in the nation's average wage.

Later, if the fund reserves exceed 32% of what is estimated to be needed for a year, recipients will be entitled to extra cost-of-living increases to compensate for losses in inflation protection resulting from having benefit increases tied to wage levels.

## C-3. Are only payments in cash counted as wages?

No, amounts paid by check, promissory note, or in other media such as goods, clothing, board or lodging usually count as wages. In a few cases, however, only cash pay is counted (see C-14; Domestic and Household Workers, B-36; Non-business or Casual Employment, B-37; and Agricultural Labor, B-38).

Ordinarily only pay actually received by the employee in a calendar year is counted as wages for that year. However, pay that is "constructively received" during the year is also counted. Wages are constructively received when they have been credited or set apart for the employee without any substantial limitation or restriction on the time or manner of payment and are available to him so that he can get them at any time. A special provision applies to pay under a nonqualified deferred compensation plan which is generally based on payments made after 1983.

### C-4. Are employer payments for group life insurance covered wages?

The employer-cost of group life insurance in excess of $50,000 is covered wages for the employee, effective January 1, 1988. Group-term life insurance provided to an individual who separated from employment before January 1, 1989, is excluded from covered wages subject to the social security tax.

Where an employer continues to provide taxable group-term life insurance to an employee who has left his employment, the former employee is required to pay the employee portion of the social security tax. The employer is required, for group life insurance coverage provided after 1990, to list separately on the former employee's W-2 form each year the amount of the payment for group-term life insurance and the amount of employer social security tax imposed on it. Instructions on IRS form 1040 will direct the employee to add this amount to his total tax liability.

### C-5. Are vacation pay and dismissal pay wages?

Yes.

### C-6. Are payments on account of sickness or accident disability counted as wages?

Payments under a plan or system made by an employer to or on behalf of an employee or any of the employee's dependents for death, or medical or hospitalization *expenses* in connection with sickness or accident disability are not wages. (Pensions and retirement pay before January 1, 1984 are not counted as wages, even when not paid under a plan or system, see C-8.) Before 1982, payments under a plan or system made by an employer to an employee or any of the employee's dependents on account of sickness or accident disability were not wages. After 1981, these payments count as wages regardless of whether made under a plan or system, including payments by a third party such as an insurance company except to the extent attributable to the employee's own contributions. After 1981, payments of state temporary disability insurance benefits are wages except to the extent attributable to the employee's own contributions.

Note, however, that the exclusion for sick pay made after the end of the sixth calendar month following the last month in which the employee worked remains in effect. Payments for sickness or accident disability are counted as wages for social security purposes if paid before the end of six calendar months after the last month in which the employee worked. Sick pay paid more than six calendar months after the calendar month in which the employee stopped working continues to be excluded from wages. Also, payments to employees under a workers' compensation law continue not to be treated as wages.

Sick pay paid to an employee by a third party is wages unless it is attributable to the employee's contributions to a sickness or accident disability plan (e.g., employee-paid insurance premiums).

For payments to be excluded under a plan or system, the plan must provide for all employees generally or for a class or classes of employees. Some or all of the following features may also be a part of the plan:

- Set a definite basis for determining who is eligible, such as length of service, occupation or salary classification; and

- Set definite standards for determining the minimum duration of payments; and

- Provide a formula for determining the minimum amount to be paid an eligible employee.

Sick pay that is not paid under a plan or system by the employer is counted as wages for social security purposes if paid before the end of six calendar months after the last month in which the employee worked.

### C-7. Are payments made under a deferred compensation plan counted as wages?

Amounts deferred under a nonqualified deferred compensation plan of an employer covered by FICA (Federal Insurance Contributions Act) are wages subject to social security taxes at the *later of* (1) when the services are performed or (2) when the employee's right to such amounts are no longer subject to a substantial risk of forfeiture. IRC Sec. 3121(v)(2).

In general, many employees would prefer to have amounts deferred treated as wages for social security purposes at the time the services are performed. At such time, their salaries, in all likelihood, already exceed the social security taxable wage base (in 1992, $55,500 for OASDI and $130,200 for HI), and the amounts deferred would thus escape any social security taxes.

If the amounts deferred are subject to a substantial risk of forfeiture, then the employee will treat such amounts as wages for social security purposes at the time the forfeiture lapses. For these purposes, a "substantial risk of forfeiture" is determined according to the regulations under Internal Revenue Code section 83. If the deferred compensation payments vest (i.e., there is no further risk of forfeiture) upon retirement, then the present value of the payments expected under the deferred compensation agreement will be treated as wages for social security tax purposes in the year of retirement and may be subject to social security taxes (if the social security taxable wage base for that year has not yet been exceeded).

The above rules generally apply to *remuneration paid* after December 31, 1983. However, if an agreement to defer compensation was in existence on March 24, 1983 (except in the case of a deferred plan for state and local government employees) then these rules apply to *services performed* after December 31, 1983. Also, an employer may elect to take remuneration paid after December 31, 1983 into account prior to 1984 if such amounts would have been taken into account at such time had these rules applied at that time. Tax Reform Act of 1984 (TRA '84), Act Sec. 2662(f)(2)(A).

Deferred compensation payments which are exempt from the social security tax are:

- Any payment by an employer to a survivor or the estate of a former employee after the calendar year in which the employee died. IRC Sec. 3121(a)(14).

- Any payment made by an employer to an employee, if at the time the payment is made the employee is entitled to disability insurance benefits under social security and became entitled prior to the calendar year in which the payment is made, provided the employee did not perform services for the employer during the period for which such payment is made. IRC Sec. 3121(a)(15).

### C-8. Are payments made to or from a qualified pension or annuity plan counted as wages?

No, neither the employer's contribution to the plan nor payments to the employee from the plan are treated as wages. They are not subject to social security tax and are not creditable for benefit purposes.

### C-9. If a teacher takes a reduction in salary to provide funds for a tax-sheltered annuity, how are his wages computed for Social Security purposes?

The salary before the reduction will be treated as wages. Rev. Rul. 65-208. In other words, the amount of reduction, although paid to the insurer by the employer, is nevertheless not considered an employer contribution to a retirement fund. For example, suppose that a teacher, whose salary is $55,500, takes a $1,000 salary cut for 1992 so that this amount can be used to purchase a tax-sheltered annuity for his benefit. Social Security taxes will still be payable on the full $55,500, and this is the amount which will be credited to his social security account for benefit purposes.

Employer payments from employer funds into such plans are excluded from wages, effective January 1, 1984. Prior to 1984, employer payments were usually wages.

### C-10. Are cash tips considered wages?

Tips received by an employee in the course of employment are usually counted as wages for social security purposes whether they are received directly from a person other than the employer or are paid to the employee by the employer. There are two exceptions, however:

- Tips received in a medium other than cash are not counted as wages.

- Cash tips received by an employee in the course of employment by a single employer are not counted as wages if they total less than $20 in a calendar month.

Payments made to employees from service charges, which some hotels, restaurants, and similar establishments charge customers for the use of their dining facilities, are wages for social security purposes.

(For method of reporting tips, see SOCIAL SECURITY TAXES, SECTION J.)

### C-11. Do wages include the portion of an employee's social security taxes paid by his employer?

Yes, beginning January 1, 1981, except for domestic service in the private home of the employer and agricultural labor. However, payments by a state or local employer are wages for social security tax purposes only if the payment is pursuant to a salary reduction agreement (whether evidenced by a written instrument or otherwise). The term salary reduction agreement includes any salary reduction arrangement, regardless of whether there is approval or choice of participation by individual employees or whether such approval or choice is mandated by state statute.

### C-12. Are salesperson's commissions wages?

They are wages if the salesperson is an employee. (For rules to determine whether a commission salesperson is an employee, see B-10.) Where the commissions are the sole pay and no advances are given, the commissions are wages in the calendar year in which they are paid. However, where advances are made against future commissions, the year in which the advances are paid is the year to which the amount advanced is credited.

### C-13. Under what circumstances are the first-year and renewal commissions of a life insurance agent treated as wages?

If the agent is an *employee* when the policy is sold, both first-year and renewal commissions are treated as wages when they are *paid* to him. (For rules to determine whether a life insurance agent is an employee, see B-11.) Thus, the commissions are subject to the employer-employee tax in each year as he receives them (see SOCIAL SECURITY TAXES, SECTION J). For retirement test purposes, however, if the agent is an employee when the policy is sold, both first-year and renewal commissions are treated as "earned" in the month and year in which the policy was sold (see LOSS OF BENEFITS BECAUSE OF EXCESS EARNINGS, SECTION H).

### C-14. Is the value of meals and lodging furnished by an employer to an employee considered wages for social security taxation purposes?

The Supreme Court has held that the value of meals and lodging furnished to an employee for the convenience of the employer is not wages for social security coverage and tax purposes. *Rowan Companies, Inc. v. U.S.*, 48 AFTR 2d 81-5115.

Such meals must be provided at the employer's place of business. The employee must accept lodging at the employer's place of business in order for the value of the lodging to be excluded from wages.

The Social Security Amendments of 1983 state, however, that the exclusion of income from income tax withholding by the employer does not necessarily affect the treatment of the income for social security coverage and taxation purposes in other cases.

## SELF-EMPLOYMENT INCOME

### C-15. What is taxable and creditable self-employment income?

It is that part of an individual's net earnings from self-employment which is subject to social security tax and counted for social security benefits. In determining what part of a person's net earnings from self-employment is creditable for social security purposes, the following rules apply:

- 92.35% of all net earnings from self-employment is taxable and creditable self-employment income unless the trade, business or profession is not covered by the Social Security Act. The 92.35% factor has been used only in 1990 and after (when the self-employed first began paying the full employer-employee tax rate).

- If such amount for the taxable year is less than $400, the net earnings are not treated as self-employment income. That is, no social security tax is paid on the net earnings, and they are not credited to the person's social security account. (But see C-18.)

- The maximum amount of self-employment income for a taxable year that is subject to the Old-Age, Suvivors, and Disability Insurance tax (OASDI) and used to determine benefits cannot exceed:

| | |
|---|---|
| $55,500* | 1992 |
| $53,400 | 1991 |
| $51,300 | 1990 |
| $48,000 | 1989 |
| $45,000 | 1988 |
| $43,800 | 1987 |
| $42,000 | 1986 |
| $39,600 | 1985 |
| $37,800 | 1984 |
| $35,700 | 1983 |
| $32,400 | 1982 |
| $29,700 | 1981 |
| $25,900 | 1980 |
| $22,900 | 1979 |
| $17,700 | 1978 |
| $16,500 | 1977 |
| $15,300 | 1976 |
| $14,100 | 1975 |
| $13,200 | 1974 |
| $10,800 | 1973 |
| $9,000 | 1972 |
| $7,800 | 1968-1971 |
| $6,600 | 1966-1967 |
| $4,800 | 1959-1965 |
| $4,200 | 1955-1958 |
| $3,600 | 1951-1954 |

*After 1992, the maximum amount may increase automatically each January following a cost-of-living benefit increase (See C-2).

The maximum amount of self-employment income subject to the Medicare Hospital Insurance tax (HI) in 1992 is $130,200. The maximum amount subject to the HI tax was the same as for OASDI for all years before 1991 (back to 1966, when the HI tax was first applicable).

Net earnings in excess of the maximum amount for a particular taxable year are not considered self-employment income for social security purposes. No maximum amounts are given for years prior to 1951 since no self-employment was covered before 1951. (See B-16.)

### C-16. How is the amount of self-employment income figured if a person has both wages and net earnings from self-employment in the same year?

If a person has both wages (as an employee) and net earnings from self-employment in a taxable year, his *self-employment income* is only the difference, if any, between his wages and the maximum social security earnings base for that year (see C-15).

*Example.* Mr. Herman, an attorney, is employed as an instructor in a law school. In 1992, he draws a salary of $15,000 from the school and also earns $50,000 in private practice, which counts as $46,175 for Social Security purposes (i.e., 92.35% of $50,000). His self-employment income for OASDI purposes for 1992 is $40,500 ($55,500 maximum less $15,000 wages). Only $40,500 is subject to self-employment social security tax. $15,000 is subject to the employer-employee tax. Note, however, that $46,175 of the $50,000 earned in private practice is subject to the Medicare Hospital Insurance tax for self-employed individuals. In addition, Mr. Herman must pay the Medicare Hospital Insurance for employees on the $15,000 he earned as a law school instructor.

### C-17. In general, what constitutes net earnings from self-employment?

Net earnings from self-employment may be the net income from a trade, business or profession carried on by the individual alone, or it may be his distributive share of the ordinary net income of a partnership. In computing net earnings from self-employment, gross income and deductions are, for the most part, the same as for income tax purposes. However, the following differences must be taken into account:

- Rentals from real estate are excluded in determining net earnings from self-employment unless: (1) the rentals are received in the course of a trade or business by a real estate dealer; or (2) services are rendered primarily for the convenience of the occupants of the premises, as in the case of hotels, motels, etc. (but income from renting property for business or commercial use, such as a store, factory, office space, etc. is excluded regardless of the amount of services rendered to the tenant); (3) in the case of farm rentals, the farm landlord materially participates in the management or in the production of farm commodities on land rented to someone else.

- Dividends on stock and interest on bonds do not count for social security unless they are received in the course of business by a dealer in stocks or securities. The term "bond" includes debentures, notes, certificates, and other evidence of indebtedness issued with interest coupons or in registered form by a corporation. Bonds also include government bonds. Other interest received in the course of a trade or business does count for social security. For example, interest received by a merchant on his account or notes receivable are included in computing net earnings from self-employment.

- Partnerships are treated as individuals when it comes to the dividend and interest exclusion. Dividends and interest on securities held for investment are excluded from net earnings of the partners. However, if a partnership is in business as a securities dealer, income on the securities held for resale by the partnership is included as net earnings of the partners.

- Capital gains and losses, and gains and losses from the sale or exchange of property which is not inventory or stock in trade, are excluded in computing net earnings from self-employment.

- Retirement payments received by a retired partner from a partnership of which the individual is a member or a former member are excluded from net earnings from self-employment if the following conditions are met:

  A. The payments are made under a written plan of the partnership which provides for periodic payments on account of retirement, to partners generally or to a class or classes of partners, to continue at least until the partner's death; and

  B. The partner rendered no services in any business conducted by the partnership (or its successors) during the taxable year of the partnership ending within or with the taxable year in which such payments were received; and

C.  At the end of the partnership's taxable year there is no ob-
    ligation from the other partners to the retired partner other
    than for the retirement payments under the plan; and

D.  The partner's share in the capital of the partnership has
    been paid in full by the end of the partnership's taxable year.

• No deductions for net operating losses of other years are permitted in determining net earnings from self-employment.

• Ministers (unless granted an exemption from coverage) must
  include in net earnings from self-employment:

A.  The rental value of a home furnished as part of his or her
    compensation.

B.  A rental allowance paid as part of his compensation.

C.  The value of any meals or lodging furnished in connection
    with services performed in the exercise of his ministry. Rev.
    Rul. 77-80, 1977-1 C.B. 36.

However, the Internal Revenue Code excludes these items from
gross income for income tax purposes.

• Income taxable as "dividends" to shareholders of a Subchapter S corporation (a corporation electing not to be taxed as a
  corporation) is not considered "net earnings from self-
  employment." (But see B-7.)

## C-18. If an individual's earnings from self-employment are quite low, is there a special provision available?

Yes. If the individual had at least $400 per year of earnings from non-
farm self-employment (after reduction by the 92.35% factor mentioned in C-15) in two of the preceding three years and his gross
income from self-employment for the taxable year is $2,400 or less,
he can report either his actual net income or two-thirds of his gross
income.

If the individual's gross income from nonfarm self-employment
is over $2,400, and his net income is over $1,600, he reports his actual net income. But if his gross income is over $2,400, and his net in-
come is less than $1,600, he may report either his actual net income
or $1,600. This provision also applies to partnerships.

Note that a non-farmer may use this method only if his net earnings from self-employment are less than $1,600 *and* less than two-
thirds of gross income from *all* trades and businesses carried on by
him. In addition, this option can only be used five times in nonfarm self-employment by one individual.

**C-19. How does a self-employed life insurance agent report his first-year and renewal commissions?**

If the agent is self-employed *when the policy is sold*, he treats the commissions as earnings from self-employment in the year they are paid to him. It is immaterial whether he is an employee or self-employed when he *receives* the commissions. For retirement test purposes, renewal commissions paid to a self-employed agent after retirement are not included as earnings after the initial month of retirement if they were the result of services rendered prior to retirement. (For rules to determine whether a life insurance agent is an employee or self-employed, see B-11.) (For treatment of commissions as "earnings" for "retirement test" purposes, see LOSS OF BENEFITS BECAUSE OF EXCESS EARNINGS, SECTION H.)

# INSURED STATUS

### D-1. How does a person become qualified for Social Security benefits for himself and his family?

By becoming "insured." Most types of benefits are payable if the person is *fully* insured. Some types of benefits are payable if the person is either *fully* or *currently* insured. A special insured status is required for disability benefits (D-18).

A person becomes insured by acquiring a certain number of *quarters of coverage*.

## QUARTERS OF COVERAGE

### D-2. What is meant by a "calendar quarter?"

A "calendar quarter" means a period of three calendar months ending March 31, June 30, September 30, or December 31 of any year.

### D-3. How are quarters of coverage determined for an employee?

1. **For 1992, an employee receives one quarter of coverage for each $570 of earnings up to a maximum of four.**

   *Example.* Mrs. Hall works for two months in 1992 and earns $1,200. She is credited with two quarters of coverage for the year because she receives one quarter of coverage for each $570 of earnings, up to a maximum of four. In order to receive four quarters of coverage in 1992, Mrs. Hall would have needed earnings totaling $2,280 ($570 × 4 = $2,280).

   This method of determining quarters of coverage will be used for years after 1992 also, but the measure of earnings ($570 in 1992) will automatically increase each year to take account of increases in average wages.

   However, see D-6 for quarters that cannot be counted as quarters of coverage regardless of whether the earnings requirement has been met.

2. For years prior to 1978, an employee receives one quarter of coverage for each quarter in which wages paid were $50 or more in

covered employment. In addition, each quarter of the year is counted as a quarter of coverage if the employee's total wages (or wages and self-employment income) for any calendar year equal or exceed the maximum social security earnings base for that year. This is true even if the employee receives no wages in some of the quarters. (Maximum earnings creditable for calendar years before 1978 are shown in C-2.)

*Example.* Mr. Brown is unemployed from January 1, 1977 to May 1, 1977. During the last eight months of the year he worked in covered employment and was paid over $16,500 (the maximum social security earnings base for 1977). He is credited with four quarters of coverage for 1977 even though he received no wages in the first quarter.

3. For years after 1977 and before 1992, the amount of earnings needed for one quarter of coverage is as follows:

| Year | Earnings for Quarter of Coverage |
|------|----------------------------------|
| 1991 | $540 |
| 1990 | 520 |
| 1989 | 500 |
| 1988 | 470 |
| 1987 | 460 |
| 1986 | 440 |
| 1985 | 410 |
| 1984 | 390 |
| 1983 | 370 |
| 1982 | 340 |
| 1981 | 310 |
| 1980 | 290 |
| 1979 | 260 |
| 1978 | 250 |

### D-4. How are quarters of coverage determined for a self-employed person?

Quarters of coverage for self-employed persons are determined by using two different methods; one for years prior to 1978 and another for 1978 and after.

1. In 1992, a self-employed person receives one quarter of coverage for each $570 of earnings, up to a maximum of four.

2. The amount of earnings needed for one quarter of coverage between 1978 and 1991 is as follows:

| Year | Earnings for Quarter of Coverage |
|------|----------------------------------|
| 1991 | $540 |
| 1990 | 520 |
| 1989 | 500 |
| 1988 | 470 |
| 1987 | 460 |
| 1986 | 440 |
| 1985 | 410 |
| 1984 | 390 |
| 1983 | 370 |
| 1982 | 340 |
| 1981 | 310 |
| 1980 | 290 |
| 1979 | 260 |
| 1978 | 250 |

3. For years prior to 1978, a self-employed person acquires 4 quarters of coverage for each calendar year in which he has been credited with $400 or more of self-employment income. A self-employed person must have at least $400 in net earnings from covered self-employment in a taxable year before any of such net earnings can be counted as self-employment income. (For definition of the terms "net earnings from self-employment" and "self-employment income," see SECTION C.)

The method of determining quarters of coverage described in items 1 and 2 will be used for years after 1992 also, but the measure of earnings ($570 in 1992) will automatically increase each year to take account of increases in average wages.

(For calendar quarters that cannot be counted as quarters of coverage in any event, see D-6.)

## D-5. How does a farm employee acquire quarters of coverage?

For years prior to 1978, a farm employee is credited with quarters of coverage based on total cash wages paid to him for farm work during a calendar year rather than on the amount of wages paid to him during a calendar quarter. He is credited with one quarter of coverage for each $100 in cash wages paid to him during the year as follows:

| If the cash wages in a year prior to 1978 amount to: | The number of quarters of coverage credited is: |
|---|---|
| $400 or more | 4 |
| $300-$399.99 | 3 |
| $200-$299.99 | 2 |
| $100-$199.99 | 1 |
| Under $100 | 0 |

In 1992, a farm employee receives one quarter of coverage for each $570 of earnings, up to a maximum of four.

The amount of earnings needed for one quarter of coverage prior to 1992 and after 1977 is as follows:

| Year | Earnings for Quarter of Coverage |
|---|---|
| 1991 | $540 |
| 1990 | 520 |
| 1989 | 500 |
| 1988 | 470 |
| 1987 | 460 |
| 1986 | 440 |
| 1985 | 410 |
| 1984 | 390 |
| 1983 | 370 |
| 1982 | 340 |
| 1981 | 310 |
| 1980 | 290 |
| 1979 | 260 |
| 1978 | 250 |

This method of determining quarters of coverage will be used for years after 1992 also, but the measure of earnings ($570 in 1992) will automatically increase each year to take account of increases in average wages.

### D-6. What calendar quarters cannot be counted as quarters of coverage even though the earnings requirement has been met?

A calendar quarter cannot be a quarter of coverage if:

- It begins after the calendar quarter in which the person died.

- It has not started yet.

- It is within a period of disability that is excluded in figuring benefits (see SECTION F). (However, the beginning and ending quarters of a prior disability period may be counted as quarters of coverage if the earnings requirement is met in these quarters.)

*Example.* Mr. Stegman dies on June 24, 1992 after having earned $55,500 (the maximum earnings base for 1992). Normally he would be credited with four quarters of coverage for that year (see D-3). However, he is credited with only two because the quarters after his death cannot be counted.

### D-7. Can quarters of coverage be acquired at any age?

Yes, quarters of coverage can be acquired even before age 21 or after retirement age.

### D-8. Are quarters of coverage used in determining the size of a person's social security benefits?

No, quarters of coverage are used only to determine insured status. The law provides an exact method for computing benefits based on the person's average monthly earnings or average indexed monthly earnings. Calendar years are used in making the computation. (See SECTION F.)

## FULLY INSURED

### D-9. How does a person become fully insured?

By acquiring a sufficient number of quarters of coverage to meet either of these two tests:

1. A person is fully insured if he has 40 quarters of coverage (a total of 10 years in covered work). Once a person has acquired 40 quarters of coverage he is fully insured for life, even if he spends no further time in covered employment or covered self-employment.

2. A person is fully insured if: (a) he has at least six quarters of coverage, and (b) he has acquired at least as many quarters of coverage as there are years elapsing *after* 1950 (or, if later, after the year in which he reaches age 21) and *before* the year in which he dies, becomes disabled, or reaches, or will reach age 62, whichever occurs first. (However, if a year, or any part of a year, fell within an established period of disability, that year need not be counted.) Note that prior to 1975, there is a transition period in effect for men. See D-11 and D-15.

The two tests above serve only to determine the *number* of quarters of coverage needed to be fully insured. It is immaterial when these quarters of coverage were acquired (but they can be acquired only after 1936). Also, in applying test No. 2, it is not necessary that the quarters of coverage be acquired during the elapsed period. All quarters of coverage, whether within or outside the elapsed period, are counted to determine whether the person has the required number.

(For method of determining fully insured status for retirement benefits, see D-10 to D-14. For method of determining fully insured status for survivors' benefits, see D-15. For method of determining fully insured status for disability benefits, see D-18.)

### D-10. Must a person be fully insured to qualify for retirement benefits?

Yes, in addition to other requirements (see SECTION E), he must be fully insured.

### D-11. How do you determine the number of quarters of coverage needed for a person to be fully insured for retirement benefits?

Count the number of years *after* 1950 (or, if later, after the year in which he attained age 21), and *before* attaining age 62. (But do not count a year any part of which was in an established period of disability.) Generally, this is the minimum number of quarters of coverage he will need to be fully insured. However, the person must have at least six quarters of coverage to be fully insured; and a person is fully insured in any event if he has 40 or more quarters of coverage.

The 1972 amendments provided for a change in the retirement benefit computation point for men from age 65 to age 62 (the computation point in effect for women). The change became fully effective for men born in 1913 and reaching age 62 in 1975. For those born in 1911, the computation point is age 64 and for those born in 1912, it is age 63.

See TABLE 2, for minimum numbers of quarters of coverage needed to be fully insured for retirement benefits.

*Example (1)*. Mr. Gray applies for retirement benefits in 1992; he attains age 62 in 1990. He needs 39 quarters of coverage to be fully insured (there are 39 years between 1950 and 1990, the year he attained age 62).

*Example (2)*. Mr. Brown applied for retirement benefits in 1979, the year he attained age 65. He needed 25 quarters of coverage to be fully insured (there are 25 years between 1950 and 1976, the year he attained age 62).

*Example (3)*. Miss Black applies for retirement benefits in 1992, the year she attains age 65. She needs 38 quarters of coverage to be fully insured (there are 38 years between 1950 and 1989, the year she attained age 62).

*Example (4)*. Mr. Green was born in 1930 and will be 62 in 1992. Normally, he would need 40 quarters of coverage to be fully insured for retirement benefits. Suppose, however, that Mr. Green has a period of disability lasting from August 1966 to February 1968. He would need only 37 quarters of coverage to be fully insured for retirement benefits (the three years, 1966-1968, would not be counted in determining the number of quarters of coverage required.)

**D-12. Does a woman need fewer quarters of coverage than a man to be fully insured for retirement benefits?**

No, the determination for men and women is the same. However, women who reached age 62 before 1975 needed fewer quarters of coverage than men to be fully insured for retirement benefits. (see D-11.)

**D-13. Can a person be fully insured for retirement benefits even though he has not worked in covered employment since 1950?**

Yes. To be fully insured for retirement benefits a person needs at least as many quarters of coverage as there are years after 1950 (or, if later, the year of his 21st birthday) and before the year when he reaches age 62. However, it is immaterial when these quarters of coverage were acquired.

*Example.* Mrs. Luck was born in 1927. In 1992 (at age 65) she applied for reduced retirement benefits. She needs 38 quarters of coverage to be fully insured (1 quarter of coverage for each year between 1950 and 1989). Mrs. Luck worked in covered employment for 10 years (acquired 40 quarters of coverage) prior to her marriage in 1951. Mrs. Luck is fully insured—she has more than the required 38 quarters of coverage.

**D-14. Can a person become fully insured after retirement age?**

Yes. A person can acquire quarters of coverage after age 62.

**D-15. How do you determine the number of quarters of coverage needed for a person to be fully insured at death?**

Count the number of years *after* 1950 or, if later, after the year in which he reached age 21, and *before* the year in which he dies. (But do not count a year any part of which was in an established period of disability.) He needs at least this many quarters of coverage to be fully insured at death. However, no person can be fully insured if he has less than six quarters of coverage; and a person is fully insured in any event if he has 40 quarters of coverage.

NOTE: A person born in 1929 reached age 21 in 1950. Consequently, for persons born in 1929 or before, count the years after 1950 and before the year of death. For persons born after 1929, see TABLE 3 for year of 21st birthday.

*Example (1)*. Mr. Luck, who was born in 1930, dies in 1992. He is fully insured if he has 40 quarters of coverage (there are 40 years between 1951 and 1992, the year in which he died).

*Example (2)*. Mr. Anderson, who was born in 1950, dies in 1992. He is fully insured if he has 20 quarters of coverage (there are 20 years between 1971, the year in which he reached age 21, and 1992, the year in which he died).

The above rule applies to persons who die before age 62. If a person dies after he reaches age 62, count only the years between 1950 (or the year of attainment of age 21, if later) and age 62.


## CURRENTLY INSURED


### D-16. What benefits are payable if a person is only currently insured at death?

Child's benefits, mother's or father's benefits, and the lump sum death payment. Benefits for a widow(er) age 60 or over, and benefits for a dependent parent, are payable only if the worker was *fully insured* at death.

### D-17. When is a person currently insured?

A person is currently insured if he has acquired at least six quarters of coverage during the full 13-quarter period ending with the calendar quarter in which he (1) died, or (2) most recently became entitled to disability benefits, or (3) became entitled to retirement benefits.

The six quarters of coverage need not be consecutive, but they must be acquired *during* the 13-quarter period. Since insured status is based on quarters of coverage, one can work for as little as two months in two different years and be currently insured. (Calendar quarters any part of which are in an established prior period of disability are not counted in figuring the 13 quarter period, except that the first and last quarters of the disability period are counted if they are quarters of coverage.)

*Example*. Mrs. Helcher, who reached age 21 in 1975, dies in February, 1992. Mrs. Helcher had started to work in covered employment on October 1, 1988 and worked until her death. During that period, she acquired nine quarters of coverage. Mrs. Helcher was currently insured at death because she had over the required six quarters of coverage in the 13-calendar-quarter period.

## INSURED STATUS FOR DISABILITY BENEFITS AND DISABILITY "FREEZE"

**D-18. What insured status requirements must be met to qualify a person for disability benefits?**

A person is insured for disability benefits if he is fully insured (see D-15) and:

1. At least 20 of the quarters in the 40-calendar-quarter period ending with the quarter in which his disability begins are quarters of coverage; or

2. Where disability begins before age 31, at least one-half of the quarters after age 21 and the quarter in which disability begins are quarters of coverage or, if there are less than 12 quarters in such period, at least six in the last 12 quarters (including the quarter in which disability begins) are quarters of coverage.

In order to meet the 20-out-of-40 quarters requirement, the 20 quarters of coverage need not be consecutive, but they must all be acquired during the 40-quarter period. (A quarter any part of which was included in a prior period of disability is not counted as one of the 40 quarters unless it was a quarter of coverage and was either the first or last quarter of the period.) Generally speaking, this requirement is met if the person has worked five years in covered employment or covered self-employment out of the last 10 years before his disability.

If the person meets the statutory definition of blindness, provisions 1 and 2 above are waived. The only requirement is that he be fully insured.

If a disability period is established for a person, his earnings record is frozen, and the period of disability may be excluded in determining his insured status when he becomes eligible for retirement benefits or dies. The disability period may also be excluded in figuring his Primary Insurance Amount for benefit purposes (see COMPUTING BENEFITS, SECTION F). The same insured status is required to qualify a person for a disability "freeze" as is required for disability benefits.

## ALTERNATE METHOD FOR DETERMINING
## QUARTERS OF COVERAGE BEFORE 1951

### D-19. What alternate method can be used in determining the number of quarters of coverage earned before 1951?

One quarter of coverage can be counted for each $400 of total wages earned before 1951. This alternate method cannot be used, however, unless: (1) the person will be fully insured on the basis of quarters of coverage before 1951 (derived by this method) plus quarters of coverage, if any, acquired after 1950; and (2) the individual's "elapsed years" are not less than seven (see D-9).

# BENEFITS

## RETIREMENT AND DISABILITY BENEFITS

**E-1. What Social Security benefits are available for retired or disabled workers and their families?**

- A monthly Retirement benefit for a retired worker, (see E-2 to E-11).

- A monthly Disability benefit for a disabled worker, (see E-12 to E-26).

- A monthly Spouse's benefit for a retired or disabled worker's spouse if he or she is: (a) at least 62 years old, or (b) caring for at least one child (under age 16, or over age 16 and disabled if disability began before age 22) of the retired or disabled worker (see E-27 to E-35).

- A monthly Child's benefit for a retired or disabled worker's child if the child is: (a) under age 18, or (b) age 18 and a full-time high school or elementary school student, or (c) age 18 or over and disabled if the disability began before age 22 (see E-36 to E-51).

## RETIREMENT BENEFIT

**E-2. In general, what requirements must be met to qualify a person for retirement benefits?**

An individual is entitled to a retirement benefit if he or she: (1) is fully insured; (2) has reached age 62; and (3) has filed application for benefits.

**E-3. Must a person be fully insured to qualify for retirement benefits?**

Yes. (But a small monthly benefit is payable to some men who became age 72 before 1972 and some women who became age 72 before 1970—see E-106).

### E-4. What is the earliest age at which a person can start to receive retirement benefits?

Age 62. A retired worker who is fully insured can elect to start receiving a reduced benefit at any time between ages 62 and 65, or wait until age 65 and receive the full benefit rate (but see next paragraph as to later age for full benefits in 2003 and after). A person does not have to be completely retired to receive retirement benefits. He is considered "retired" if he meets the "retirement" test (see SECTION H). A fully insured person age 70 or over can receive retirement benefits even if he is not retired and regardless of the amount he earns.

The Social Security Amendments of 1983 increase the retirement age when unreduced benefits are available (presently age 65) by two months a year for workers reaching age 62 in 2000-2005; maintains age 66 for workers reaching age 62 in 2006-2016; increases by two months a year the retirement age for workers reaching age 62 in 2017-2022; and maintains age 67 for workers reaching age 62 after 2022 (i.e., reaching age 67 in 2027). The Normal Retirement Age for spouse's benefits moves upward in exactly the same way as that for workers; the Normal Retirement Age for widow(er)'s benefits also rises but in a slightly different manner (beginning for widow(er)s who attain age 60 in 2000 and reaching a Normal Retirement Age of 67 in 2029).

The 1983 amendments do not change the availability of reduced benefits at 62 but revise the reduction factors so that there is a further reduction (up to a maximum of 30% for workers entitled at age 62 after the retirement age is increased to age 67, rather than only 20 percent for entitlement at age 62 under previous law and for those reaching age 62 before 2000 under current law.) See Table, F-28.

### E-5. Must a person file application for retirement benefits?

Yes. He can file application within three months before the first month in which he becomes entitled to benefits. The earliest date for filing would be three months before the month of attaining age 62.

As evidence of his age, a claimant must ordinarily submit one or more of the following: birth certificate; church record of birth or baptism; Census Bureau notification of registration of birth; hospital birth record; physician's birth record; family Bible; naturalization record; immigration record; military record; passport; school record; vaccination record; insurance policy; labor union or fraternal record; marriage record; other evidence of probative value.

However, if a person is receiving social security disability benefits for the month before the month he or she reaches age 65 (or, in 2003 and after, such higher age as applies for receipt of full benefits), no application is required. The disability benefit is ended and the retirement benefit is begun automatically. For an explanation of how to file for benefits, see FILING FOR BENEFITS, SECTION L.

### E-6. What is the amount of a retirement benefit?

A retirement benefit which starts at Normal Retirement Age equals the worker's PIA (primary insurance amount). But a worker who elects to have benefits start before Normal Retirement Age will receive a monthly benefit equal to only a percentage of his PIA (the PIA will be reduced by 5/9 of 1% (1/180) for each of the first 36 months he is under Normal Retirement Age when payments commence and by 5/12 of 1% (1/240) for each such month in excess of 36). (See Table 9 for reduced retirement benefits.)

As a general rule, if a person takes reduced retirement benefits before Normal Retirement Age, he will continue to receive a reduced rate after Normal Retirement Age.

An individual can obtain higher retirement benefits by working past Normal Retirement Age. See F-27.

### E-7. What is the first month for which a retired person receives a retirement benefit?

A monthly benefit is available to a retired worker when he reaches age 62, provided he is fully insured.

Workers and their spouses (including divorced spouses) do not receive retirement benefits for a month unless they meet the requirements for entitlement throughout the month. The major effect of this provision is to postpone, in the vast majority of cases, entitlement to retirement benefits for persons who claim benefits in the month in which they reach age 62 to the next month, which currently means reduction for early-retirement benefits based on the 35 months before age 65, instead of on 36 months. (See F-29 and F-30.) Only in the case of a person who attains age 62 on the first day of a month can benefits be paid for the month of attainment of age 62. Note that a person attains his or her age on the day preceding the anniversary of his or her birth. For example, if an individual is born on May 2, he attains his age on May 1.

Most entitlement requirements (other than the entitlement of the worker) affecting young spouses or children of retired or disabled workers are deemed to have occurred as of the first of the month in which they occurred; however, in the case of a child who is born in or after the first month of entitlement of a retired or disabled worker, benefits are not payable for the month of birth (unless born on the first day of the month).

Retroactive benefits are usually prohibited if permanently reduced benefits (as compared with what would be payable for the month the application is filed) would occur in the initial month of eligibility. However, retroactive benefits may be applied for if: (1) with respect to widow(er)'s benefits, the application is for benefits for the month of death of the worker, if filed for in the next month; and (2) retroactive benefits for any month before attaining age 60 are applied for by a disabled widow(er) or disabled surviving divorced spouse.

### E-8. Can a person receive retirement benefits regardless of the amount of his wealth or the amount of his retirement income?

Yes, he is entitled to retirement benefits regardless of how wealthy he is. Also, the amount of retirement income he receives (e.g. dividends, interest, rents, etc.) is immaterial. He is subject to loss of benefits only because of excess earnings arising from his personal services (see E-9 and LOSS OF BENEFITS BECAUSE OF EXCESS EARNINGS, SECTION H).

### E-9. Can a person lose his retirement benefits by working?

Yes, he can lose some or all of his monthly benefits if he is under age 70 but over age 64 and earnings exceed $10,200 in 1992; or if he is under age 65 for all of 1992 and earnings exceed $7,440. The amount of loss depends on the amount of earnings in excess of these earnings limits, but in the initial year of retirement in which occurs a non-work month, no retirement benefits for a person age 65-69 will be lost for any month in which he neither (1) earned over $850 as an employee nor (2) performed any substantial services in self-employment. If his initial year of retirement is between age 62-64, the monthly earnings limit is $620.

The several dollar exempt amounts mentioned in the previous paragraph will be increased automatically after 1992 as wage levels rise. (See LOSS OF BENEFITS BECAUSE OF EXCESS EARNINGS, SECTION H.)

### E-10. When do retirement benefits end?

At the worker's death. No retirement benefit is paid for the month of death.

### E-11. Can a husband and wife both receive retirement benefits?

Yes. If each is entitled to receive benefits based on his own earnings record, each can receive retirement benefits independently of the

other's benefits. However, a woman or man who is entitled to a retirement benefit and a spouse's benefit cannot receive both in full. (For
details of how benefits are determined, see E-30.)

## DISABILITY BENEFITS

### E-12. In general, what requirements must be met to qualify a person for disability benefits?

A worker is entitled to disability benefits if he: (1) is insured for disability benefits; (2) is under age 65; (3) has been disabled for 12
months, or is expected to be disabled for at least 12 months, or has
a disability which is expected to result in death; and (4) has filed
application for disability benefits.

### E-13. What insured status is required for disability benefits?

Generally, a person is insured for disability benefits if he (a) is fully
insured, and (b) has worked under social security for at least five
of the 10 years (20-out-of-40 quarters) just before becoming disabled,
or if disability begins before age 31 but after age 24, for at least one-
half of the quarters after reaching age 21 and before becoming disabled (but not less than six). Thus, if a person becomes disabled before the quarter in which he or she attains age 24, he must have 6
quarters of coverage in the 12 quarter period ending with the quarter in which the disability began.

However, a person who had a period of disability that began before age 31, who subsequently recovered, and then became disabled
again at age 31 or later, is again insured for disability benefits if he
has one quarter of coverage for every two calendar quarters elapsing after age 21 and through the quarter in which the later period
of disability began (up to a maximum of 20 quarters of coverage out
of the last "countable" 40 calendar quarters), but excluding from such
elapsed quarters any quarters in the previous period of disability
which were not quarters of coverage. Quarters acquired during the
first period of disability are excluded in counting the "elapsed" quarters, however, and the quarters of coverage must be acquired during
the measuring period. This provision of the Social Security Amendments of 1983, effective after April 1983, provides relief to those workers who could otherwise not get disability benefits because they
did not have time following recovery from an earlier disability to work
long enough before a second disability to meet the 20-out-of-40 quarters insured status test.

**E-14. How disabled must a person be to qualify for disability benefits?**

Disability is defined as the inability to engage in any substantial gainful activity by reason of any medically determinable physical or mental impairment which can be expected to result in death or which has lasted or can be expected to last for a continuous period of not less than 12 months. A person must be not only unable to do his previous work or work commensurate with the previous work in amount of earnings and utilization of capacities but cannot, considering age, education, and work experience, engage in any other kind of substantial work which exists in the national economy. It is immaterial whether such work exists in the immediate area, or whether a specific job vacancy exists, or whether the worker would be hired if he applied for work.

In making a determination, the worker's impairment or impairments must be the primary reason for his inability to engage in substantial gainful activity, although age, education, and work experience are also taken into consideration.

The term "substantial gainful activity" is used to describe a level of work activity that is both substantial and gainful. Substantial work activity involves the performance of significant physical or mental duties, or a combination of both, which are productive in nature. Gainful work activity is activity for remuneration or profit to the individual performing it or to the persons, if any, for whom it is performed.

Impairments related to the commission of a felony for which the individual is subsequently convicted, or related to confinement in a correctional facility for conviction of a felony, may not be used to establish a disability for social security benefits.

**E-15. Does blindness qualify a person for disability benefits?**

A special definition of the term "disability" is provided for an individual age 55 or over who is blind. Such an individual is disabled for the purpose of disability benefits if he is unable to engage in substantial gainful activity requiring skills or abilities comparable to those of any gainful activity in which he has previously engaged with some regularity and over a substantial period of time.

A blind individual is considered to be engaging in substantial gainful activity if earnings exceed the monthly limitation that applies to beneficiaries at Normal Retirement Age or over who are receiving retirement benefits. See SECTION H, "Loss of Benefits Because of Excess Earnings."

Blindness, for social security purposes, means either central visual acuity of 20/200 or less in the better eye with the use of a correcting lens, or a limitation in the fields of vision such that the widest diameter of the visual field subtends an angle of 20 degrees or less. However, no benefits will be payable for any month in which the individual engages in substantial gainful activity.

### E-16. At what age can a person receive disability benefits?

At any age under 65. If a person is receiving disability benefits when he reaches Normal Retirement Age, the disability benefit automatically ends and a retirement benefit begins.

### E-17. Is there a waiting period for disability benefits?

There is a full five month waiting period. Generally, benefits will start with the 6th full month of disability. However, if application is not made until later, benefits are payable retroactively for up to 12 months, beginning with the first month after the waiting period.

Ordinarily, no benefits are payable for the first five full months of disability. Under some circumstances, however, where the person has had a prior period of disability, benefits will begin with the first full month of disability. Benefits will begin with the first full month of disability if: (1) the new disability arises within five years after the previous one ended, and (2) the new disability is expected to last for at least 12 months, or to result in death.

### E-18. When must an application for disability benefits be filed?

An application for disability benefits may be filed before the first month for which the person can be entitled to benefits. An application filed before the first month in which the applicant satisfies the requirements for disability benefits is valid only if the applicant satisfies the requirements at some time before a final decision on his application is made. If the applicant is found to satisfy the requirements, the application is deemed to have been filed in the first month in which he satisfied the requirements. An application for disability benefits may be made retroactively effective for as many as 12 months before the one which application is filed. For an explanation of how to file for benefits, see FILING FOR BENEFITS, SECTION L.

Social security disability benefits may be reinstated without a new disability application if, during the 15-month period following a trial work period, a person who has not recovered medically no longer engages in substantially gainful activity. (See E-25).

## E-19. What is the amount of a disability benefit?

The amount of a disabled worker's benefit generally equals his PIA (primary insurance amount), determined as if the worker were at Normal Retirement Age and eligible for retirement benefits in the first month of his waiting period.

However, the formula for determining a disabled worker's AIME (Average Indexed Monthly Earnings) and PIA differs from the formula used for a retiring worker. See Primary Insurance Amount, SECTION F. There are also different limits on the amount of family benefits that can be paid to a disabled worker and his family. See Maximum Family Benefits, SECTION F.

Disability benefits may be reduced before the worker attains age 65 to fully or partially offset a workers' compensation benefit or disability benefit under a federal, state, or local public law. This reduction will be made only if the total benefits payable to the worker (and dependents) under both programs exceed the higher of 80% of his or her "average current earnings" before the onset of disability, or the family's total social security benefit.

"Average current earnings" is defined as the highest of: (1) the average monthly wages used for computing primary insurance amounts for some beneficiaries, even though not used for this particular one, or (2) the average monthly earnings from covered employment and self-employment during the highest 5 consecutive years after 1950, or (3) the average monthly earnings based on the one calendar year of highest earnings from covered employment during a period consisting of the year in which disability began and the 5 preceding years.

Different factors are used in determining whether there is an offset and the amount of the offset. The factors used are determined by the date the worker first became disabled and the date the worker first became entitled to benefits. For workers who first became disabled after February 1981, and who first became entitled to disability benefits after August 1981, benefits paid as workers' compensation and received under a federal, state, or local public program will be considered in determining the amount of the offset.

Specifically excluded are all VA disability benefits, needs-based benefits, federal benefits based on employment covered for social security purposes, and state and local benefits based on covered state and local employment. Private pension or insurance benefits will also not be considered in determining the amount of the offset. The offset of benefits will continue until the worker reaches Normal Retirement Age.

For a worker disabled and receiving benefits prior to the above dates, only benefits paid as workers' compensation are considered in determining the amount of the offset. The offset of benefits stops when the worker reached age 62 (rather than age 65).

The amount of the reduction is the amount by which social security benefits plus workers' compensation and, where applicable, public disability benefits exceeds 80% of the average current earnings. The combined payments after the reduction will never be less than the total social security benefits were before the reduction. However, the amount of social security benefits can fluctuate based on the decrease or increase in the amount of workers' compensation. In addition, the amount of the reduction is adjusted periodically to take into account increases in national earnings levels as applied to the initially-determined average current earnings, but this adjustment will never decrease the amount of benefits payable on the worker's earnings record.

When a worker receives a lump-sum settlement under state workers' compensation law or under federal, state, or local public disability benefit law, the lump-sum settlement amount is subject to the offset provisions. In this situation, the lump-sum is distributed to reflect, as accurately as possible, the monthly rate that would have been paid had the lump-sum award not been made.

### E-20. Is a person entitled to disability benefits regardless of his wealth?

Yes, benefits are not payable on a "needs" basis. If a person meets the requirements for entitlement, he can receive benefits regardless of how wealthy he is.

### E-21. Can a disabled person receive disability benefits even though his spouse is employed?

Yes, if the person is entitled to benefits based on his own earnings record. Entitlement to benefits as a worker is entirely independent of a spouse's employment.

### E-22. What is the trial work period?

A trial work period is provided as an incentive for personal rehabilitation efforts for disabled workers who are still disabled but return to work. It allows them to perform services in as many as 9 months, not necessarily consecutive, without affecting their right to benefits if their impairment does not improve during this period. (Since benefits will continue for the month the disability is determined to have ceased and the two months after that, benefits may continue as much as 12 months from the beginning month of employment.)

Work and earnings during the trial work period are disregarded in determining whether the disability has ceased. However, work done in or after the trial work period is considered in determining whether the disability ceased after the end of the trial work period. Moreover, the trial work period does not prevent the consideration of any medical evidence which may demonstrate recovery before the ninth month of trial work. Thus, it is possible for benefits to terminate before the ninth month of trial work. Only one trial work period is allowed in any one period of disability.

Beginning January 1, 1992, all beneficiaries will have an opportunity to test their capacity to engage in substantial gainful activity over a sustained period of time. A disabled beneficiary will exhaust his nine-month trial work period only if he performed services in any nine months within a rolling 60-month period (that is, within any period of 60 consecutive months). Also, re-entitled disabled workers will be eligible for the trial work period.

### E-23. Can a person become entitled to disability benefits after becoming entitled to some other type of Social Security benefit?

Yes. For example, a person who is receiving a reduced retirement benefit before Normal Retirement Age can become entitled to disability benefits. However, the disability benefit is actuarially reduced for the months that the person has already received retirement benefits.

### E-24. Will a disabled person lose his benefits if he refuses to accept rehabilitation services?

A person will lose the disabled worker's benefit if he or she refuses without good cause to accept vocational rehabilitation services.

Good cause for refusing vocational rehabilitation services exists if, for example, the person is a member of any recognized church or religious sect which teaches reliance solely upon prayer or spiritual means for the treatment of any impairment, and refusal to accept vocational rehabilitation services is based solely on adherence to these teachings.

### E-25. When do a person's disability benefits end?

The last month of entitlement to a disabled worker's benefit generally is whichever of the following occurs earliest: (1) the second month after the month in which the disability ceases, (2) the month before the month the worker attains Normal Retirement Age (at which time benefits are automatically converted to retirement benefits), or (3) the month before the month in which the worker dies.

However, there are certain conditions under which benefits may continue or reentitlement to benefits may be established after disability ceases:

1. *Benefits for persons in vocational rehabilitation programs.* Benefits for disabled workers participating in a vocational rehabilitation program may continue until completion of the program or for a specified period of time in certain situations where disability ceases prior to completion of the program. This provision applies only to disabled individuals not expected to recover medically before the end of the program and who began the program before his or her disability ended.

2. *Extended period of eligibility for reentitlement to benefits following trial work period.* Disabled workers who complete the 9-month trial work period and who continue to have a disabling impairment may receive an extended period of eligibility of 36 consecutive months. If a person's work attempts fail during the extended period, payments may be reinstated without the need of a new application and disability determination. Benefits for the family of the worker are suspended during this period if the worker's benefits are suspended.

The Social Security Disability Amendments of 1984 establish a medical improvement standard under which the Social Security Administration may terminate disability benefits. Benefits can be terminated only if (1) there is substantial evidence that there has been medical improvement in the individual's impairment or combination of impairments (other than medical improvement which is not related to the person's ability to work), *and* the individual is now able to engage in substantial gainful activity (see E-14); or (2) there is substantial evidence which demonstrates that although there is no medical improvement, the person has benefited from advances in medical or vocational therapy or technology related to the ability to work, *and* he or she is now able to perform substantial gainful activity; or (3) there is substantial evidence that although there is no medical improvement, the person has benefited from vocational therapy, *and* the beneficiary can now perform substantial gainful activity; or (4) there is substantial evidence that, based on new or improved diagnostic techniques or evaluations, the person's impairment or combination of impairments is not as disabling as it was considered to be at the time of the prior determination, and, therefore, the individual is able to perform substantial gainful activity; or (5) there is substantial evidence either in the file at the original determination or newly obtained showing that the prior determination was in error; or (6) there is substantial evidence that the original decision was fraudently obtained; or (7) if the individual is engaging in substantial gainful activity and fails without good cause to cooperate in the review or follow prescribed treatment or cannot be located.

### E-26. Are benefits payable to the family of a disabled worker?

Yes. (See SPOUSE'S BENEFIT and CHILD'S BENEFIT.)

## SPOUSE'S BENEFIT

### E-27. Is the spouse of a retired or disabled worker entitled to benefits?

An individual is entitled to spouse's benefits on a worker's social security record if: (1) the worker is entitled to retirement or disability benefits, and (2) the individual has filed an application for spouse's benefits, and (3) the individual is not entitled to a retirement or disability benefit based on a primary insurance amount equal to or larger than one-half of the worker's primary insurance amount, and (4) the individual is either age 62 or over, or has in care a child under age 16, or disabled, who is entitled to benefits on the worker's social security record.

The spouse of a worker must also meet *one* of the following conditions: (1) he or she must have been married to the worker for at least one year just before filing an application for benefits, or (2) he or she must be the natural mother or father of the worker's biological child, or(3) he or she was entitled or potentially entitled to spouse's, widow(er)'s, parent's, or childhood disability benefits in the month before the month of marriage to the worker, or (4) he or she was entitled or potentially entitled to a widow(er)'s, parent's, or child's (over 18) annuity under the Railroad Retirement Act in the month before the month of marriage to the worker. A spouse is "potentially entitled" if he or she meets all the requirements for entitlement other than the filing of an application and attaining the required age.

### E-28. What is meant by having a child "in care"?

Having a child in care is a basic requirement for spouse's benefits when the spouse is under age 62. "In care" means that the mother or father (1) exercises parental control and responsibility for the welfare and care of a child under age 16 or mentally incompetent child age 16 or over, or (2) performs personal services for a disabled mentally competent child 16 years of age or over.

### E-29. Is the divorced spouse of a retired or disabled worker entitled to a spouse's benefits?

The spouse is entitled to a divorced spouse's benefit on the worker's social security record if: (1) the worker is entitled to retirement or disability benefits, (2) the spouse has filed an application for divorced spouse's benefits, (3) the spouse is not entitled to a retirement or disability benefit based on a primary insurance amount which equals or exceeds one-half the worker's primary insurance amount, (4) the spouse is age 62 or over, (5) the spouse is not married, and (6) the spouse has been married to the worker for 10 years before the date the divorce became final.

Beginning in 1985, a divorced spouse who is age 62 or over and who has been divorced for at least two years is able to receive benefits based on the earnings of a former spouse who is eligible for retirement benefits, regardless of whether the former spouse has retired or applied for benefits. However, this two-year waiting period for independent entitlement to divorced spouse's benefits is waived if the worker was entitled to benefits prior to the divorce. A spouse whose divorce took place after the couple had begun to receive retirement benefits, and whose former spouse (the worker) returned to work after the divorce (thus causing a suspension of benefits), will not lose benefits (on which he or she had come to depend).

Prior to 1985, a divorced spouse could not qualify for benefits based on the earnings of a former spouse until the former spouse had filed an application for benefits. If the former spouse became entitled to benefits but continued to work, a divorced spouse could have had some or all benefits withheld due to the former spouse's earnings.

### E-30. What is the amount of a spouse's benefit?

If the spouse of a retired or disabled worker is caring for the worker's under-age-16 or disabled child, the monthly benefit equals 1/2 of the worker's PIA regardless of his age. If the spouse is not caring for a child, monthly benefits starting at Normal Retirement Age likewise equal 1/2 of the worker's PIA; but if the spouse chooses to start receiving benefits at or after age 62, but before Normal Retirement Age, the benefit is reduced. (See Table 9 for spouse's reduced benefits.)

If the spouse chooses to receive, and is paid, a reduced spouse's benefit for months before Normal Retirement Age, he is not entitled to the full spouse's benefit rate upon reaching Normal Retirement Age. A reduced benefit rate is payable for as long as he remains entitled to spouse's benefits. (But see F-34, Recomputation of Benefits.)

A spouse will not always receive a spouse's full benefit; under the following circumstances he will receive a smaller amount:

(1) If the total amount of monthly benefits payable on the worker's social security account exceeds the Maximum Family Benefit,

all benefits (except the worker's benefit) will be reduced proportionately to bring the total within the family maximum limit. (See SECTION F, Maximum Family Benefits.)

(2) If a spouse who is not caring for a child elects to start receiving a spouse's benefit at age 62 (or at any time between the ages 62 and Normal Retirement Age), the benefit will be reduced by 25/36 of 1 percent (1/144) for each of the first 36 months that the spouse is under Normal Retirement Age when benefits commence and by 5/12 of 1 percent (1/240) for each such month in excess of 36.

(3) If the spouse is entitled to a retirement or disability benefit which is smaller than the spouse's benefit rate, he will receive a spouse's benefit equal to only the difference between the retirement or disability benefit and his full spouse's benefit rate.

(4) The amount of a spouse's monthly benefit is usually reduced if the spouse receives a pension based on his own work for a federal, state, or local government that is not covered by social security on the last day of such employment. (See E-35.)

If a spouse is entitled to a retirement or disability benefit which is larger than the spouse's benefit rate, he will receive only the retirement or disability benefit.

### E-31. What is the amount of a divorced spouse's benefit?

The amount of a divorced spouse's benefit is the same as a spouse's benefit amount. As a general rule, it will equal 1/2 of the beneficiary's former spouse's PIA and will be reduced if he or she elects to start receiving benefits before Normal Retirement Age. However, a divorced spouse's benefit is paid independently of other family benefits. In other words, it will not be subject to reduction because of the family maximum limit, and will not be taken into account in figuring the maximum limit for the former spouse's family.

### E-32. Must a spouse be dependent upon the worker for support to be eligible for a spouse's benefits?

No, a spouse is entitled to benefits if the worker is receiving benefits and the spouse is otherwise qualified. A spouse need not be dependent upon the worker, and may be independently wealthy.

### E-33. May a spouse lose benefits if the worker works or if the spouse works?

Yes, a spouse can lose some or all of his or her monthly benefits if the worker is under age 70 but over age 64 and earns over $10,200 in 1992, or the worker is under age 65 for all of 1992 and earns over

$7,440. Similarly, if the spouse is under age 70 but over age 64 and has earnings over $10,200 in 1992 (or is under age 65 for all of 1992 and has earnings of over $7,440), some or all benefits can be lost. (See LOSS OF BENEFITS BECAUSE OF EXCESS EARNINGS, SECTION H.)

When both the worker and the spouse have earnings in excess of the earnings limitation, (1) 50% of the worker's "excess" earnings are charged against the total monthly family benefits if the worker is under age 65 and 33 1/3 if the worker is under age 70 but over age 64, and then (2) the spouse's "excess" earnings are charged against his own benefits in the same manner depending upon the age of the spouse, but only to the extent that those benefits have not already been charged with the worker's excess earnings.

*Example.* Mr. Nagel, age 62, is entitled to a monthly retirement benefit of $346, and his wife, also age 62, is entitled to a monthly spouse's benefit of $162.70. Mr. Nagel had earnings that were $4,069.60 in excess of the earnings limitation. His wife had earnings which were $1,627 in excess of the earnings limitation. Mr. Nagel's earnings are charged against the total monthly family benefit of $508.70 ($346 + $162.70), so neither Mr. Nagel nor his wife receives payments for January through April (50% of $4,069.60 = $2,034.80, and 4 × $508.70 = $2,034.80). The wife's excess earnings are charged only against her own benefit of $162.70. Since her benefits for January through April were charged with the worker's excess earnings, the charging of her own earnings cannot begin until May; she thus receives no benefits for May through September (50% of $1,627 = $813.50, and 5 × $162.70 = $813.50).

*Exception.* The excess earnings of the worker do not cause deductions from the benefits of an entitled divorced spouse who has been divorced from the worker at least 2 years.

### E-34. When does a spouse's benefit end?

A spouse's benefits end when: (1) the spouse dies; or (2) the worker dies (in this case the spouse will be entitled to widow(er)'s, or mother's, or father's benefits); or (3) the worker's entitlement to disability benefits ends and he or she is not entitled to retirement benefits; or (4) the spouse is under age 62 and there no longer is a child of the worker under 16 or disabled who is entitled to child's benefits; or (5) the spouse becomes entitled to retirement or disability benefits and his or her PIA is equal to or larger than one-half of the worker's PIA; or (6) the spouse and the worker are divorced before the spouse reaches age 62 and before the spouse and worker had been married for 10 years; or (7) the divorced spouse marries someone other than the worker. However, the divorced spouse's benefit will not be terminated by marriage to an individual entitled to widow(er)'s, mother's, father's or parent's monthly benefits, or to an individual age 18 or over who is entitled to childhood disability benefits.

A spouse is not entitled to a spouse's benefit for the month in which any of the above events occurs. The last payment will be the payment for the preceding month.

### E-35. Will a spouse's benefit be reduced if the spouse is receiving a government pension?

Social security benefits payable to spouses—including surviving spouses and divorced spouses—are reduced by two-thirds of the amount of any governmental (federal, state, or local) retirement benefit payable to the spouse based on *his own earnings* in employment not covered by social security on the last day of such employment. The reduction is two-thirds of the pension. Thus, for the affected group, the spouse's benefit is reduced $2 for every $3 of the government pension.

This offset against social security benefits did not apply prior to December 1977, or if the individual (1) met all the requirements for entitlement to social security benefits that existed and were applied in January 1977, and (2) received or was eligible to receive a government pension between December 1977 and December 1982. In addition, it does not apply to those first eligible to receive a government pension prior to July 1983 if they also meet the one-half support test.

Generally, federal workers hired before 1984 are part of the Civil Service Retirement System (CSRS) and are not covered by social security. Most Federal workers hired after 1983 are covered by the Federal Employees' Retirement System Act of 1986 (FERS), which includes coverage by Social Security. The FERS law provided that employees covered by the CSRS could, from July 1, 1987 to December 31, 1987, make a one-time election to join FERS (and thereby obtain social security coverage). Thus, a CSRS employee who switched to FERS during this period immediately became exempt from the government pension offset. Also, an employee who elected FERS on or before December 31, 1987 is exempt from the government pension offset even if that person retired from government service before his FERS coverage became effective.

However, federal employees who elect to become covered under FERS during any election period which may occur on or after January 1, 1988, are exempt from the government pension offset only if they have 5 or more years of federal employment covered by Social

Security after January 1, 1988. This rule also applies to certain legislative branch employees who first become covered under FERS on or after January 1, 1988.

## CHILD'S BENEFITS
### (Child of Retired or Disabled Worker)

**E-36. Is a child, grandchild or great-grandchild of a retired or disabled worker entitled to Social Security benefits?**

Yes, if: (1) the worker is receiving benefits; and (2) the child is under age 18, or between the ages of 18 and 19 and a full-time elementary or high school student, or disabled and the disability began before age 22; and (3) the child is (or was) dependent upon the worker (but see E-38 to E-41); and (4) the child is not currently married (but see E-47); and (5) an application for the child's benefit has been filed.

In the case of the grandchild, stepgrandchild, great-grandchild or step great-grandchild of a worker: (1) the child's parents must have died or become disabled and the child must have been living with and receiving one-half of his support from his grandparent or great-grandparent for the year preceding the month of the grandparent's or great-grandparent's entitlement to benefits (or the month the grandparent's or great-grandparent's period of disability began); or (2) the child was adopted by his grandparent or great-grandparent who was the spouse of a worker who had died and the child's parent is not living with the spouse or making regular contributions toward the support of the child, provided the child was living with and receiving one-half of his support from the worker at the time of the worker's death or at the time the worker became entitled to benefits.

An illegitimate child is eligible for child's benefits if he has the right under state law to inherit the worker's intestate personal property; was acknowledged in writing by the worker; was decreed by the court to be the child's parent; or was ordered by the court to contribute to the child's support. An illegitimate child may also qualify if other evidence establishes a biological relationship, and the worker was living with or contributing to the child's support at applicable times.

**E-37. Who is considered a "child" of a retired or disabled worker for benefit purposes?**

The worker's: (1) child or legally adopted child; (2) stepchild, provided he has been a stepchild of the worker for at least one year before his application for a child's benefit is filed. Divorce of a child's parent and stepparent ends the stepparent-stepchild relationship; but if the child's entitlement to benefits has already been established at the time of divorce, his benefits are not terminated because of the divorce. (If a child is entitled to a child's benefits on both his father's and stepfather's social security accounts, he will receive only the higher benefit.)

### E-38. Must a child be dependent upon the worker to qualify for child's benefits?

Yes, but in most cases a child is deemed to be dependent upon his parent and actual dependency is immaterial. The factors that determine whether a child is "dependent" vary depending upon whether the parent is the natural or legally adopting father or mother or the stepfather or stepmother (see E-39 to E-41). Other rules also apply to grandchildren and stepgrandchildren (See E-36).

### E-39. Is a child considered to be dependent upon his father or mother regardless of actual dependency?

A child is deemed to be dependent upon his parent (father or mother). The fact that the parent and child are not living together, or the parent is not contributing to the child's support, is not a factor unless the child has been adopted by another person.

### E-40. Under what circumstances is a child considered to be dependent upon his stepfather or stepmother?

If: (1) the child is living with his stepfather or stepmother; or (2) the stepfather or stepmother is contributing at least one-half of the child's support.

### E-41. Can a child receive benefits based on one parent's Social Security account even though the other parent is working and furnishing his support?

Yes. A good example would be where the child is entitled to benefits due to the death of his mother who was a covered worker. The fact that the child's father was supporting him would not matter.

### E-42. Under what circumstances can a retired or disabled worker's child receive benefits between the ages of 18 and 22?

Benefits for full-time students between the ages of 18 and 22 who attend college or other post-secondary schools were completely phased out in April 1985.

Benefits paid to non-phaseout students age 18 or over who attend elementary or secondary schools end at age 19.

### E-43. Is the disabled child of a retired or disabled worker entitled to benefits past age 22?

Yes, if the disability began before the child reached age 22 and continued until the filing date of the application. The definition of "disability" is the same as for a worker applying for disability benefits (see E-14).

### E-44. What is the amount of the benefit for a retired or disabled worker's child?

The child of a retired or disabled worker is entitled to a monthly benefit equal to 50% of his parent's PIA. Usually this is an amount equal to one-half of the worker's benefit; but if the worker has elected to receive a reduced retirement benefit before Normal Retirement Age, the child's benefit will be based on one-half of his parent's PIA, not on one-half of the reduced benefit; and if the worker receives a larger benefit than the PIA, due to delayed retirement beyond Normal Retirement Age, the child's benefit is still only 50% of the PIA.

Although a child's full benefit is equal to one-half his parent's PIA, in many cases the benefit actually paid to a child will be smaller because of the "family maximum" limit. Thus, if the total amount of benefits based on the parent's social security account exceeds the family maximum, all benefits (except the worker's benefit) will be reduced to bring the total within the family maximum. (See Maximum Family Benefits, SECTION F, and Table 10.)

Notice that the benefit for a retired or disabled worker's child is less than the benefit for a deceased worker's child. The child of a deceased worker is entitled to a benefit equal to 75% of his deceased parent's PIA (see Child's Benefit, Child of Deceased Worker).

### E-45. Can a child lose his benefits by working?

Yes, a child can lose some or all of his benefits if he works and earns over $7,440 in 1992. (See LOSS OF BENEFITS BECAUSE OF EXCESS EARNINGS, SECTION H.)

### E-46. If the retired or disabled parent loses benefits, will the child lose benefits also?

Yes. For example, if a disabled worker loses his benefits because he refuses to accept rehabilitation services, his child's benefits will be stopped also. Or, if the disabled worker recovers and is no longer entitled to benefits, the child's benefits will end.

### E-47. Will a child lose his benefits if he marries?

Yes, with one exception: a disabled child age 18 or over will not lose his benefits because of marriage to another disabled child age 18 or over who is receiving child's benefits, or because of marriage to a person entitled to retirement, widow(er)'s, mother's, father's, parent's, disability, or spouse's benefits.

### E-48. When does a child's benefit end?

(1) When he dies; (2) when he reaches age 18 if he is neither disabled nor a full-time student; (3) when he ceases to be a full-time elementary or secondary school student or, despite being such a student, reaches age 19; (4) when he married (but not if he is a disabled child over 18 and he marries another social security beneficiary); (5) when the worker's entitlement to retirement or disability (see E-47 for exception) benefits ends for a reason other than death or attainment of age 65. (See also, E-46.)

### E-49. If a child is neither disabled nor a full-time elementary or secondary student, when does his benefit end?

When he reaches age 18, unless he marries before then. The last benefit is the benefit for the month preceding the month when he reaches age 18.

### E-50. Who files application for a child's benefits?

If the child is at least age 18 and physically and mentally competent, he must execute his own application form. Otherwise, an application may be filed on his behalf by his legal guardian or by the person (e.g. parent or relative) who is caring for him. (See FILING FOR BENEFITS, SECTION L.)

### E-51. Who receives a child's benefits?

A representative payee, such as a parent or relative, will be appointed to receive the child's benefits. However, if the child is over age 18 and competent, payment will be made directly to him. Also, if the child is under 18, away from home (e.g. in the Army), and is deemed mature enough to handle his benefit, payment may be made directly to him.

### SURVIVOR'S BENEFITS

### E-52. What benefits are payable to the survivors of a deceased insured worker?

- Mother's or Father's benefit (monthly benefit for widow(er), regardless of age, who is caring for at least one child, under 16 or disabled before age 22, of the deceased worker)—see E-53 to E-66.

- Child's benefit (monthly benefit for each child who is: under age 18; or over age 18 and disabled before age 22; or age 18 and attending elementary or high school)—see E-67 to E-80.

- Widow(er)'s benefit (monthly benefit for widow(er), or surviving divorced widow(er), age 60 or older)—see E-81 to E-90.

- Disabled Widow(er)'s benefit (monthly benefit for a disabled widow(er), age 50-60)—see E-92.

- Parent's benefit (monthly benefit for parent age 62 or older who was dependent upon deceased worker for support)—see E-93 to E-102.

- Lump-sum death payment—see E-103 to E-105.

## MOTHER'S OR FATHER'S BENEFIT

### E-53. Is the surviving spouse of an insured worker entitled to a monthly Mother's or Father's benefit at any age?

Yes, if caring for a child under age 16 or disabled before age 22. Otherwise a surviving spouse is not eligible for benefits until age 60 (or age 50-59 if disabled).

The surviving spouse of a fully or currently insured worker is entitled to a mother's or father's benefit at any age if: (1) caring for a child under age 16 or disabled before age 22 who is entitled to a child's benefit on the deceased worker's account; (2) the surviving spouse is unmarried; (3) no widow's or widower's benefit is available; (4) no retirement benefit is available based on the surviving spouse's own work record which is equal to or larger than the mother's or father's benefit; (5) application has been filed for benefits.

Prior to a 1975 Supreme Court decision, only widows were eligible for this benefit.

The Social Security Act had granted benefits to widows with minor children in their care, but denied them to widowers under the same circumstances. The court noted that the mother's benefit unjustifiably discriminated against women wage earners required to pay social security taxes by affording them less protection for their survivors than was provided male wage earners. *Weinberger v. Wiesenfeld* (43 L. Ed. 2d 514 1975).

A surviving spouse must have been married to the worker for a period of not less than nine months before his or her death. The nine-month duration-of-marriage requirement is waived if the insured person's death was accidental, or if it occurred in the line of duty while he or she was a member of a uniformed service serving on active duty, or if the widow(er) who was married to the insured person at the time of his or her death, was previously married to and divorced from him or her and the previous marriage had lasted nine months. The insured person's death is defined as accidental only if he or she received bodily injuries solely through violent, external, and accidental means and, as a direct result of the bodily injuries and independently of all other causes, died within three months after the day he or she received the injuries. The exception to the nine-month duration-of-marriage requirement does not apply if, at the time of the marriage, the insured person could not reasonably have been expected to live for nine months.

### E-54. Can a divorced spouse qualify for a survivor's benefit?

Yes, a husband or wife is entitled to a "surviving divorced mother's or father's benefit" if caring for his or her natural or adopted child who is entitled to child's benefits on the deceased divorced wife's or husband's earnings record. Prior to a 1979 court case, this benefit was provided to surviving divorced mothers only.

### E-55. Must a worker be fully insured at death to qualify a widow(er) for this benefit?

No; the mother's or father's benefit is payable if the worker was *either* fully or currently insured (See D-15 to D-17).

### E-56. What is the amount of a mother's or father's benefit?

The amount of a mother's or father's benefit is equal to 75 percent of the deceased spouse's PIA (primary insurance amount). However, because of the "family maximum" limit, the monthly benefit actually received by the surviving spouse may be less. (If the total benefits payable on one worker's social security account exceed the family maximum, all benefits are reduced proportionately to bring the total within the family maximum.) (See Maximum Family Benefits, Section F.) A surviving divorced mother's or father's benefit is the same amount. However, benefits paid to a divorced mother or father will not be reduced because of the limit on total family benefits; and such benefits are not counted in figuring the total benefits payable to others on the basis of the deceased worker's account.

If the surviving spouse is entitled to a smaller retirement or disability benefit based on his own earnings record, he will receive the benefit based on his own account, and will receive as a mother's or father's benefit only the difference between the mother's or father's benefit rate and the other benefit rate.

**E-57. What are the differences between a mother's or father's benefit and a widow(er)'s benefit?**

A *mother's or father's* benefit is payable to a surviving spouse at any age, but he or she must be caring for at least one under-age 16 or disabled child of the deceased spouse. A *widow(er)'s* benefit is not payable until the surviving spouse reaches age 60 unless disabled at age 50-59.

A surviving spouse will qualify for a *mother's or father's* benefit if the deceased spouse was either fully or currently insured at death. However, a surviving spouse will not qualify for a *widow(er)'s* benefit unless the deceased spouse was fully insured at death.

A full *mother's or father's* benefit is equal to only 75% of the deceased spouse's PIA. A full *widow(er)'s* benefit (at the Normal Retirement Age, currently age 65) is equal to 100% of the deceased spouse's PIA.

**E-58. Is a mother's or father's benefit payable regardless of the surviving spouse's need?**

Yes, if the surviving spouse qualifies (see E-53), he or she will receive benefits regardless of wealth.

**E-59. Can a surviving spouse lose some or all of the benefits by working?**

Yes, in 1992, by earning over $7,440 a year if under age 65 or $10,200 if age 65-69. (See LOSS OF BENEFITS BECAUSE OF EXCESS EARNINGS, SECTION H.) However, this loss of benefits will not cause the children to lose their benefits.

**E-60. If the only child in a surviving spouse's care loses his benefits by working, will this cause his mother or father to lose benefits?**

No. (See LOSS OF BENEFITS BECAUSE OF EXCESS EARNINGS, SECTION H.)

**E-61. Must a surviving spouse file application for a mother's or father's benefit?**

Yes, unless receiving a spouse's benefit before the worker's death. The application should be filed within six months after the worker's death because no more than six month's benefit will be paid retroactively.

**E-62. When do a mother's or father's benefits begin?**

If a surviving spouse qualifies, benefits will begin with a payment for the month in which his or her spouse died (but see E-61).

### E-63. When do a mother's or father's benefits end?

A mother's or father's benefit ceases when the youngest child reaches age 16 (unless a child is disabled). The surviving spouse can receive no further benefits until he becomes entitled to a widow(er)'s benefit at age 60 (or a disabled widow's or widower's benefits at age 50). The period during which the surviving spouse is entitled to no benefits is known as the BLACK-OUT PERIOD. The fact that a child's benefits will continue after age 16 does not entitle his mother or father to a continuation of benefits.

Generally, the mother's or father's benefit will cease if the surviving spouse dies or remarries before the youngest child is 16. Remarriage will prevent the surviving spouse from becoming entitled to mother's or father's benefits on the prior deceased spouse's social security record except where the subsequent marriage ends, whether by death, divorce, or annulment. If the subsequent marriage ends, he may become entitled or reentitled to mother's or father's benefits on the prior deceased spouse's (or former spouse's) earnings record beginning with the month the subsequent marriage ends.

Note, however, that the mother's or father's benefit will not be cut off because of remarriage to a person who is entitled to retirement, disability, wife's, husband's, widow(er)'s, father's, mother's, parent's, or childhood disability benefits.

### E-64. Will a mother's or father's benefit be reduced if he or she is receiving a government pension?

Social security benefits payable to spouses—including surviving spouses and divorced spouses—are reduced by two-thirds of the amount of any governmental (federal, state, or local) retirement benefit payable to the spouse based on *his or her own earnings* in employment not covered by social security on the last day of such employment. The reduction is two-thirds of the pension. Thus, for the affected group, the spouse's benefit is reduced $2 for every $3 of the government pension.

Prior to June 1983, the social security spouse's benefit was reduced dollar for dollar by the amount of the government pension.

This offset against social security benefits did not apply prior to December 1977, or if the individual (1) met all the requirements for entitlement to social security benefits that existed and were applied in January 1977, and (2) received or was eligible to receive a government pension between December 1977 and December 1982.

**E-65. Will a mother's or father's benefits stop when the youngest child (or only child) reaches age 16?**

Yes (unless the child is disabled and was disabled before age 22), and he or she will not become eligible for widow(er)'s benefits until age 60 (unless disabled at ages 50-59). The time in between when a surviving spouse is not entitled to any social security benefits is commonly called the *black-out period*. (But if the surviving spouse is caring for a disabled child whose disability began before age 22, mother's or father's benefits will not stop so long as the child continues to be disabled and entitled to a child's benefits.) If the surviving spouse is disabled, he or she may qualify for a disabled widow(er)'s benefit at age 50. (See E-91.)

**E-66. Does a mother or father continue to receive benefits until the youngest child (or only child) is age 22 if the child is attending school?**

No. A mother's or father's benefits are payable only so long as the child in his or her care is under age 16 or disabled. Benefits for children age 18-21 who attend college or a post-secondary school were completely phased out in April 1985. (See E-42.)

### CHILD'S BENEFIT
### (Child of Deceased Worker)

**E-67. Is a child of a deceased worker entitled to Social Security benefits?**

If a worker dies either fully *or* currently insured, each child who meets the relationship requirements is entitled to a child's benefit if: (1) under age 18, or over age 18 and disabled by a disability that began before age 22, or under age 19 and a full-time elementary or secondary school student; (2) not married; and (3) an application has been filed for benefits.

**E-68. Must a parent be fully insured at death to qualify his child for a child's benefits?**

No, the child is eligible for benefits on his parent's social security account if the parent was either fully or currently insured at death. (See D-15 to D-17.)

**E-69. Must a child have been dependent upon the deceased parent to be eligible for a child's benefit?**

The child must have been dependent upon the deceased worker.

The factors that determine whether a child is dependent upon a worker vary, depending upon whether the worker is the natural parent, the legally adopting parent, the stepparent, or the grandparent.

A child is "deemed" dependent upon the worker if the child has not been legally adopted by someone other than the worker and (1) is the legitimate child of the worker, or (2) an illegitimate child who would have the right under applicable state law to inherit intestate property from the worker as a child, or (3) the child of a void or voidable marriage, or (4) the child of an invalid ceremonial marriage, or (5) the legally adopted child of the worker adopted prior to the worker's death.

**E-70. Under what circumstances is a child considered dependent upon his grandparent, step-grandparent, great-grandparent, or step great-grandparent?**

A child is dependent upon a grandparent, step-grandparent, great-grandparent, or step great-grandparent if the child began living with such person before he or she reached age 18, and lived with the person in the U.S. and received at least one-half support from the person (1) for the year before the month the person died, or (2) for the year immediately before the month in which a period of disability began, provided the period of disability lasted until the person died. Both parents must be deceased or disabled.

**E-71. Under what circumstances is a child considered dependent upon his stepfather or stepmother?**

If: (1) the child is living with the stepfather or stepmother; or (2) the stepfather or stepmother is contributing at least one-half of the child's support.

A stepchild must have been the stepchild of the insured worker for at least 9 months immediately preceding the day the worker died, unless the worker and the child's natural or adopting parent were previously married, divorced, and then remarried at the time of the worker's death, and the 9-month duration-of-relationship requirement was met at the time of the divorce. If the death of the worker was accidental or occurred in the line of duty while a member of a uniformed service serving on active duty, the 9-month requirement may be considered satisfied, unless at the time of the marriage, the worker could not have been expected to live for 9 months. A child who was not legally adopted by the worker will nevertheless be treated as his legally adopted child if he was living in the worker's home or receiving at least one-half of his support from the worker at the time of the worker's death, and the child is adopted by the worker's surviving spouse after the worker's death (but only if adoption proceedings were instituted by the worker before his death or adoption by the surviving spouse occurs within two years after the worker's death). However, such a child will not be treated as the worker's legally adopted child if at the time of the worker's death he was receiving regular contributions toward his support from someone other than the worker or his spouse or a public or private welfare organization.

A child is eligible for benefits based on his father's social security account even if he was supported by his stepfather when his father died.

### E-72. Can a child receive benefits based on a deceased parent's Social Security account even though the other parent is still living and supporting the child?

Yes.

### E-73. Is a child age 18 or over entitled to benefits if he is attending school?

Benefits for students attending college or other post-secondary schools were completely phased out in April 1985.

Benefits paid to students age 18 who attend elementary or secondary school end at age 19.

### E-74. What is the amount of the monthly benefit for a child of a deceased worker?

The surviving child's benefit is equal to 75% of the deceased parent's PIA (primary insurance amount). However, because of the "family maximum" limit, the monthly benefit actually received by the child may be less. (If the total amount payable in benefits based on one worker's social security account exceeds the "family maximum," all benefits are reduced proportionately to bring the total within the "family maximum." (See Maximum Family Benefits, SECTION F.)

A child entitled to benefits based on more than one worker's record will get the benefit based on the record that provides him the highest amount, if the payment does not reduce the benefits of any other individual who is entitled to benefits based on the same earnings record.

### E-75. Will a child lose benefits if he or his parent works?

The child can lose part or all of his benefits if he earns over $7,440 in 1992. However, none of the child's benefits will be lost because his surviving parent works. Also, the child's work will not affect his parent's benefits. (See LOSS OF BENEFITS BECAUSE OF EXCESS EARNINGS, SECTION H.)

### E-76. If a child is entitled to benefits on more than one person's Social Security account, will he receive both benefits?

No, he will receive only the higher benefit. (But see F-35.)

### E-77. When does a child's benefit begin?

Ordinarily, the first benefit is payable for the month in which the parent died. However, unless the child was receiving benefits before the parent's death, an application should be filed within six months after death. Benefits will be paid retroactively for not more than six months.

### E-78. When does a child's benefit end?

A child's benefit ends: (1) at death; or (2) at age 18 (age 19 if full-time elementary or secondary school student); or (3) when disability ceases if benefits are being received only because the child was disabled before age 22 (but further benefits may be available if disability occurs again within seven years after childhood disability benefits terminate); or (4) when married. However, marriage of a disabled child age 18 or over to another social security beneficiary over age 18 (other than to a person receiving child's benefits under age 18 or age 18 as a full-time elementary or secondary school student) will ordinarily not terminate the child's benefits.

The benefits of a childhood disability beneficiary, regardless of sex, continue after the child's spouse is no longer eligible for benefits as a childhood disability beneficiary or disabled worker beneficiary.

The child is not entitled to a payment for the month in which any of the foregoing events occur, but benefits will be continued through the second month after the month that a disabled child's disability ceases.

### E-79. Will a child's benefits end if he marries?

Yes, as a general rule. However, marriage of a disabled child over age 18 to another social security beneficiary over age 18 will ordinarily not terminate the child's benefits (see E-78).

### E-80. Who files application for a child's benefits and who receives the benefits?

See E-50 and E-51.

## WIDOW(ER)'S BENEFIT

### E-81. Is the widow(er) of an insured worker entitled to benefits if there are no children in his or her care?

A widow(er) is entitled to a widow(er)'s benefit based on the deceased spouse's earnings if: (1) the widow(er) is age 60 or over, or is between the ages of 50 and 60 and disabled; (2) the widow(er)'s spouse was fully insured at his or her death; (3) the widow(er) is not entitled to a retirement benefit that is equal to or larger than the worker's primary insurance amount (PIA); (4) the widow(er) has filed an application for widow(er)'s benefits; and (5) the widow(er) is not married except under special circumstances discussed below.

In addition, one of the following conditions must be met: (1) the widow(er) was married to the deceased worker for at least 9 months just before he or she died (see exceptions below); or (2) the widow(er) is the natural mother or father of the worker's child (this requirement is met if a live child was born to the worker and the widow(er), although the child need not still survive); or (3) the widow(er) legally adopted the worker's child during their marriage and before the child reached age 18; or (4) the widow(er) was married to the worker when they both legally adopted a child under age 18; or (5) the worker legally adopted the widow(er)'s child during their marriage and before the child reached age 18; or (6) the widow(er) was entitled or potentially entitled to wife's, husband's, parent's, or childhood disability benefits, or to a widow(er)'s, child's (age 18 or over) or parent's annuity under the Railroad Retirement Act, in the month before the month the widow(er) married the deceased worker.

The 9-month duration of marriage requirement is waived if the insured person's death was accidental or it occurred in the line of duty while he or she was a member of a uniformed service serving on active duty, or if the widow(er) who was married to the insured person at the time of his or her death, was previously married to and divorced from him or her and the previous marriage had lasted 9 months.

The insured person's death is defined as accidental only if he or she received bodily injuries solely through violent, external, and accidental means and, as a direct result, died within 3 months after the day he or she received the injuries. The exception to the 9-month duration of marriage requirement does not apply if, at the time of marriage, the insured person could not reasonably have been expected to live for 9 months.

An application for widow(er)'s benefits is not required if the man or woman was age 65 or over and entitled to spouse's benefits for the month immediately preceding the month in which the worker died, or if he or she was entitled to father's or mother's benefits for the month immediately preceding the month in which he or she attained age 65. If an entitled spouse is between ages 62 and 65 when the worker dies and he or she is not also entitled to a disability or retirement benefit, the spouse's benefits will automatically be converted to widow(er)'s benefits.

### E-82. Must the worker be fully insured at death to qualify the widow(er) for a widow(er)'s benefit?

Yes, the widow(er) will not be entitled to a widow(er)'s benefit at age 60 or over if the worker was only currently insured at death (see D-16, D-17, E-57).

### E-83. Can the divorced spouse of a deceased worker qualify for a widow(er)'s benefit?

A widow(er) is entitled to surviving divorced spouse's benefits on the worker's social security record if: (1) the widow(er) is age 60 or over, or is between ages 50 and 60 and disabled; (2) the deceased spouse was fully insured at his or her death; (3) the widow(er) is not married (but see E-86 below); (4) the widow(er) is not entitled to a retirement benefit that is equal to or greater than the deceased worker's primary insurance amount (PIA); and (5) the widow(er) has filed an application for widow(er)'s benefits.

### E-84. What is the earliest age at which a widow(er) can receive a widow(er)'s benefit?

A widow(er) can elect to start receiving a reduced widow(er)'s benefit at age 60 (see E-85). But a disabled widow(er) can start receiving benefits at age 50.

### E-85. What is the monthly rate of a widow(er)'s benefit?

A widow(er) who is eligible for a widow(er)'s benefit may apply for a reduced benefit at any time between 60 and Normal Retirement Age, or may wait until Normal Retirement Age to receive a full widow(er)'s benefit. If the widow(er) is Normal Retirement Age or older when benefits commence, the monthly benefit is equal to 100% of the deceased worker's PIA (the amount the worker would have been entitled to receive upon retirement at Normal Retirement Age) plus any additional amount the deceased worker was entitled to because of delayed retirement credits (the delayed retirement credit is discussed at E-88 and F-27). If the worker was actually receiving benefits that began before Normal Retirement Age, the widow(er) would be entitled to an amount equal to the reduced benefit the worker would have been receiving had he lived (but not less than 82.5% of the PIA).

If the widow(er) chooses to receive, and is paid, a reduced widow(er)'s benefit for months before Normal Retirement Age, he or she is not entitled to the widow(er)'s full benefit rate upon reaching Normal Retirement Age. A reduced benefit is payable for as long as he or she remains entitled to widow(er)'s benefits.

Currently, the widow(er)'s benefit is reduced by 19/40 of 1% for each month that the widow(er) is under age 65 when the benefits commence. A benefit beginning at age 60 will equal 71.5% of the deceased worker's PIA; one beginning at age 62 will equal 82.9% of the PIA. When Normal Retirement Age is more than 65, the 71.5% at age 60 will remain unchanged, but the reduction factor will be different (based on 71.5% at age 60 and 100% at Normal Retirement Age).

The monthly payment amount of a widow(er) who remarries after attaining age 60 is not reduced.

If there are other survivors entitled to benefits based on the deceased worker's earnings record, the widow(er) could receive a smaller benefit because of the family maximum limit. (See Maximum Family Benefits SECTION F, and Table 10.)

If the widow(er) has in care the deceased spouse's child, under 16 or disabled, who is entitled to child's benefits, for some months while he or she is under 65, his or her widow(er)'s benefits are not reduced for those months below 75% of the deceased spouse's PIA.

The Social Security Amendments of 1983 provide a new way of figuring benefits for a widow(er) who becomes eligible for benefits in 1985 or later and whose spouse dies before reaching age 62. The new benefit computation method will provide higher benefits for most widow(er)s whose spouses die before age 62. (See Computing Benefits, SECTION F.)

The surviving divorced spouse's benefit is the same amount as a widow(er)'s benefit. However, it is paid independently of benefits for the former spouse's family. In other words, it is not subject to reduction because of the family maximum limit, and does not affect the family maximum for the former spouse's family.

A widow(er) who files an application for actuarially reduced widow(er)'s benefits in the calendar month following the month his or her spouse died is entitled to one month of retroactive benefit payments.

### E-86. How does remarriage affect a widow(er)'s benefits?

A widow(er)'s remarriage after age 60 will not prevent him or her from becoming entitled to widow(er)'s benefits on his or her prior deceased spouse's earnings.

Remarriage does not prevent entitlement for disabled surviving spouses who marry at age 50-59, disabled divorced surviving spouses who marry at age 50-59, and divorced surviving spouses who marry at age 60 or older.

A widower is entitled to benefits even when he or she remarries prior to the death of the former spouse.

Prior to 1984, the remarriage of a surviving divorced spouse, disabled surviving spouse, or disabled divorced surviving spouse prevented his or her entitlement except where his or her subsequent marriage ended, whether by death, divorce, or annulment. If the subsequent marriage ended, the widow(er) could become entitled or reentitled to widow(er)'s benefits on his or her prior deceased spouse's (or former spouse's) earnings record beginning with the month the subsequent marriage ended.

A widow(er) who has remarried prior to attaining age 60 but is not married at the time he or she applies for benefits is entitled to a widow(er)'s benefit.

There is a distinct advantage in being able to receive the widow(er)'s benefit instead of the spouse's benefit. Part or all of a spouse's benefit could be lost if the new spouse is under age 70 and loses some of his or her benefits by working. The widow(er)'s benefit, on the other hand, will be unaffected by the new spouse's work.

### E-87. If a widow(er) is entitled to a retirement benefit and a widow(er)'s benefit, will he or she receive both benefits?

No, the widow(er) will receive the retirement benefit plus the difference if the widow(er)'s benefit is greater. In other words, the widow(er) will receive only the larger benefit. (See also Reduction in Benefits, SECTION F.)

### E-88. How does the delayed retirement credit affect a widow(er)'s benefit?

A widow(er) whose spouse reached age 65 in 1982-89 receives an increase in benefits equal to 3% for each year (1/4 of 1% per month) in which his or her spouse deferred retirement benefits between age 65 and 70. A widow(er) whose spouse reached age 65 before 1982 receives a benefit increase equal to 1% for each year (1/12 of 1% per month) that his or her spouse defers receiving retirement benefits between age 65 and 70.

Beginning in 1990, the delayed retirement credit is gradually increased by 1/2 of 1% every other year from 3% per year for workers age 65 before 1990 until reaching 8% per year for workers reaching the Normal Retirement Age after 2008 (in 2009, the Normal Retirement Age will be 66). The delayed retirement credit is based on the year of attainment of age 62, not the year of work, and it can be earned only after Normal Retirement Age. (See F-27 for further information.)

A surviving divorced spouse is entitled to the same increase that had been applied to the benefit of the deceased worker or for which the deceased was eligible at the time of death.

### E-89. Can a widow(er) lose benefits by working?

Yes. Although benefits are payable regardless of how wealthy the widow is, she will lose some or all of her benefits if she is under age 70 but over age 64 and earnings exceed $10,200 in 1992; or if she is under age 65 for all of 1992 and earnings exceed $7,440. (See LOSS OF BENEFITS BECAUSE OF EXCESS EARNINGS, SECTION H.)

### E-90. Will a widow(er)'s benefits be reduced if he or she is receiving a government pension?

Social security benefits payable to spouses—including surviving spouses and divorced spouses—are reduced by two-thirds of the amount of any governmental (federal, state, or local) retirement benefit payable to the spouse based on *his or her own earnings* in employment not covered by social security on the last day of such employment. The reduction is two-thirds of the pension for people eligible for a government pension. Thus, for the affected group, the spouse's benefit is reduced $2 for every $3 of the government pension.

This offset against social security benefits did not apply prior to December 1977, or if the individual (1) met all the requirements for entitlement to social security benefits that existed and applied in January 1977, and (2) received or was eligible to receive a government pension between December 1977 and December 1982.

Generally, federal workers hired before 1984 are part of the Civil Service Retirement System (CSRS) and are not covered by social security. Federal workers hired after 1983 are covered by the Federal Employees' Retirement System Act of 1986 (FERS), which includes coverage by social security. The FERS law provided that employees covered by the CSRS be given the opportunity from July 1, 1987 to December 31, 1987 to make a one-time election to join FERS (and thereby obtain social security coverage). Thus, a CSRS employee who switched to FERS during this period immediately became exempt from the government pension offset.

However, federal employees who switch from CSRS to FERS during any election period which may occur on or after January 1, 1988, are exempt from the government pension offset only if they have 5 or more years of federal employment covered by social security beginning January 1, 1988. This rule also applies to certain legislative branch employees who first become covered under FERS on or after January 1, 1988.

### E-91. When do a widow(er)'s benefits end?

The widow(er)'s benefit ends: (1) when the widow(er) dies; (2) when the widow(er) becomes entitled to a retirement benefit which is as large as or larger than the deceased worker's PIA; or (3) when the widow(er)'s disability ceases.

Benefits are paid until the second month after the month in which the disability ceased, except that entitlement continues if the widow(er) reaches Normal Retirement Age on or before the last day of the third month after the disability ends.

## DISABLED WIDOW(ER)'S BENEFIT

### E-92. Is a disabled widow(er) entitled to benefits starting before age 60?

A disabled widow(er) (or surviving divorced widow(er)) who otherwise qualifies for a widow(er)'s benefit can start receiving a disabled widow(er)'s benefit at any time after attaining age 50 and before attaining age 60. The monthly benefit will be based on 100% of the deceased spouse's PIA, but will be reduced by 28.5% so that the benefit equals 71.5% of the deceased spouse's PIA at age 60. The monthly benefit remains at 71.5% of the deceased spouse's PIA for disabled widow(er)'s between ages 50 and 59. Once established, the benefit rate remains the same; it will not be increased when the widow(er) reaches age 60 or Normal Retirement Age. Benefits are payable only after a waiting period of five months.

To be eligible for a disabled widow(er)'s benefit, the widow(er) must become totally disabled within seven years of the spouse's (or former spouse's) death, or in the case of a widowed mother or father, before or within seven years after the mother's or father's benefit ends. The widow(er) must be unable to engage in any gainful activity, must have become disabled no later than 7 years after the worker died or 7 years after the widow(er) was previously entitled to benefits on the worker's earnings record, and must have been disabled throughout a 5 month waiting period (unless previously entitled to disabled widow(er)'s benefits).

Prior to 1991, the test of disability was more restrictive than that for disabled workers and childhood disability beneficiaries, and was based solely on the level of severity of impairment without regard to nonmedical factors such as age, education, and work experience. Beginning with disability applications filed or pending on or after January 1, 1991, widow(er)s must only meet the definition of disability used to determine if workers are entitled to disability benefits. In other words, the widow(er) must be unable to engage in any substantial gainful activity by reason of physical or mental impairment. The impairment must be medically determinable and expected to last for at least 12 months or result in death.

## PARENT'S BENEFITS

### E-93. Under what circumstances is a deceased worker's parent entitled to benefits?

The parent of an individual who died fully insured is entitled to a parent's benefit if he or she: (1) has attained age 62; (2) was receiving at least one-half of his or her support from the worker; (3) has filed application for benefits; (4) is not entitled to a retirement benefit that is equal to or larger than the amount of the unadjusted parent's benefit; and (5) has filed proof of support within the specified time limit.

The support requirement must be met at (1) the time that the insured person died, or (2) the beginning of a period of disability that was established for the deceased if it continued up until the month in which he or she died. Evidence of support must be filed within the two-year period (1) after the date of the death of the insured person, if the support requirement was met at the time of death, or (2) after the month in which the insured person had filed an application to establish a period of disability if the support requirement was met at the time the disability began. Evidence of support must be filed within the appropriate period even though the parent may not be eligible for benefits at that time (e.g., has not reached retirement age). The time limit may be extended for good cause.

The insured provides one-half of a parent's support if (1) he or she makes regular contributions for the parent's ordinary living costs; (2) the amount of these contributions equals or exceeds one-half of the parent's ordinary living costs; and (3) any income (from sources other than the insured person) for support purposes is one-half or less of the parent's ordinary living costs.

The insured is not providing at least one-half of the parent's support unless he or she has done so for a reasonable period of time. Ordinarily, the Social Security Administration will consider a reasonable period to be the 12-month period immediately preceding the time when the one-half support requirement must be met.

### E-94. Who is a parent for the purpose of receiving a parent's benefit?

For the purpose of this benefit, a "parent" is the natural father or mother of the worker, a stepparent by a marriage contracted before the worker reached age 16, or a person who adopted the worker before age 16.

### E-95. What is the amount of a parent's monthly benefit?

A parent's benefit is equal to 82-1/2% of the deceased worker's PIA (primary insurance amount), if there is only one eligible parent. If two parents are entitled to benefits, the benefit for each is 75% of the worker's PIA. The full benefit is payable at age 62 (to father or mother). However, because of the maximum family limit, the monthly benefit actually received by a parent (parents) may be less. (If total monthly benefits payable on the basis of one worker's earnings record exceeds the family maximum, all benefits are reduced proportionately to bring the total within the family maximum.) (See Maximum Family Benefits, SECTION F.)

### E-96. Can a parent receive benefits even if the worker's widow(er) and children are eligible for benefits?

Yes. (But see E-97.)

### E-97. May benefits payable to a parent reduce the benefits payable to the worker's widow(er) and children?

Yes, because the total amount of monthly benefits based on one worker's social security account is limited by a maximum family benefit ceiling. If total benefits computed separately would exceed this limit, all benefits are reduced proportionately to bring the total within the family maximum. (See Maximum Family Benefits, SECTION F.)

**E-98. Is a parent's benefit starting at age 62 smaller than one starting at age 65?**

No, the full parent's benefit is payable (to a father or mother) at age 62.

**E-99. If a person is entitled to a parent's benefit and a retirement benefit, will he receive both full benefits?**

If the parent is also eligible for a retired worker's benefit based on his own earnings record, he will receive the retired worker's benefit if it equals or exceeds the parent's benefit. However, he is not compelled to take a reduced retired worker's benefit before age 65. He can receive the parent's benefit; then switch to a full retired worker's benefit at age 65.

**E-100. Can a person lose his parent's benefit by working?**

Yes, he can lose some or all of his benefits if he is under age 70 but over age 64 and earnings exceed $10,200 in 1992; or if he is under age 65 for all of 1992 and earnings exceed $7,440. (See LOSS OF BENEFITS BECAUSE OF EXCESS EARNINGS, SECTION H.)

**E-101. When do a parent's benefits end?**

When the parent dies or remarries after the worker's death (but see E-102), or when the parent becomes entitled to a retirement benefit or disability benefit equal to or larger than the unadjusted parent's benefit.

**E-102. If a parent remarries after the worker's death, will he lose his benefits?**

Yes, unless the parent marries an individual who is receiving widow(er)'s, mother's, father's, spouse's, parent's, or disabled child's benefits.

## LUMP-SUM DEATH PAYMENT

**E-103. What is the amount of the Social Security lump sum death payment?**

A lump sum death benefit of $255 is paid upon the death of an insured worker, provided he is survived by a spouse who was living in the same household as the deceased at the time of death, or a spouse or dependent child eligible to receive social security benefits for the month of death based on his earnings record. Different rules apply for deaths prior to September 1, 1981.

The lump-sum death payment is paid in the following order of priority:

(a) The widow(er) of the deceased wage earner who was living in the same household as the deceased wage earner at the time of death;

(b) The widow(er) (excluding a divorced spouse) who is eligible for or entitled to benefits based on the deceased wage earner's record for the month of death;

(c) Children who are eligible for or entitled to benefits based on the deceased wage earner's record for the month of death.

If no surviving widow(er) or child as defined above survives, no lump sum is payable.

However, beginning on or after January 1, 1989, if an otherwise eligible widow(er) dies before making application for the lump-sum death payment or before negotiating the benefit check, the legal representative of the estate of the deceased widow(er) may claim the lump-sum payment. Where the legal representative of the estate is a state or political subdivision of a state, the lump-sum death benefit is not payable.

The lump-sum death benefit is not payable to an otherwise ineligible child of the wage earner after the wage earner's widow, who applied for the benefit, died before it could be paid. (*Social Security Ruling* 85-24a, October 1985).

### E-104. Is the lump-sum death benefit payable only if the worker was fully insured at death?

No, it is payable if the worker was either fully or currently insured.

### E-105. Must an application be made for the lump-sum death benefit?

An application need not be made by the widow(er) if he or she was receiving a spouse's benefit when the insured person died. Otherwise, an application must be filed within two years after the insured person's death unless good cause can be shown why the application was not filed within the two-year period.

## UNINSURED PERSONS AGE 72

**E-106. What special benefit is payable to uninsured persons age 72?**

A special cash payment may be made to a person who attained age 72 before 1968 even though having no quarters of coverage. This special cash payment may also be made to a man who attained age 72 after 1967 and before 1972 and a woman who attained age 72 after 1967 and before 1970 and who have too few quarters of coverage to be fully insured, but sufficient to meet a special test. This special benefit is $173.60 a month for January-November 1992, or $347.20 a month if both spouse's qualify. These monthly benefits are generally available regardless of need; but they are not payable to persons who are receiving benefits under certain federally funded public assistance programs, and are reduced by the amount of any federal, state or local government-employee pensions. The cost of the benefits does not come from social security taxes but from the general revenues.

The special monthly payment terminates with the month before the month the individual dies.

## SUSPENSION OF BENEFITS FOR INMATES AND WAR CRIMINALS

**E-107. Can benefits payable to an inmate in a penal institution or a deported war criminal be suspended?**

The Social Security Amendments of 1983 suspended payment of social security benefits to convicted felons while in prison; but benefits to auxiliaries based on an incarcerated individual's earnings are not affected. This provision of the 1983 amendments became effective for benefits payable after April 1983.

In addition, benefits to individual's deported as Nazi war criminals under the Immigration and Nationality Act are automatically terminated.

# COMPUTING BENEFITS

### F-1. In general, how are social security benefits determined?

Benefits payable under the retirement, survivors, and disability benefits program are almost always based on the insured's social security earnings since 1950. (Under some circumstances—where an individual has little or no earnings since 1950—benefits may be computed based on earnings since 1937.)

The wage indexing formula is used to compute benefits if disability, death or age 62 occurs after 1978. (See F-4.)

If disability, death or age 62 occurred before 1979, benefits are determined using the simplified old-start benefit computation method. (See F-2.)

A transition period took place from 1979 through 1983. A worker who became 62, or a worker who died after reaching age 62 during this period, is guaranteed that the method producing the larger benefit will be used.

To be eligible for the guarantee the worker must (1) have had income credited for one year prior to 1979, and (2) must not have been disabled prior to 1979.

The transitional guarantee does not apply to disability computations—even if disability occurs after reaching age 62. It does, however, apply to benefits for survivors if the insured becomes 62—then dies—during the transition period. (See F-19.)

### THE SIMPLIFIED OLD-START BENEFIT COMPUTATION METHOD

### F-2. How are benefits computed under the simplified old-start benefit computation method?

The simplified old-start benefit computation method must be used if disability, death, or age 62 occurred before 1979.

**Step I.** Count the number of years elapsed after 1950 (or after year the insured reached age 21, if later) and before (not including) the year of death, disability, or year of attaining age 62 (65 for worker born before 1911—64 if born in 1911—63 if born in 1912).

**Step II.** Subtract five. (Also subtract any years that fell wholly or partly in a period of disability.) The result is the number of years of earnings (but not less than two) to be used in computing Average Monthly Earnings (AME).

**Step III.** List earnings for each year starting with 1951 and including the year in which the worker died—or the year *prior* to disability or application for old-age benefits. Earnings listed can't exceed $3,600 (1951-1954); $4,200 (1955-1958); $4,800 (1959-1965); $6,600 (1966-1967); $7,800 (1968-1971); $9,000 (1972); $10,800 (1973); $13,200 (1974); $14,100 (1975); $15,300 (1976); $16,500 (1977); $17,700 (1978); $22,900 (1979); $25,900 (1980); $29,700 (1981); $32,400 (1982); $35,700 (1983); $37,800 (1984); $39,600 (1985); $42,000 (1986); $43,800 (1987); $45,000 (1988); $48,000 (1989); $51,300 (1990); $53,400 (1991); and $55,500 (1992).

**Step IV.** From this list, select years of highest earnings (same number found in step I).

**Step V.** Total the earnings in the selected years—divide by the number of months in those years (drop cents). This is the worker's Average Monthly Earnings.

A worker's Average Monthly Earnings are subject to recalculation if earnings in his year of retirement or year of disability are higher than the lowest year of earnings used in the original calculation. Earnings in the last year are substituted for earnings in the lowest year if this results in higher Average Monthly Earnings.

**Step VI.** Determine the insured's Primary Insurance Amount (PIA) from Table 12.

## PRIMARY INSURANCE AMOUNT

### F-3. What is the Primary Insurance Amount (PIA)?

The Primary Insurance Amount is the basic unit used to determine the amount of each monthly benefit payable under social security. It applies to both the old and new method of computing benefits.

A disabled worker—or a retired worker whose retirement benefits start at Normal Retirement Age—receives monthly benefits equal to the PIA. Retired workers who are fully insured and whose retirement benefits start *after* Normal Retirement Age also receive an additional delayed retirement credit. (See F-27.)

Monthly benefits for members of an insured worker's family (dependent's and survivor's benefits) are all figured as percentages of the worker's PIA. (See Table 1.)

The total amount of monthly benefits payable on a worker's social security account is limited by a "maximum family benefit" which is also related to the worker's PIA.

In some instances, monthly benefits will be reduced if the insured elects to receive benefits before a specified age. (See F-29.)

The retirement benefit is reduced if the retired worker (man or woman) elects to start receiving a benefit at or after age 62 but before Normal Retirement Age. The benefit for the spouse of a retired worker is also reduced if received before Normal Retirement Age. (See F-29, F-30 and Table 9.)

The benefit for a widow(er) is reduced if he or she elects to start receiving benefits at or after age 60 but before Normal Retirement Age. (See F-31 and Table 10.)

Disabled widower's benefits are payable beginning at age 50 for disability occurring before age 60, and are always reduced from what would have been payable at Normal Retirement Age. (See E-92.)

The law provides a minimum benefit for insured workers and for survivors of insured workers when the worker had many years of coverage. (See F-20 and F-21.)

## THE "WAGE INDEXING" BENEFIT COMPUTATION METHOD

### F-4. Why did Congress require a new method for computing benefits in 1979 and after?

Benefits had traditionally been based on a worker's average earnings during his working life. As the worker's earnings increased, his potential future benefits also increased. Since the 1972 amendments, benefits for future beneficiaries had also been increased whenever the Consumer Price Index had risen, and price rises exceeded the rates expected by Congress. Thus, as wages increased to reflect price increases and as prices have increased to reflect wage increases, there was an upward spiraling of benefit levels which placed a much heavier burden on the social security trust funds than was intended by Congress.

The benefit computation method used prior to the 1977 amendments was flawed under certain economic conditions. As a result, over the years, benefit amounts would increase greatly in relative terms, *and* eventually many workers would have received retirement benefits greater than their wage levels when they retired.

### F-5. How is the relationship between earnings levels and benefit levels stabilized under the "wage indexing" method?

The method for stabilizing the relationship between benefit levels and earnings levels is known as "decoupling." Decoupling means that cost-of-living increases will continue to apply to keep benefits inflation-proof, but only after a person either becomes eligible for benefits, or dies before becoming eligible.

### F-6. In general, how is the PIA computed under the "wage indexing" method?

It is based on "indexed" earnings over a fixed number of years after 1950. (Indexing is a mechanism for expressing prior years' earnings in terms of their current dollar value.) Previous computations used actual earnings and a PIA Table. The "wage indexing" method uses a formula to determine the PIA.

Step I. Index the earnings record

Step II. Determine the Average Indexed Monthly Earnings (AIME)

Step III. Apply the PIA formula to the AIME.

### F-7. Who should use the "wage indexing" benefit computation method?

The "wage indexing" method applies where first eligibility is after 1978. First eligibility is the earliest of (1) the year of death; (2) the year disability begins; or (3) the year the insured becomes 62.

However, if the worker was entitled to a disability benefit before 1979—and that benefit terminated more than 12 months before death, another disability, or age 62—the new method will be used in determining the PIA for the subsequent entitlement. (See F-14.)

### F-8. What earnings are used in computing a person's Average Indexed Monthly Earnings (AIME)?

The AIME is based on social security earnings for years after 1950. This includes wages earned as an employee and/or self-employment income. (For an explanation of the terms wages and self-employment income, see SECTION C.)

Only earnings credited to the person's social security account can be used and the maximum earnings creditable for specific years are as follows:

$55,500 for 1992

$53,400 for 1991

$51,300 for 1990

$48,000 for 1989

$45,000 for 1988

$43,800 for 1987

$42,000 for 1986

$39,600 for 1985

$37,800 for 1984

$35,700 for 1983

$32,400 for 1982

$29,700 for 1981

$25,900 for 1980

$22,900 for 1979

$17,700 for 1978

$16,500 for 1977

$15,300 for 1976

$14,100 for 1975

$13,200 for 1974

$10,800 for 1973

$9,000 for 1972

$7,800 for years 1968-1971

$6,600 for years 1966-1967

$4,800 for years 1959-1965

$4,200 for years 1955-1958

$3,600 for years 1951-1954

## F-9. How is the earnings record indexed for the AIME computation?

The AIME is based on the earnings record after wages have been indexed. Indexing creates an earnings history which more accurately reflects the value of the individual's actual earnings in comparison to the national average wage level at the time of eligibility. Earnings for each year are indexed up to the "indexing year," the second year before the worker reaches age 62, or dies or becomes disabled before age 62.

Wages are indexed by applying a ratio to the worker's earnings for each year beginning with 1951. The ratio is the "indexing average wage" for the second year before the year of the worker's eligibility for benefits or death, divided by the "indexing average wage" for the year being indexed. Thus, indexed earnings for each year are computed as follows:

| Worker's Actual Earnings (Up to the Social Security Maximum) for Year to be Indexed | | Average Earnings of All Workers in Indexing Year (Second year before Eligibility or Death) *indexing year* Average Earnings of All Workers for Year being Indexed |
|---|---|---|
| | X | |

*Example.* Mr. Martin earned $4,000 in 1957 and reached age 62 in 1992. The indexing average wage for 1990 (his "indexing year") was $21,027.98 and the indexing average wage for 1957 was $3,641.72. Indexed earnings for 1957 are computed as follows:

$$\$4,000 \ \ X \ \ \frac{\$21,027.98}{\$\ 3,641.72} = \$23,096.76$$

Indexed earnings of $23,096.76 are used in place of actual earnings for 1957 in Mr. Martin's AIME computation.

The indexing formula must be applied to earnings in each year after 1950—up to, but not including, the "indexing year." Actual earnings are used for the indexing year and all later years.

The list below shows the indexing average wages for each year beginning with 1951. These amounts must be used in 1992 to index earnings from 1951 through the "indexing year."

| | | | | |
|---|---|---|---|---|
| 1951 | $2,799.16 | | 1957 | $3,641.72 |
| 1952 | $2,973.32 | | 1958 | $3,673.80 |
| 1953 | $3,139.44 | | 1959 | $3,855.80 |
| 1954 | $3,155.64 | | 1960 | $4,007.12 |
| 1955 | $3,301.44 | | 1961 | $4,086.76 |
| 1956 | $3,532.36 | | 1962 | $4,291.40 |

| 1963 | $4,396.64 | 1977 | $9,779.44 |
| 1964 | $4,576.32 | 1978 | $10,556.03 |
| 1965 | $4,658.72 | 1979 | $11,479.46 |
| 1966 | $4,938.36 | 1980 | $12,513.46 |
| 1967 | $5,213.44 | 1981 | $13,773.10 |
| 1968 | $5,571.76 | 1982 | $14,531.34 |
| 1969 | $5,893.76 | 1983 | $15,239.24 |
| 1970 | $6,186.24 | 1984 | $16,135.07 |
| 1971 | $6,497.08 | 1985 | $16,822.51 |
| 1972 | $7,133.80 | 1986 | $17,321.82 |
| 1973 | $7,580.16 | 1987 | $18,426.51 |
| 1974 | $8,030.76 | 1988 | $19,334.04 |
| 1975 | $8,630.92 | 1989 | $20,099.55 |
| 1976 | $9,226.48 | 1990 | $21,027.98 |

Each year before November 1, the Department of Health and Human Services publishes the indexing average wage for the next indexing year. The indexing average wage for 1991—the "indexing year" for those reaching age 62, or dying or becoming disabled before age 62 in 1993—will be published by November 1992.

It's important to remember that the "indexing year" is related to the year of first *eligibility* and not necessarily to the year of *entitlement*. A person filing for a retirement benefit in 1992 at age 64 is first *eligible* in 1990—at age 62—and his earnings record will be indexed based on the indexing year 1988 (two years prior to first eligibility).

### F-10. How do you determine a person's Average Indexed Monthly Earnings (AIME)?

Earnings listed in the records of the Social Security Administration—up to the annual wage limitation—are the basis for computing the AIME.

**Step I.** Count the *number* of years *after* 1950 (or after year person reached age 21, if later) and *up to* (not including) the year of attaining age 62 (or the year of disability or death, if before age 62). The number of years counted is the number of *computation elapsed years*.

**Step II.** Subtract five from the number of computation elapsed years when computing the AIME for *retirement* or *death benefits*. The number remaining (if less than two, use two) is the *number of computation base years* to be used in computing the AIME.

The number of years to be subtracted for *disability benefits* is scaled accordingly to the worker's age, under the following schedule:

| Worker's Age in year of disability | Number of dropout years |
|---|---|
| Under 27 | 0 |
| 27 through 31 | 1 |
| 32 through 36 | 2 |
| 37 through 41 | 3 |
| 42 through 46 | 4 |
| 47 and over | 5 |

Up to 3 additional years—actually 2 because it is impossible to have more than 2 years—are subtracted from the elapsed years if a disabled individual had no earnings in those years and had been living with a child under age 3. However, total dropout years—when child-care years are used—may not exceed 3.

**Step III**. List social security earnings in the *computation base years* (See F-8 for social security earnings limits.) Computation base years are years *after* 1950, up to and *including* the year of death, or the year *before* entitlement to retirement or disability benefits. (A person is not entitled to benefits until an application for benefits is filed.)

Notice that the year of death is included as a computation base year—but the year in which an application is made for retirement or disability benefits is not included. However, for benefits payable for the next year after application is made for retirement or disability benefits, the AIME for retirement or disability benefits will be recomputed, and earnings for this final year substituted for lowest year if result is a higher AIME.

Where benefits are being estimated for entitlement at some future time, use anticipated earnings (but not over the social security maximum) for future computation base years.

**Step IV**. Index earnings in each computation elapsed year up to but not including the "indexing year." (See F-9 for instructions on how to index earnings.)

**Step V**. From the list of indexed earnings (and nonindexed earnings for and after the "indexing year"), select years of highest earnings (same number as found in Step II). Selected years need not be in consecutive order.

**Step VI**. Total indexed and nonindexed earnings for the selected years are divided by the number of months in the number of years found in Step II, dropping cents. This is the person's Average Indexed Monthly Earnings (AIME).

If a person does not have earnings covered by social security in as many years as are required to be used as benefit computation years, total earnings must nevertheless be divided by the number of months in the required number of years. In other words, one or more years of zero earnings must be used. (See F-11.)

A special minimum PIA of $122.00 originally (actually much higher now due to cost-of-living adjustments) may be used for workers first eligible for benefits on or before December 31, 1981, when it is higher than the one the worker's AIME would produce. There is no special minimum PIA for workers first eligible for benefits on or after January 1, 1982. (See F-21.) (The special minimum PIA remains applicable until January 1, 1992 for a few vow-of-poverty members of religious orders.)

**AIME for Widow(er)'s Benefits**. In computing aged widow(er)'s benefits for the spouse of a worker who died before age 62 and is eligible for benefits after December 1984, the deceased worker's earnings are indexed to wages up to the earliest of: (1) two years before the worker would have reached age 62, (2) two years before the survivor becomes eligible for aged widow(er)'s benefits, or (3) two years before the survivor becomes eligible for disabled widow(er)'s benefits. This computation applies only if it results in a higher benefit than the standard computation above (including applicable cost-of-living adjustments for the deferred period before benefits start). It will provide higher benefits for many widow(er)s whose spouses died before age 62 and will assure that the widow(er)'s initial benefit reflects wage levels prevailing nearer the time she (or he) comes on the rolls.

## EXAMPLES

In each of the three examples provided below, the worker earned at least the social security maximum each year. Therefore, social security earnings in the computation base years are as follows: $3,600 (1951-1954); $4,200 (1955-1958); $4,800 (1959-1965); $6,600 (1966-1967); $7,800 (1968-1971); $9,000 (1972); $10,800 (1973); $13,200 (1974); $14,100 (1975); $15,300 (1976); $16,500 (1977); $17,700 (1978); $22,900 (1979); $25,900 (1980); $29,700 (1981); $32,400 (1982); $35,700 (1983); $37,800 (1984); $39,600 (1985); $42,000 (1986); $43,800 (1987); $45,000 (1988); $48,000 (1989); $51,300 (1990); $53,400 (1991); $55,500 (1992).

**Example I. Computation of AIME for person entitled to retirement benefits.**

Mr. Graves, born 1930, reaches age 62 on November 1, 1992. On November 1st he retires and applies for retirement benefits. Earnings and months in 35 years must be used in computing his AIME (40 computation elapsed years, 1952-1991, minus 5). Mr. Graves has worked in covered employment and earned at least the social security maximum in every year after 1950. Earnings are indexed from 1952-1989. Mr. Graves' earnings in 1990-1991, his "indexing year" and the next year are not indexed.

Indexed earnings which apply to each example in-whole or in-part are as follows:

| | | | | | |
|------|----------|------|----------|------|----------|
| 1951 | $27,044  | 1965 | $21,665  | 1979 | $41,948  |
| 1952 | $25,460  | 1966 | $28,103  | 1980 | $43,523  |
| 1953 | $24,112  | 1967 | $26,620  | 1981 | $45,344  |
| 1954 | $23,989  | 1968 | $29,437  | 1982 | $46,885  |
| 1955 | $26,751  | 1969 | $27,829  | 1983 | $49,260  |
| 1956 | $25,002  | 1970 | $26,513  | 1984 | $49,262  |
| 1957 | $24,251  | 1971 | $25,244  | 1985 | $49,499  |
| 1958 | $24,039  | 1972 | $26,528  | 1986 | $50,986  |
| 1959 | $26,177  | 1973 | $29,960  | 1987 | $49,983  |
| 1960 | $25,188  | 1974 | $34,563  | 1988 | $48,942  |
| 1961 | $24,697  | 1975 | $34,352  | 1989 | $50,217  |
| 1962 | $23,520  | 1976 | $34,870  | 1990 | $51,300  |
| 1963 | $22,957  | 1977 | $35,478  | 1991 | $53,400  |
| 1964 | $22,055  | 1978 | $35,259  |      |          |

Mr. Graves' highest AIME is obtained by selecting the 35 years 1951-1953, 1955-1957, 1959-1961 and 1966-1990. His AIME is $2,985 ($1,254,001 ÷ 420).

His AIME will later be recomputed to include earnings in 1992, and if this results in a higher AIME, the higher benefit will be paid beginning the following year. Thus, if Mr. Graves earned at least $55,500 in 1992, recomputation will be based on the 35 years 1951-1952, 1955-1957, 1959-1961 and 1966-1992, giving him an AIME of $3,060.

**Example II. Computation of AIME for disability benefits.**

Mr. Prather, born in 1946, is disabled as a result of an accident on October 15, 1992. He applies for disability benefits on December 1, 1992. In computing his AIME for disability benefits, 20 benefit computation years must be used (24 years in 1968-91, less 4). Mr. Prather has worked in covered employment every year since 1967 and in each year (including the year in which he became disabled) was paid at least the maximum social security earnings base for that year.

Earnings in 1967-1989 are indexed. Earnings in 1990-1991 are not adjusted because they were paid in and after his "indexing year" (1990).

Mr. Prather's highest AIME is obtained by selecting the 20 years, 1968 and 1973-1991. His AIME is $3,601 ($864,475 ÷ 240).

The AIME will be recomputed to include earnings in 1992, and if this results in a higher AIME, the higher benefit will be paid beginning the following year. If Mr. Prather earned at least $55,500 in 1992, recomputation will be based on the 20 years 1973-1992, giving him an AIME of $3,710 ($890,538 ÷ 240).

**Example III. Computation of AIME for person who dies before retirement age.**

Mr. Wagner dies in November, 1992, at age 61 (he was born in 1931). In computing his AIME, 34 benefit computation years must be used (39 years in 1953-91, less 5). Mr. Wagner has worked in covered employment every year since 1951 and in each year (including the year of death) was paid at least the maximum social security earnings base for that year. Earnings in Mr. Wagner's computation base years through 1990 are indexed. Actual earnings in 1990-1992 are not adjusted since 1990 is his "indexing year."

Mr. Wagner's highest AIME is obtained by selecting the following 34 years of highest earnings: 1951-1952, 1955-1956, 1959-1961, and 1966-1992. Mr. Wagner's AIME is $3,091 ($1,261,136 ÷ 408).

**F-11. How are Average Indexed Monthly Earnings (AIME) computed for a self-employed individual whose self-employment came under social security after 1951?**

The same formula and starting date (1951) are used as in the computation for employees. In many cases, this will mean that years of zero earnings must be used in the AIME contribution.

*Example.* Dr. Baumgartner, a physician, came under social security in 1965. He applies for retirement benefits in 1992 when he reaches age 62. Earnings and months in 35 years must be used in computing his AIME (40 elapsed years, 1952-1991, less 5). Social security earnings in his elapsed years are as follows: $0 (1951-1964); $4,800 (1965); $6,600 (1966-1967); $7,800 (1968-1971); $9,000 (1972); $10,800 (1973); $13,200 (1974); $14,100 (1975); $15,300 (1976); $16,500 (1977); $17,700 (1978); $22,900 (1979); $25,900 (1980); $29,700 (1981); $32,400

(1982); $35,700 (1983); $37,800 (1984); $39,600 (1985); $42,000 (1986); $43,800 (1987); $45,000 (1988); $48,000 (1989); $51,300 (1990); $53,400 (1991); $55,500 (1992).

Although Dr. Baumgartner has covered earnings in only 27 of these years, the total earnings for these 27 years must be divided by the number of months in 35 years (420). His AIME is computed by indexing his earnings from 1965-1989, adding actual earnings in 1990 and 1991 to total indexed earnings, and dividing by 420. Thus, his AIME is $2,492 ($1,046,980 ÷ 420).

Recomputation to include Dr. Baumgartner's earnings in 1992 (assuming they are at least $55,500) will give him an AIME of $2,624.

### F-12. How do you determine a person's Primary Insurance Amount (PIA) for 1992?

The Primary Insurance Amount is determined by applying a formula to the person's Average Indexed Monthly Earnings (AIME). Where first eligibility is in calendar year 1992, the primary insurance amount is the sum of three separate percentages of portions of the AIME. It is found by taking 90 percent of the first $387 or less of the AIME, 32 percent of the AIME in excess of $387 through $2,333, and 15% of the AIME in excess of $2,333.

If the PIA is not an even multiple of 10¢, it is rounded to the next lower multiple of 10¢.

The percentage figures and the dollar figures in the PIA formula will remain constant for computations and recomputations where first eligibility is in 1992, no matter when entitlement is established.

The PIA is subject to cost-of-living increases beginning with the year of first eligibility. (See F-23.)

*Example.* Mr. Bell, born May 18, 1930, filed an application for retirement benefits on March 31, 1992. His AIME is $2,400.00. His PIA is calculated as follows:

> 90 percent of $387 = $348.30
> 32 percent of $1,946 = $622.72
> 15 percent of $67 = $10.05
>
> $348.30 + $622.72 + $10.05 = $981.07 = PIA of $981.00

*Example.* Mr. Jones, born February 13, 1930, filed an application for retirement benefits on February 10, 1992. His AIME is $300. His PIA is $270.00 (90 percent of $300 = $270.00).

Note, however, that the Primary Insurance Amount is calculated differently when eligibility begins prior to 1992. The percentages in the PIA formula remain constant but the dollar amounts differ each year. The dollar amounts in the formula prior to 1992 are as follows:

| Eligibility Begins | AIME Dollar Amounts |
|---|---|
| 1979 | $180 and $1,085 |
| 1980 | $194 and $1,171 |
| 1981 | $211 and $1,274 |
| 1982 | $230 and $1,388 |
| 1983 | $254 and $1,528 |
| 1984 | $267 and $1,612 |
| 1985 | $280 and $1,691 |
| 1986 | $297 and $1,790 |
| 1987 | $310 and $1,866 |
| 1988 | $319 and $1,922 |
| 1989 | $339 and $2,044 |
| 1990 | $356 and $2,145 |
| 1991 | $370 and $2,230 |

*Example.* Mr. Meder, born March 12, 1927, filed an application for retirement benefits on August 19, 1992. His AIME is $2,100.00. Since he became eligible for retirement benefits in 1989 (the year he reached age 62), his PIA is calculated as follows:

90 percent of $339 = $305.10
32 percent of $1,705 = $545.60
15 percent of $56 = $8.40

$305.10 + $545.60 + $8.40 = $859.10 = PIA of $859.10

This amount is subject to a 4.7 percent cost-of-living increase in December 1989, a 5.4 percent cost-of-living increase in December 1990, and a 3.7 percent cost-of-living increase in December 1991.

### Formula For Workers Receiving A Pension From Work Not Covered By Social Security

If a worker receives a pension from a job not covered by Social Security, and the worker also has enough social security credits to be eligible for retirement or disability benefits, a different formula may be used to figure his social security benefit. This formula results in a lower benefit. But the worker's pension from the job not covered by Social Security is not affected by this change.

The reason a different formula is used is that social security benefits are weighted in favor of low earners (i.e., low earners' benefits represent a higher percentage of their prior earnings than do the benefits of workers with higher earnings). If the benefits of people who work for only a portion of their careers in jobs covered by Social Security were computed as if they had been long-term, low-wage workers, these individuals would receive the advantage of the weighted benefit formula. Instead, a modified formula eliminates this unintended windfall.

The modified formula does not affect survivor benefits. It affects only workers who reach age 62 or become disabled after 1985 and first become eligible after 1985 for a monthly pension based in whole or in part on work not covered by Social Security. A worker is considered eligible to receive a pension if he meets the requirements of the pension, even if he continues to work.

The modified formula does not apply if:
- the worker is a federal worker hired after December 31, 1983.

- the worker was employed on January 1, 1984, by a nonprofit organization that was mandatorily covered under Social Security on that date.

- the worker has 30 or more years of substantial earnings under Social Security.

- the worker's only pension is based solely on railroad employment.

- the worker's only work not under Social Security was before 1957.

The modified formula is used in figuring the social security benefit beginning with the first month for which the worker receives both a social security benefit and a pension from work not covered under Social Security.

Social security benefits are based on the worker's Average Indexed Monthly Earnings (AIMEs). In figuring benefits, the first part of the average earnings is multiplied by 90 percent; the second part is multiplied by 32 percent; and any part of the AIME remaining is multiplied by 15 percent. In the modified benefit formula, the 90 percent used in the first factor is reduced.

The formula for workers first eligible in 1992 provides that benefits are determined by taking 40 percent of the first $387 of Average Indexed Monthly Earnings; 32 percent of AIMEs from $387 to $2,333; and 15 percent of AIMEs above $2,333.

The reduction was phased in gradually for workers who reached 62 or became disabled in 1986 through 1989. The phase-in applies as follows:

| Year You Became 62 or Disabled | First Factor |
|---|---|
| 1986 | 80 percent |
| 1987 | 70 percent |
| 1988 | 60 percent |
| 1989 | 50 percent |
| 1990 or later | 40 percent |

Workers with 30 or more years of substantial social security coverage are not affected by the modified benefit formula. Workers with 21-29 years of social security coverage (as defined in F-20) will have the first factor reduced as follows:

| Years of Coverage | First Factor |
|---|---|
| 30 or more | 90 percent |
| 29 | 85 percent |
| 28 | 80 percent |
| 27 | 75 percent |
| 26 | 70 percent |
| 25 | 65 percent |
| 24 | 60 percent |
| 23 | 55 percent |
| 22 | 50 percent |
| 21 | 45 percent |
| 20 or less | 40 percent |

In this formula, a worker is credited with a year of coverage if his earnings equal or exceed the figures shown for each year in the following chart.

In this formula, you are credited with a year of coverage if your earnings equal or exceed the figures shown for each year in the following chart.

| Year | Earnings | Year | Earnings |
|---|---|---|---|
| 1937-50 | $ 900[1] | 1979 | $4,725 |
| 1951-54 | 900 | 1980 | 5,100 |
| 1955-58 | 1,050 | 1981 | 5,550 |
| 1959-65 | 1,200 | 1982 | 6,075 |
| 1966-67 | 1,650 | 1983 | 6,675 |
| 1968-71 | 1,950 | 1984 | 7,050 |
| 1972 | 2,250 | 1985 | 7,425 |
| 1973 | 2,700 | 1986 | 7,875 |
| 1974 | 3,300 | 1987 | 8,175 |
| 1975 | 3,525 | 1988 | 8,400 |
| 1976 | 3,825 | 1989 | 8,925 |
| 1977 | 4,125 | 1990 | 9,525 |
| 1978 | 4,425 | 1991 | 9,900 |

[1]Total credited earnings from 1937-50 are divided by $900 to get the number of years of coverage (maximum of 14 years).

A guarantee is provided to protect workers with relatively low pensions. It provides that the reduction in the social security benefit under the modified formula cannot be more than one-half of that part of the pension attributable to earnings after 1956 not covered by Social Security. Effective for benefits based on applications filed in or after November 1989, the amount of the pension considered when determining the windfall guarantee is the amount payable in the first month of concurrent entitlement to both Social Security and the pension from noncovered employment.

### F-13. How do you determine the Primary Insurance Amount (PIA) after 1992?

For individuals who attain age 62, or become disabled or die before age 62 in any calendar year after 1992, the PIA will be determined by formulas using the same percentage amounts listed in F-12 above. However, the bend points (dollar amounts) will be adjusted yearly as average wages rise or fall.

On or before November 1st of each year the Social Security Administration must publish in the Federal Register the bend points (dollar amounts) that will be used in computing the PIA for those eligible in the year after publication.

Remember that the bend points used in calculating an individual's PIA apply to the year the individual first became *eligible* for the benefits and not necessarily to the year he was first *entitled* to benefits.

### F-14. How is the PIA computed for an individual who was previously entitled to a disability benefit?

The PIA is not always computed under the "wage indexing" benefit computation method when a worker reaches age 62 or becomes disabled after 1978. Other benefit computations may be required if the worker was previously entitled to a disability benefit.

The PIA will be computed or recomputed under the simplified old-start benefit computation method if the individual was entitled to a disability benefit before 1979 and fewer than 12 months have passed between the prior entitlement to the disability benefit and current entitlement to benefits.

If an individual has been entitled to a disability benefit either before or after 1979—but within 12 months of current entitlement to retirement, disability, or death benefits—the PIA is the largest of the following:

(a) The PIA (including one computed under the simplified old-start benefit computation method) which was used in figuring the individual's previous disability benefit—increased by any cost-of-living or general benefit increases which occurred since the individual was last entitled; or

(b) The special minimum PIA; or

(c) A recomputation of the former PIA to take into account earnings after the disability entitlement ended.

If an individual's entitlement to a disability benefit ended more than 12 months before his current entitlement to benefits, a new PIA must be computed under the "wage indexing" method. The PIA will be the higher of the recalculated PIA or the individual's PIA during the last month of his former entitlement to disability benefits (without regard to any interim cost-of-living increases).

### MAXIMUM FAMILY BENEFITS

### F-15. How do you determine the Maximum Family Benefit under the wage indexing method in 1992?

The following formula determines the Maximum Family Benefit for those reaching age 62 or dying before age 62 in 1992:

(1) 150 percent of the first $495 of PIA, plus

(2) 272 percent of PIA over $495 through $714, plus

(3) 134 percent of PIA over $714 through $931, plus

(4) 175 percent of PIA over $931.

The result is the family maximum. (The final figure should be rounded to the next lower multiple of $.10 if not an even multiple of $.10.)

The Maximum Family Benefit is calculated differently when eligibility begins prior to 1992. The percentages in the Maximum Family Benefit formula remain constant but the dollar amounts differ each year. The dollar amounts in the formula prior to 1992 are as follows:

| Eligibility Begins | PIA Dollar Amounts |
|---|---|
| 1979 | $230, $332, and $433 |
| 1980 | $248, $358, and $467 |
| 1981 | $270, $390, and $508 |
| 1982 | $294, $425, and $554 |
| 1983 | $324, $468, and $610 |
| 1984 | $342, $493, and $643 |
| 1985 | $358, $517, and $675 |
| 1986 | $379, $548, and $714 |
| 1987 | $396, $571, and $745 |
| 1988 | $407, $588, and $767 |
| 1989 | $433, $626, and $816 |
| 1990 | $455, $656, and $856 |
| 1991 | $473, $682, and $890 |

## DISABILITY

For a disabled worker and his family, family benefits may not exceed the lesser of 85 percent of the Average Indexed Monthly Earnings (AIME) on which the worker's disability benefit is based, or 150 percent of the disability benefit payable to the worker alone. However, in no case will a family's benefit be reduced below 100 percent of the benefit which would be payable to the worker alone.

This limit on family disability benefits applies to workers who first become entitled to disability benefits after June 30, 1980. A worker who first becomes entitled to disability benefits in the first six months of 1980 will compute his maximum family benefit in the same manner as those who reach age 62 or die in 1980.

*Example.* Mr. Placke becomes entitled to disability benefits on October 1, 1992. His AIME is $1,800.00 and he would be eligible to receive $800.40 a month in disability payments on his own. However, Mr. Placke has a wife and a 10 year-old child. His maximum family benefit is the lesser of 85 percent of his AIME (85% × $1,800.00 = $1,530.00), or 150 percent of his disability benefit (150% × $800.40 = $1,200.60). Since 150 percent of his benefit is less than 85 percent of his AIME, his maximum family benefit is $1,200.60.

**F-16. How is the Maximum Family Benefit determined under the simplified old-start benefit computation method?**

Maximum Family Benefits applicable under the law in December 1978 remain in effect for those individuals who attained age 62, became disabled, or died before January 1979. Maximum Family Benefits—based on the worker's Average Monthly Earnings (AME)—are listed in the June 1978 benefit table of the Social Security Administration. (See Table 12—Consumer Price Index increases after June 1978 must be applied to Maximum Family Benefits listed in Table 12.)

**F-17. How are individual benefit rates reduced to bring the total amount payable within the family maximum limit?**

Whenever the total of monthly benefits payable on one social security account exceeds the maximum family benefit for that account, all benefit rates, except the old-age or disability benefit of a living worker, must be reduced to bring the total monthly benefits payable within the maximum family benefit amount. This means that even though a beneficiary's benefit rate is set by law as a percentage of the insured person's PIA, the actual benefit paid may be less when the total monthly benefits payable for any month exceed the family maximum. Where the total monthly benefits payable on one social security account exceed the family maximum, individual benefits are figured in the following manner.

(1) If the insured person is alive, his benefit is subtracted from the applicable family maximum. The remainder is then divided proportionately among those entitled to benefits.

(2) If the insured worker is dead, each beneficiary is paid a proportionate share of the applicable family maximum, based on the beneficiaries' full benefit rates.

*Example.* Mr. Edwards dies before age 62 in 1992, leaving a widow age 35 and two small children. His AIME is $2,000, and his PIA is $864.40. The full benefit for the widow and each child is $648.30 (75% of $864.40). However, the sum of the full benefits is $1,944.90 (3 × $648.30) which exceeds $1,539.70—the maximum family benefit for a PIA of $864.40. Thus, the benefit actually payable to each beneficiary is $513.00 (1/3 of $1,539.70, rounded to the next lower dollar).

However, a divorced spouse's benefits are paid independently of other family benefits. They do not affect, nor are they affected by, the family maximum. (See E-29 and E-83.)

**F-18. If one or more members of a family cease to be entitled to benefits, will the benefits of the remaining beneficiaries be increased?**

Yes, if their benefits have been reduced because of the family maximum limit.

*Example*. Mr. Hillman dies in 1992, leaving a widow and two children aged 6 and 12 entitled to survivor's benefits. His AIME is $1,800; his PIA, $800.40; and the maximum family benefit is $1,453.90. Since the full benefit for each family member is $600.30 (75% of $800.40), the total of all three benefits exceeds the family maximum of $1,453.90 because 3 × $600.30 = $1,800.90. Initially, then, each beneficiary receives only $484.00 (1/3 of $1,453.90, rounded down to the next lower dollar). Eventually, the older child reaches age 18, and his benefits end. The widow and younger child then receive their full benefits (the widow until the child attains age 16, and the child until attaining age 18) since the sum of these two benefits does not exceed the maximum family benefit.

## TRANSITIONAL GUARANTEE BENEFIT METHOD

### F-19. What is the transitional guarantee benefit method?

To provide a degree of protection for workers nearing retirement when decoupling was implemented, those who reach age 62 after 1978 and before 1984 are guaranteed a retirement benefit no lower than they would have received under the simplified old-start benefit computation method as of December 1978. The benefit computed under this method is known as the transitional guarantee PIA.

Those eligible for retirement benefits in the transition period are eligible for the larger of the PIA under the "wage indexing" benefit computation method or the transitional guarantee method.

The PIA under the transitional guarantee method is based on the June 1978 benefit table. (See Table 12.) The benefit table will not be subject to future automatic benefit increases, but an individual's retirement benefits will automatically increase beginning with age 62 for cost-of-living adjustments.

To be eligible for the guarantee, an individual must (1) have had income credited for one year prior to 1979, and (2) must not have been disabled prior to 1979.

The transitional guarantee does not apply to disability computations even when the disability begins after age 62. It does apply to survivors of individuals who attain age 62 in the transition period and who die in or after the month they reach age 62.

The transitional guarantee method is basically the same as the simplified old-start benefit computation method, but earnings in the year in which the worker reached age 62 and any year thereafter may not be included in the benefit computation.

*Example.* Mr. White, born 1917, reaches age 62 on October 7, 1979. He retires one day later and applies for retirement benefits. Earnings and months in 23 years must be used in computing his AME (28 computation elapsed years, 1951-1978, less 5). Mr. White has worked in covered employment and earned at least the social security maximum in every year after 1950. Social security earnings in his computation base years are therefore as follows: $3,600 (1951-1954); $4,200 (1955-1958); $4,800 (1959-1965); $6,600 (1966-1967); $7,800 (1968-1971); $9,900 (1972); $10,800 (1973); $13,200 (1974); $14,100 (1975); $15,300 (1976); $16,500 (1977); $17,700 (1978). Mr. White's highest AME is obtained by selecting the 23 years 1956-1978. His AME is $678 ($187,200 ÷ 276), and his PIA is $486.10.

The PIA computed above under the transitional guarantee method will be used if it's higher than Mr. White's PIA computed under the "wage indexing" method.

The PIA under the transitional guarantee method is subject to cost-of-living increases beginning with the month applicable for the year of first eligibility. A worker who attains age 62 in 1982, is entitled to a transitional guarantee PIA determined from the PIA Table printed in 1978. The PIA will not be affected by cost-of-living benefit increases in 1979, 1980 or 1981, but the June 1982 cost-of-living increase and subsequent ones will apply.

## MINIMUM AND MAXIMUM SINGLE BENEFITS

### F-20. What is the special minimum benefit?

The special minimum benefit, which applies to individuals who worked for many years under social security for very low wages, guarantees a benefit of at least $11.50 for each "year of coverage" over

10 and up to 30, adjusted for cost-of-living increases in 1979 and after. The special minimum benefit is used if it is higher than the one the worker's AIME would produce.

A "year of coverage" is defined as having earnings equal at least to 25% of the maximum taxable earnings base for years in 1951-1978, about 18.7% of such base in 1979-90, and about 11.2% of such base in subsequent years.

The maximum special PIA is $230 ($11.50 × 20 Years), before adjustment for cost-of-living increases in 1979 and after, and is $478.70 for benefits for December 1991 through November 1992. A worker and spouse, if both are 65 at initial claim, are entitled to a maximum special benefit of $718.00 per month in 1992.

The special minimum benefit was recomputed in January 1979 for pre-1979 beneficiaries to take into account the increase in the base figure from $9.00 to $11.50. Cost-of-living increases apply automatically each year, so that the special minimum applicable for December 1991 through November 1992 is at a rate of approximately $23.90 per year of coverage.

### F-21. What is the frozen minimum PIA?

Legislation in 1981 eliminated the frozen minimum PIA for workers first eligible for benefits on or after January 1, 1982.

The frozen minimum PIA is $122 a month for workers first eligible for benefits on or before December 31, 1981. Hence, $122 is the minimum amount payable as a disability benefit or as a retirement benefit if the worker is 65 or over when benefits commence. The minimum benefit for a sole survivor of an insured worker is also $122. Benefits based on the minimum have been updated for increases in the cost-of-living (as measured by the Consumer Price Index) beginning with the year the person became entitled to benefits and will continue to be so updated in the future.

### F-22. What is the maximum benefit payable under present law?

The maximum benefit payable in 1992 at 65 (person born in 1926) who did not have a prior period of disability is $1,088 a month. This benefit amount is computed under the "wage indexing" computation method.

The maximum benefit at the Normal Retirement Age in the future *before* any cost-of-living increases is $1,314 a month. A person born in 1962 who earns the social security maximum each year for 35 years up through age 66 (assuming it remains at $55,500 each year after 1992 and that the 1992 PIA formula does not change) would be entitled to this amount at age 67 under the "wage indexing" computation method. Increases in the social security earnings base after 1992 and future revisions in the bend points in the AIME computation method will increase this amount dramatically before the worker reaches Normal Retirement Age.

## INCREASE IN BENEFITS

### F-23. Do benefits increase when the cost-of-living increases?

The Social Security Act provides for automatic increases in benefits and in the maximum earnings base (earnings subject to social security taxes) due to changing economic conditions.

The automatic increases are determined by increases in the Consumer Price Index for All Urban Wage Earners and Clerical Workers prepared by the Department of Labor. (But see F-25.)

Benefits have been raised by the following percentages since 1977:

| Month/Year | Increase in Benefits |
| --- | --- |
| July 1977 | 5.9% |
| July 1978 | 6.5% |
| July 1979 | 9.9% |
| July 1980 | 14.3% |
| July 1981 | 11.2% |
| July 1982 | 7.4% |
| January 1984 | 3.5% |
| January 1985 | 3.5% |
| January 1986 | 3.1% |
| January 1987 | 1.3% |
| January 1988 | 4.2% |
| January 1989 | 4.0% |
| January 1990 | 4.7% |
| January 1991 | 5.4% |
| January 1992 | 3.7% |

There can be no cost-of-living computation quarter in any calendar year if in the year prior to that year a general benefit increase has been enacted or become effective.

Automatic cost-of-living benefit increases are based on the rise in the Consumer Price Index for All Urban Wage Earners and Clerical Workers from the third quarter of one year to the third quarter of the following year.

Benefits are automatically increased by the same percentage (rounded to the nearest 1/10 of 1%) as the percentage by which the Consumer Price Index for the cost-of-living computation quarter exceeds the Consumer Price Index for the later of: (1) the most recent cost-of-living computation quarter, or; (2) the most recent calendar quarter in which a general benefit increase became effective.

The Secretary must notify the House Ways and Means Committee and the Senate Finance Committee of the proposed increase within 30 days after the close of the "cost-of-living computation quarter," and must publish an announcement of it in the Federal Register within 45 days after the close of the quarter.

The maximum earnings base will be automatically adjusted each January after 1992 if nationwide (covered and non-covered) wages have increased and there has been a cost-of-living increase in benefits for the preceding December.

All benefits would be increased, including the special benefits payable to persons age 72 or over who are not fully insured. Also, the amount of excess earnings that results in loss of benefits will be increased whenever there is an automatic cost-of-living benefit increase and nationwide average wages have risen (the increase being based on the percentage rise in average wages). (See H-2)

### F-24. Who is entitled to a cost-of-living benefit increase?

Individuals using the "wage indexing" benefit computation method are entitled to cost-of-living increases beginning with the year of first eligibility (the year of attaining age 62, disability or death). The PIA is calculated for the year of first eligibility and the cost-of-living increases in that year and subsequent years will be added. As long as eligibility exists in any month of the year, the PIA will be increased by the automatic benefit increase percentage applicable to the check sent in January of the following year.

*Example.* Mr. Jones attains age 62 in November 1990, and waits until January 1992 to apply for benefits. The PIA is calculated and will be increased by the automatic cost-of-living benefit increase applicable to December 1990 and December 1991. The resultant PIA will be payable in the benefit paid in January 1992.

The automatic cost-of-living increase provisions in effect in December 1978 continue to apply for those who reached age 62, became disabled or died before January 1979. A revised benefit table is published each year by the Social Security Administration. These revised tables are *not* applicable to individuals who become eligible for benefits *after* 1978.

Beneficiaries using the transitional guarantee will also receive cost-of-living increases beginning with the year of first eligibility. (See F-19.)

## F-25. How will the cost-of-living stabilizer affect future cost-of-living benefit increases?

The Social Security Amendments of 1983 include a provision designed to protect the system from the kinds of trust-fund depletions that occur when price increases outpace wage gains. This stabilizer provision goes into effect if reserves in the trust fund providing retirement, disability and survivor benefits fall below 20% of what is needed to provide benefits for a year. When the stabilizer takes effect, automatic cost-of-living benefit increases are based on the lower of the percentage increase in the Consumer Price Index or the percentage rise in the nationwide average wage.

Later, if the fund reserves exceed 32% of what is estimated to be needed for a year, recipients will be entitled to extra cost-of-living increases to compensate for losses in inflation protection resulting from having benefit increases tied to wage levels in the past (if this occurred).

## YEAR OF RETIREMENT

## F-26. If age 62 is the computation age, is there any advantage to waiting until age 65 to collect benefits?

Yes, remember that the full PIA is payable at age 65 for those attaining age 65 before 2003, with a reduced amount paid in case of an earlier retirement age. Age 62 is used to determine the computation elapsed years but earnings are counted to age 65. Thus, early retirement usually affects the benefit in two ways. The PIA usually will be smaller (because fewer years of possibly higher earnings will be used in computing the AIME), and the lower PIA will be subject to reduction (5/9 of 1% for each month under 65 when benefits commence).

## F-27. Can a person obtain higher retirement benefits by working past retirement age?

Yes, in two ways. First, workers who continue on the job receive an increase in retirement benefits for each year they work between age 65 and 70. Note that this is *not* an increase in the worker's PIA. Other benefits based on his PIA, such as those payable to a spouse, are not affected.

This delayed retirement credit is also payable to a worker's surviving spouse receiving a widow(er)'s benefit.

Beginning in 1990, the delayed retirement credit payable to workers who attain age 62 after 1986 and who delay retirement past the full-benefit age (currently 65) is gradually increased. The delayed retirement credit is increased by 1/2 of one percent every other year until reaching 8 percent per year in 2009 or later. The higher delayed retirement credits are based on the year of attaining age 62 and are payable only at and after Normal Retirement Age.

Prior to 1990, workers who continued on the job received an increase in retirement benefits usually equal to 3% for each year (1/12 of 3% for each month) they worked between age 65 and 70.

Second, work past retirement age frequently results in a higher AIME. The reason: In figuring the *number* of years to be used in the computation, the year in which the person reaches age 62, and succeeding years, are not counted. (See F-10). But those years can be selected as years of highest earnings.

| Delayed Retirement Credit Rates | | |
|---|---|---|
| Attain Age 62 | Monthly Percentage | Yearly Percentage |
| 1979-1986 | 1/4 of 1% | 3% |
| 1987-1988 | 7/24 of 1% | 3.5% |
| 1989-1990 | 1/3 of 1% | 4% |
| 1991-1992 | 3/8 of 1% | 4.5% |
| 1993-1994 | 5/12 of 1% | 5% |
| 1995-1996 | 11/24 of 1% | 5.5% |
| 1997-1998 | 1/2 of 1% | 6% |
| 1999-2000 | 13/24 of 1% | 6.5% |
| 2001-2002 | 7/12 of 1% | 7% |
| 2003-2004 | 5/8 of 1% | 7.5% |
| 2005 or after | 2/3 of 1% | 8% |

**F-28. Will the retirement age when unreduced benefits are available (currently age 65) ever be increased?**

Yes, the Social Security Amendments of 1983 increase the retirement age when unreduced benefits are available (presently age 65) by two months a year for workers reaching age 62 in 2000-2005—to age 66;

maintains age 66 for workers reaching age 62 in 2006-2016; increases by two months a year the retirement age for workers reaching age 62 in 2017-2022; and maintains age 67 for workers reaching age 62 after 2022. It does not change the age of eligibility for Medicare.

The 1983 amendments do not change the availability of reduced benefits at 62 (60 for widow(er)s) but revise the reduction factors so that there is a further reduction (up to a maximum of 30 percent for workers entitled at age 62 after the Normal Retirement Age is increased to age 67, rather than only up to 20 percent for entitlement at age 62 under current law). There is no increase in the maximum reduction in the case of widow(er)s, but some increases in the reduction occur at ages above 60 and below Normal Retirement Age.

### Effects of Retirement-Age Provision in Social Security Amendments of 1983*

| Year of Birth | Attainment of Age 62 | Normal Retirement Age (Year/ Months) | Date of Attainment of Normal Retirement Age[1] | Age-62 Benefit as Percent of PIA[2] |
|---|---|---|---|---|
| 1938 | 2000 | 65/2 | March 1, 2003 | 79.2 |
| 1939 | 2001 | 65/4 | May 1, 2004 | 78.3 |
| 1940 | 2002 | 65/6 | July 1, 2005 | 77.5 |
| 1941 | 2003 | 65/8 | September 1, 2006 | 76.7 |
| 1942 | 2004 | 65/10 | November 1, 2007 | 75.8 |
| 1943 | 2005 | 66/0 | January 1, 2009 | 75.0 |
| 1943-1954 | 2005-2016 | 66/0 | January 1, 2009-2020 | 75.0 |
| 1955 | 2017 | 66/2 | March 1, 2021 | 74.2 |
| 1956 | 2018 | 66/4 | May 1, 2022 | 73.3 |
| 1957 | 2019 | 66/6 | July 1, 2023 | 72.5 |
| 1958 | 2020 | 66/8 | September 1, 2024 | 71.7 |
| 1959 | 2021 | 66/10 | November 1, 2025 | 70.8 |
| 1960 and after | 2022 and after | 67/0 | January 1, 2027 and after | 70.0 |

* Normal Retirement Age is for worker and spouse benefits only. Normal Retirement Age for widow(er)s is based on attainment of age 60 in 2000 or later, so that Normal Retirement Age is age 67 beginning in 2029.

[1] Birth date assumed to be January 2 of year (for benefit-entitlement purposes, Social Security Administration considers people born on the first day of a month to have attained a given age in the prior month). For later months of birth, add number of months elapsing after January up to birth month.

[2] Applies present-law reduction factor (5/9 of 1 percent per month) for the first 36 months' receipt of early retirement benefits and new reduction factor of 5/12 of 1 percent per month for additional months.

## REDUCTION IN BENEFITS

**F-29. When a person elects to start receiving his retirement benefit before Normal Retirement Age, how is the benefit reduced?**

A fully insured worker can start receiving retirement benefits the month after he reaches age 62 (or the month he reaches age 62 if his birthday is on the first day of the month), or for any month thereafter. (See E-7.) However, if he elects to start receiving benefits before Normal Retirement Age, the benefit is reduced.

In making the reduction, the worker's PIA must first be determined. The PIA is then reduced by 5/9 of 1% (1/180) for each of the first 36 months that the worker is under Normal Retirement Age when the benefits commence and by 5/12 of 1% (1/240) for each such month in excess of 36. (The amount of the reduction, if not an even multiple of 10¢, is increased to the next higher multiple of 10¢.) For example, if the worker's PIA is $1,000, and he elects to retire and start receiving benefits 24 months before age 65, his Normal Retirement Age, his benefit will be reduced by $133.40 (24 × 1/180 × $1,000), giving him a monthly benefit of $866.60. If the worker's benefits start in the month he reaches age 62, his benefit under this formula will equal 80% of his full PIA. (See Table 9.) Ordinarily, he will continue to receive the reduced benefit even after Normal Retirement Age (but see Recomputation of Benefits, F-34).

**F-30. If the spouse of a retired worker starts receiving a spouse's benefit before Normal Retirement Age, how is the benefit reduced?**

First, the spouse's full benefit is determined. This is one-half of the retired worker's PIA. (Where the retired worker is receiving a reduced retirement benefit starting before Normal Retirement Age, the spouse's full benefit is computed as 50% of the retired worker's PIA, not 50% of the reduced benefit.) The spouse's full benefit is then reduced by 25/36 of 1 percent (1/144) for each of the first 36 months that the spouse is under Normal Retirement Age when benefits commence and by 5/12 of 1% (1/240) for each month in excess of 36. (The amount of the reduction, if not an even multiple of 10¢, is increased to the next higher multiple of 10¢.)

For example, suppose that the retired worker's PIA is $1,000, and the spouse's full benefit is $500 (1/2 of $1,000). If the spouse takes the benefit exactly 24 months before age 65, his or her Normal Retirement Age, the full benefit will be reduced by $83.40 (24 × 1/144 × $500), giving the spouse a monthly benefit of $416.60 ($500 − $83.40). If a spouse starts receiving benefits for the month 36 months before

Normal Retirement Age (currently age 62), the benefit under this formula will be 75% of the full benefit, or 37.5% of the retired worker's PIA. Ordinarily, the spouse will continue to receive the reduced benefit even after Normal Retirement Age (but see Recomputation of Benefits, F-34). (See also Table 9.)

### F-31. If a widow(er) elects to start receiving a widow(er)'s benefit before Normal Retirement Age, how is the benefit reduced?

The widow(er)'s full benefit must first be determined. The full benefit (to which he or she would be entitled by waiting until Normal Retirement Age) is 100% of the deceased spouse's PIA. At present, this benefit is reduced by 19/40 of one percent (19/4000) for each month that the widow(er) is under Normal Retirement Age when benefits begin.

For example, suppose that the deceased spouse's PIA is $1,000. The widow(er)'s full benefit would be $1,000. However, if the widow(er) elects to receive benefits starting with the month of his or her 60th birthday (60 months before age 65), the full widow(er)'s benefit will be reduced by $285 (60 × 19/4000 × $1,000), resulting in a benefit of $715 ($1,000 – $285). The amount of the reduction, if not an even multiple of 10¢, is increased to the next higher multiple of 10¢. A benefit beginning with the month of a widow(er)'s 60th birthday accordingly will equal 71.5% of the spouse's PIA.

When the Normal Retirement Age is more than 65, the 71.5% reduction at age 60 will remain unchanged, but the reduction factor will be different (based on 71.5% at age 60 and 100% at Normal Retirement Age). Ordinarily, the widow(er) will continue to receive the reduced benefit even after Normal Retirement Age (but see Recomputation of Benefits, F-34). (See Table 10 for widow(er)'s reduced benefits.)

If the widow(er)'s deceased spouse retired before Normal Retirement Age, the widow(er)'s benefit cannot exceed the deceased spouse's reduced benefit or, if larger, 82-1/2% of his or her PIA.

The benefit of a disabled widow(er) who starts receiving benefits before age 60 is equal to 71.5% of his or her spouse's PIA. (See E-92.)

### F-32. How are a beneficiary's benefits figured when he is entitled to a reduced retirement benefit and a larger spouse's benefit simultaneously?

The beneficiary will receive the retirement benefit, reduced in the regular manner. (See F-29.) That is, the PIA is reduced by 1/180 for each of the first 36 months that he is under Normal Retirement Age when benefits commence and 5/12 of 1% (1/240) for each month in excess of 36. The beneficiary will also receive a spouse's benefit based on the difference between the full spouse's benefit (1/2 of his or her spouse's PIA) and his or her PIA. This spouse's benefit is reduced by 25/36 of 1% (1/144) for each of the first 36 months that he is under Normal Retirement Age when benefits commence and 5/12 of 1% (1/240) for each month in excess of 36. (See F-30.)

**F-33. How are benefits figured if a beneficiary starts receiving a reduced retirement benefit and later becomes entitled to a larger spouse's benefit?**

The beneficiary will continue to receive the retirement benefit reduced in the regular manner. (See F-29.) When he becomes entitled to the larger spouse's benefit, he will receive, in addition, a partial spouse's benefit. This benefit will be based on the difference between a spouse's full benefit (1/2 of his or her spouse's PIA) and the beneficiary's PIA. If he becomes entitled to the spouse's benefits at or after Normal Retirement Age, the spouse's benefit will equal this difference. If he becomes entitled to the spouse's benefit before Normal Retirement Age, this difference must be reduced by 25/36 of 1% (1/144) for each of the first 36 months that he is under Normal Retirement Age when the spouse's benefits commence and 5/12 of 1% (1/240) for each month in excess of 36.

## RECOMPUTATION OF BENEFITS

**F-34. Under what circumstances are benefits recomputed?**

Automatic recomputation of benefits is provided each year to take account of any earnings a beneficiary might have that would increase his benefit amount. Also, the recomputation takes into account the final year's earnings in the case of retirement and disability benefits. The recomputation for a living beneficiary is effective with January of the year following the one in which the earnings were received. A recomputation affecting survivor's benefits is effective with the month of death.

The "wage indexing" computation method must be used to recompute the PIA for an individual who has earnings after 1978, if the PIA was originally computed or could have been computed under this method.

The actual dollar amounts in the records of the Social Security Administration for the year of entitlement and each later year will annually be compared with the earnings in the base years which were used in the last computation. Higher earnings in any year that was not used in the last computation will be substituted for one or more years of lower earnings that were used, and the PIA will be recomputed.

The PIA will be recomputed using the same "bend points" and "indexing year" that applied when current eligibility was established. (See F-12.) Recomputation must result in a PIA increase of at least $1 to be effective.

A PIA computed using the transitional guarantee benefit computation method or the simplified old-start benefit computation method—based on eligibility after 1978—cannot be recomputed to include earnings in or after the year of current eligibility.

Ordinarily, if a person elects to receive reduced benefits before Normal Retirement Age, the beneficiary will continue to receive the reduced amount even after Normal Retirement Age. However, a recomputation will be made at Normal Retirement Age and an adjustment will be made for any months' benefits that have been withheld because of substantial employment. Retirement benefits will now be reduced by 1/180 of the PIA for each of the first 36 months actually lost; a spouse's benefits will now be reduced by 1/144 of 50% of the PIA for each of the first 36 months actually lost; and a widow or widower's benefit will now be reduced by 19/4000 of the PIA for each of the first 36 months actually lost. In addition, each of the above will be reduced by 1/240 for each month in excess of 36.

Benefits are usually lost because of the "retirement test" (see LOSS OF BENEFITS BECAUSE OF EXCESS EARNINGS, SECTION H), but other factors may result in an increase in benefits at Normal Retirement Age. For example, in the case of retirement benefits, there will be an increase for any months in which the individual received disability benefits. Or, there will be an increase for any months in which a beneficiary was entitled to unreduced benefits because he or she had a child in care. Or, if a beneficiary's benefits were based on a spouse's disability, there will be an increase for months lost because of the worker's refusal to accept rehabilitation services, or because the worker recovered from his disability.

### F-35. If a person is simultaneously entitled to two or more benefits, which benefit will be paid?

A person may be entitled to more than one social security benefit at the same time. For example, a woman may be entitled to a parent's benefit on her deceased child's account and to a spouse's benefit on her husband's account. However, only the highest benefit will be paid, except when one of the benefits is a retirement or disability benefit. The lower benefit cannot be paid even though the higher benefit is not payable for one or more months. But if the higher benefit is terminated, the lower benefit will be reinstalled automatically.

If a person is entitled to retirement or disability benefits and to a higher benefit, he will receive the retirement or disability benefit plus the difference between this benefit and the higher one. Payment, however, may be made in a single check. If one benefit is not payable for one or more months, the other may be payable. For example, if a spouse's benefit is not payable for some months because of the worker's excess earnings, he or she will nevertheless receive a retirement benefit.

A child may be entitled to child's benefits on more than one earnings record, for example, his father's record and his mother's record. A child can receive the benefit based on the PIA which will result in the highest original benefit. However, if the highest original benefit is payable on the lowest PIA, he is paid on this account only if it would not reduce (after the reduction for the family maximum) the benefit of any beneficiary because of his entitlement.


## DISABILITY FREEZE

### F-36. How does a period of disability affect retirement and survivor's benefits?

A person who has an established period of disability will have his earnings record "frozen" during the period of disability. This means that the years of disability need not be included in computing his AIME. Otherwise, if the worker died or recovered and returned to work before he reached retirement age, the years of zero earnings in his period of disability might reduce his PIA for retirement or survivors' benefits. In figuring the number of years that must be used in computing the worker's AIME, a year which fell wholly or partly within a period of disability is not counted. However, a year which is partly within a period of disability will be used as a computation base year if inclusion of earnings for that year will produce a higher AIME.

## CALCULATING THE EXACT BENEFIT AMOUNT

**F-37. In calculating the exact amount of each monthly benefit, how must the figures be rounded?**

Benefits for members of a worker's family, if not an even multiple of $1, are rounded (after deducting the premium for Supplementary Medical Insurance, if any) to the next lower multiple of $1. For example, if the PIA of a deceased worker is $444.30, a child's survivor benefit is figured as $333.20 (75% of $444.30). However, this amount will be rounded to $333.00 (the next lower multiple of $1).

# TAXATION OF SOCIAL SECURITY BENEFITS

**G-1. Are social security benefits subject to federal income taxation?**

Up to one-half of the social security benefits received by taxpayers whose incomes exceed certain base amounts is subject to income taxation beginning in 1984.

**G-2. What are the base amounts?**

The base amounts are: (1) $25,000 for a single taxpayer; (2) $25,000 for married taxpayers filing separately who did *not* live together at any time during the year; (3) $32,000 for married taxpayers filing jointly; and (4) zero for married taxpayers filing separately who lived together at any time during the year. Income for purposes of figuring these base amounts includes adjusted gross income under present law, plus nontaxable interest income, and one-half of social security benefits.

**G-3. How is the amount of benefits includable in taxable income determined after the base amount has been exceeded?**

The amount of benefits included in taxable income once the base amount has been exceeded is the lesser of one-half of the benefits received or one-half of the excess of the taxpayer's combined income (adjusted gross income + one-half of benefits) over the base amount.

*Example.* Assume that a married couple is filing a joint income tax return.

| | |
|---|---|
| Base Amount | $32,000 |
| Adjusted Gross Income | $50,000 |
| (Includes tax-exempt interest) | |
| Annual Social Security Benefit | $11,000 |

To determine if the taxpayer is in excess of the base amount ($32,000), take one-half of the social security retirement benefit of $11,000 ($5,500) and add it to adjusted gross income of $50,000. The total of $55,500 is in excess of the base amount of $32,000. The amount of the social security benefit includable in taxable income is the lesser of one-half of the social security benefit received ($5,500) or one-half of the excess of the taxpayer's combined income ($55,500) over the base amount ($32,000). The excess of the combined income over the base amount is $23,500. One-half of $23,500 is $11,750. Since $5,500 is less than $11,750, $5,500 is to be included in the taxpayer's taxable income.

### G-4. Why is non-taxable interest income included in the taxpayer's adjusted gross income?

Nontaxable interest income is included in income to limit opportunities for manipulation of tax liability on benefits. Individuals whose incomes consist of different mixes of taxable and nontaxable income are treated the same as individuals whose total income is taxable for federal income tax purposes.

### G-5. Are workers' compensation benefits included in the definition of social security benefits for tax purposes?

Yes, also included in the definition of social security benefits for tax purposes are workers' compensation benefits to the extent they cause a reduction in social security and railroad retirement tier I disability benefits. This is intended to assure that these social insurance benefits, which are paid in lieu of social security payments, are treated similarly for purposes of taxation.

### G-6. Are nonresident aliens subject to the tax on social security benefits?

Yes, the tax applies to nonresident aliens as well as U.S. citizens. Under the Internal Revenue Code, nonresident aliens who have income from sources other than a U.S. trade or business are taxed at a flat rate of 30%, unless a tax treaty provides otherwise, and the taxes must be withheld at the source of payment. Thus, 30% of one-half of the social security benefit (15% of the total benefit) will be withheld from nonresident alien beneficiaries.

### G-7. How are overpayments and lump-sum retroactive benefits taxed?

Special rules are provided for dealing with overpayments and lump-sum retroactive benefit payments. Benefits paid to an individual in any taxable year are reduced by any overpayments repaid during the year. Taxpayers who received a lump-sum payment of retroactive benefits may treat the benefits as wholly payable for the year in which they receive them or may elect to attribute the benefits to the tax years in which they would have fallen had they been paid timely. No benefits for months before 1984 are taxable, regardless of when they are paid.

For example, assume that a taxpayer receives a $1,000 social security benefit in 1992, $400 of which is attributable to 1991. Assume also that the $1,000 benefit would increase the taxpayer's 1992 gross income by $500 (i.e., by the full 50%), but that the $400 would have increased the taxpayer's 1991 gross income by only $150 and the remaining $600 would have increased the taxpayer's 1992 gross income by $300. The taxpayer may limit his increase in 1992 gross income to only $450, the sum of the increases in gross income that would have occurred had the $400 been paid in 1991.

**G-8. What reporting requirements must be met by the Social Security Administration?**

The Secretary of Health and Human Services must file annual returns with the Secretary of the Treasury setting forth the amounts of benefits paid to each individual in each calendar year, together with the name and address of the individual. The Secretary of Health and Human Services must also furnish similar information to each beneficiary by January 31 of the year following the benefit payments. The statement will show the total amount of social security benefits paid to the beneficiary, the total amount of social security benefits repaid by the beneficiary to the Social Security Administration during the calendar year, and the total reductions in benefits to offset workers' compensation benefits received by the beneficiary.

**G-9. Are social security benefits paid after December 31, 1983, subject to income tax withholding?**

No, benefits paid to United States citizens or residents are not subject to withholding. (One-half of all social security benefits paid to non-resident aliens are subject to income tax withholding under section 1441 of the Internal Revenue Code.) Individuals who expect to be taxed on the benefits they receive and whose benefits are not subject to income tax withholding should take the taxable portion of the benefit payments into consideration in determining whether they are liable for estimated tax payments and, if so, the amount of estimated tax that is required.

**G-10. If a recipient of social security benefits elects Part B Medicare insurance and the premiums are deducted from the individual's benefits, is the whole benefit, before the deduction, a social security benefit?**

Yes, the individual is treated as if he or she received the whole benefit (and later paid separately for the Part B coverage). Both the Secretary of Health and Human Services and the Railroad Retirement Board will include the entire amount as paid to the individual in the statements they furnish.

# LOSS OF BENEFITS BECAUSE OF "EXCESS" EARNINGS

## "RETIREMENT TEST"

### H-1. Can a person lose some or all of his Social Security benefits by working?

Yes, if he is under age 70 but over age 64 and earns over $10,200 in 1992; or if he is under age 65 for all of 1992 and earns over $7,440, except that an alternative test applies in the initial year of retirement if it produces a more favorable result (see the last "bullet" of H-2).

The annual exempt amount ($10,200 in 1992) will be increased automatically after 1992 as wage levels rise. The annual exempt amount for beneficiaries under age 65 ($7,440 in 1992) will also be increased each year as wage levels rise.

A beneficiary age 70 or over can earn any amount without loss of benefits. Regardless of how much he earns in the year he attains age 70, no benefits are withheld for the month in which he reaches age 70, or for any subsequent month. Also, earnings in and after the month in which a person attains age 70 will not be included in determining his total earnings for the year.

### H-2. What are the general rules for loss of benefits because of excess earnings?

If the beneficiary is age 70 or older, no benefits will be lost because of his earnings. If he is under age 70, the following rules apply:

- If no more than $10,200 is earned in 1992 by a beneficiary over age 64, no benefits will be lost for that year.

- If more than $10,200 is earned in 1992 by a beneficiary who attains or has attained Normal Retirement Age (age 65 in 1992), $1 of benefits will ordinarily be lost for each $3 of earnings over $10,200. The age at which this withholding rate applies will increase as the Normal Retirement Age increases. Prior to 1990, beneficiaries over age 64 ordinarily lost $1 of benefits for each $2 of earnings over the annual exempt amount.

141

- If not more than $7,440 is earned in 1992 by a beneficiary under age 65 for the entire year, no benefits will be lost for that year.

- If more than $7,440 is earned in 1992 by a beneficiary under age 65 for the entire year, $1 of benefits will ordinarily be lost for each $2 of earnings over $7,440.

- But, no matter how much is earned during 1992, no *retirement* benefits in the *initial year of retirement* will be lost for any month in which he neither (1) earns over $850 as an employee if he retires at age 65-69 ($620 if he retires at age 62-64), nor (2) renders any substantial services in self-employment.

The initial year of retirement is the first year in which he is both entitled to benefits and has a month in which he does not earn over the monthly exempt wage amount (as listed above) and does not render substantial services in self-employment.

### H-3. How are "excess" earnings charged against benefits?

In determining the amount of benefits for a given year that will be lost, two factors must be taken into consideration: (1) the amount of the person's "excess" earnings for the year; and (2) the months in the year that can actually be charged with all or a portion of the excess earnings potentially chargeable in the initial year of retirement.

Both wages earned as an employee and net earnings from self-employment are combined for purposes of determining the individual's total earnings for the year. Only "excess earnings" are potentially chargeable against benefits. If a 65 year-old earns $10,200 or less in 1992, he has no "excess earnings". If his earnings for the year are more than $10,200, then one-third of the amount over $10,200 is "excess earnings".

Excess earnings are charged against retirement benefits in the following manner. They are charged first against all benefits payable on the worker's account for the first month of the year. If any excess earnings remain, they are charged against all benefits payable for the second month of the year, and so on until all the excess earnings have been charged or no benefits remain for the year. However, a month cannot be charged with any excess earnings and must be skipped if: (1) the individual was not entitled to benefits for that month; or (2) he was age 70 or over in that month; or (3) in the initial year of retirement he did not earn over $850 in wages as an employee if he retires at age 65-69 ($620 if he retires at age 62-64) and did not render substantial services as a self-employed person in that month.

If the excess earnings chargeable to a month are less than the benefits payable to the worker and to other persons on his account, then the excess is chargeable to each beneficiary in the proportion that the original entitlement rate of each bears to the sum of all their original entitlement rates.

The 1977 social security amendments eliminated the monthly earnings test for all beneficiaries except those in their initial year of retirement. Prior to 1977, many workers were able to use the monthly earnings test to limit the reduction of their benefits each year. By earning their earnings in only a few months of the year, they were allowed a full monthly benefit for each of the remaining months in which earnings were not more than 1/12 of the annual excess earnings limit and no substantial services in self-employment were performed. For example, a worker earning $10,000 in January of 1977 and no other wages the rest of the year, would have been eligible for unreduced benefits in each month of 1977 but January. This is not possible today except in the initial year of retirement.

*Example (1).* Dr. Brown partially retires in January 1992 at the age of 65, with a PIA of $800. He practices for three months in 1992 and earns $20,010. The remainder of his initial year of retirement is spent in Florida playing golf. Despite the fact that Dr. Brown has excess earnings in 1992 which would, under the annual test, cause a benefit loss of $3,270, he will lose only $2,400 in benefits for the three months during which he performed substantial services in self-employment because 1992 is his initial year of retirement.

*Example (2).* Dr. Smith, who partially retired in 1991, practices for four months in 1992 and earns $11,010. Since 1992 is his second year of retirement, the monthly earnings test does not apply. His benefit will be reduced by $1 for each $3 of earnings over $10,200. This means that Dr. Smith's benefits in 1992 will be reduced by $3,270 (1/3 of the amount in excess of $10,200).

*Example (3).* Mr. Martin is 71 years old and has not retired. He earns $15,000 a year. Mr. Martin receives retirement benefits of $550 a month. Because he is over age 70, he loses none of his benefits by working.

Prior to November 10, 1988, the annual exempt amount applicable at the time of death was prorated based on the number of months that the beneficiary lived during the year. Beginning on or after that date, the annual exempt amount is *not* prorated in the year of death. In addition, the higher exempt amount for beneficiaries age 65-69 applies to persons who die before their birthdate in the year that they otherwise would have attained age 65.

### H-4. Can a person who is receiving dependent's or survivor's benefits lose his benefits by working?

Yes, if he is under 70 but over age 64 and earns over $10,200 in 1992; or if he is under age 65 for all of 1992 and earns over $7,440. The same "retirement test" applies as applies to retirement beneficiaries (see H-2). However, the excess earnings of a person receiving dependent's or survivor's benefits are not charged against the benefits payable to other dependents or survivors. For example, a child's excess earnings are not chargeable against his mother's benefits. A retirement beneficiary's excess earnings, on the other hand, are chargeable against his dependent's benefits because those benefits are based on his social security account.

### H-5. If a widow's benefits are withheld because of work, will this necessarily reduce the total amount of benefits payable to the family?

No. Where there are several children, all survivor benefits may have to be reduced to come within the maximum family benefit. Even though the mother works and loses her benefits, the maximum may still be payable to the children. In many cases, however, loss of the mother's benefits will reduce the total amount of benefits payable to the family.

*Example (1).* Mr. Apple dies in 1992, leaving a widow and four small children. His PIA is $700. If it were not for the family maximum limit, the widow and each child would be entitled to a survivor's benefit of $525 (75% of $700). However, since the maximum family benefit for a PIA of $700 is $1,300.10, each beneficiary receives only $260.00 (1/5 of $1,300.10, rounded to the next lower even dollar, or a total of $1,300.00). Mrs. Apple goes to work and earns an amount sufficient to eliminate her mother's benefits ($1 is withheld for every $2 of excess earnings). Nevertheless, the family still receives $1,300.00 in benefits because each child's benefit is raised to $325.00 (1/4 of $1,300.00).

*Example (2).* Mr. Berry dies in 1992, leaving a widow and two small children; his PIA is $800; and the maximum family benefit is $1,453.40. If it were not for the maximum family limit, the widow and each child would be entitled to a monthly benefit of $600 (75% of $800). Because of the family maximum limit, however, each receives only $484.00 (1/3 of $1,453.40, rounded to the next lower even dollar). Mrs. Berry goes to work and earns an amount sufficient to eliminate her mother's benefits. Each child then receives a full benefit of $600.

**H-6. How is the loss of benefits figured for the year in which the worker reaches age 70?**

In the year in which a person attains age 70, his earnings in and after the month in which he attains age 70 will not be included in determining his total earnings for the year.

**H-7. What kinds of earnings will cause loss of benefits?**

*Wages* received as an employee and net *earnings* from self-employment. Bonuses, commissions, fees, and earnings from all types of work, whether or not covered by social security, count for the retirement test. For example, earnings from family employment are counted even though such employment is not covered by social security (see B-30). Earnings above the social security "earnings base" are counted. Income as an absentee owner counts as "earnings" for the retirement test. If the person renders substantial services as a self-employed person (even in another business), such income also will count as "earnings" for the taxable year in the initial year of retirement.

The following types of income are *not* counted as "earnings" for purposes of the retirement test:

- Any income from employment earned in or after the month the individual attains age 70. (Self-employment income earned in the year is not examined as to when earned, but rather is pro-rated by months, even though actually earned after age 70.)

- Any income from self-employment which is received in a taxable year after the year the individual becomes entitled to benefits, but which is not attributable to significant services performed after the first month of entitlement to benefits.

- Damages, attorneys' fees, interest, or penalties paid under court judgment or by compromise settlement with the employer based on a wage claim.

- Payments to secure release of an unexpired contract of employment.

- Certain payments made under a plan or system established for making payments because of the employee's sickness or accident disability, medical or hospitalization expenses, or death.

- Payments from certain trust funds which are exempt from income tax.

- Payments from certain annuity plans which are exempt from income tax.

- Pensions and retirement pay.
- Sick pay if paid more than 6 months after the month the employee last worked.
- Payments-in-kind for domestic service in the employer's private home, for agricultural labor, or for work not in the course of the employer's trade or business.
- Rentals from real estate which cannot be counted in earnings from self-employment because, for instance, the beneficiary did not materially participate in production work on the farm, the beneficiary was not a real estate dealer, etc.
- Interest and dividends from stocks and bonds (unless they are received by a dealer in securities in the course of business).
- Gain or loss from the sale of capital assets, or sale, exchange, or conversion of other property which is not stock in trade nor includable in inventory.
- Net operating loss carry-over resulting from self-employment activities.
- Loans received by employees unless the employees repay the loans by their work.
- Workers' compensation and unemployment compensation benefits.
- Veterans' training pay.
- Pay for jury duty.
- Prize winnings from contests, unless the person enters contests as a trade or business.
- Tips paid to an employee which are less than $20 a month or are not paid in cash.
- Payments by an employer which are reimbursement specifically for travel expenses of the employee and which are so identified by the employer at the time of payment.
- Payments to an employee as reimbursement or allowance for moving expenses, if they are not counted as wages for Social Security purposes.
- Royalties received in or after the year in which a person reaches Normal Retirement Age, to the extent that they flow from property created by the person's own personal efforts which he or she copyrighted or patented before the taxable year in which he or she reached Normal Retirement Age.

- Retirement payments received by a retired partner from a partnership provided certain conditions are met.

- Certain payments or series of payments paid by an employer to an employee or any of his or her dependents on or after the employment relationship has terminated because of death, retirement for disability, or retirement for age and paid under a plan established by the employer.

- Payments *from* Individual Retirement Accounts (IRA's) and Keogh Plans.

In other words, a person can receive most any amount of "investment" income without loss of benefits.

### H-8. What is meant by "substantial services" in self-employment?

Whether a self-employed beneficiary is rendering "substantial services" in the initial year of retirement is determined by the actual services rendered in the month. The test is whether he can reasonably be considered retired in the month. In applying the test, consideration is given to such factors as: (1) the amount of time he devoted to the business (including all time he spent at the place of business or elsewhere) in any activity related to the business (including the time spent in planning and managing as well as doing physical work); (2) the kind of services he performed; (3) how his services compare with services he performed in past years of active work; and (4) other circumstances of his particular case.

More than 45 hours of service in a month are usually considered substantial. Services of less than 45 hours would usually not be considered substantial. However, as few as 15 hours of activity in a month could be regarded as substantial if, for instance, they involve management of a sizeable business or were spent in a highly skilled occupation. The amount of earnings is not controlling. High earnings do not necessarily mean that substantial services were rendered, nor do low or no earnings mean that they were not rendered.

The "substantial services" test is used only for the initial year of retirement. After that, the amount of earnings alone determines whether benefits will be lost.

### H-9. Must a Social Security beneficiary report his earnings to the Social Security Administration?

Yes, if he is under age 70 but over age 64 and earns, or expects to earn, more than $10,200 in 1992, he should make an estimated report before the end of the year and a final report after the end of the year. An estimated report and final report should also be filed, if he is under age 65 and earns, or expects to earn, more than $7,440 in 1992. If 1992 is the initial year of retirement, and the beneficiary is working as an employee for more than $850 a month ($620 if he retires at age 62-64), or is rendering substantial services in self-employment, and expects to earn more than $10,200 ($7,440 if he retires at age 62-64), he must report this to the Social Security Administration.

Benefits will be stopped for the number of months necessary to offset excess earnings, based on the beneficiary's estimate. Adjustments will be made after the beneficiary files his annual report. If too much has been withheld, he will receive a check for the underpayment. If too little, the overpayment will be withheld from future benefits or must be refunded. For failure to file timely reports a person, in addition to normal loss of benefits because of excess earnings, may lose one or more additional months benefits as a penalty. Annual reports are due within three months and 15 days after the close of the taxable year (April 15th for a calendar year taxpayer). However, an extension of time for filing may be granted if there is a valid reason for not filing on time.

### H-10. How are a life insurance agent's first-year and renewal commissions treated for purposes of the Retirement Test?

Whether original (first year) and renewal commissions from the sale of life insurance policies are wages or earnings from self-employment depends upon the status of the agent when he completed the sale of the policy. If the agent was an employee when he consummated the sale of the policy, both original and renewal commissions from that policy are wages. If the agent was self-employed when he completed the sale of the policy, both the original and renewal commissions from the policy are earnings from self-employment.

Each insurance company normally furnishes its agents with sufficient information identifying policies on which commission payments are made, amounts of payments which are regular commissions, the commuted value of the renewals, service fees, efficiency income, etc., to enable a beneficiary to figure how much his earnings are for social security purposes.

A life insurance agent will receive his retirement benefits for the month in which he reaches age 70, and for every month thereafter regardless of whether he is still working, and regardless of how much he earns.

Moreover in his *initial year of retirement*, and regardless of the amount of his earnings for the taxable year, he will not lose his benefits for any month in which he neither (1) earns more than $850 as an employee ($620 if he is under age 65) nor (2) renders substantial services in self-employment.

It is necessary to determine whether the agent was an employee or a self-employed person when the policy was sold. (For status of a life insurance agent as an employee or as a self-employed person under social security, see B-11.) The reason is that, for retirement test purposes, "wages" of an **employee** are treated as earnings in the year in which they are **earned**. But net earnings for **self-employment** are treated as earnings in the year in which they are **received**.

Original (first-policy-year) commissions are earnings for purposes of the retirement test for the month and year in which an **employee-agent** completed the sale of the policy. As a rule an employee-agent is paid his original commission on a policy according to the way the insured person pays the premium. The entire original commission is earnings for the month in which the agent completed the sale of the policy regardless of whether he received the commission on a monthly, quarterly, semi-annual, or annual basis.

Renewal commissions of an employee-agent are earnings for purposes of the retirement test for the month in which the employee completed the sale of the life insurance policy and are includable in total earnings for the taxable year. They are deferred compensation for services rendered in completing the sale.

All of the renewal commissions which an employee-agent anticipates receiving from a life insurance policy sold while he was an employee must be reported as earnings for purposes of the retirement test for the month and year in which the original sale of the policy was completed. If the anticipated renewal commissions fail to materialize, thus making incorrect the total annual or monthly earnings, any benefit previously withheld but now due the beneficiary will be paid.

An employee-agent beneficiary must include the following in figuring his total earnings for purposes of the retirement test for a taxable year:

- All original commissions on life insurance policies sold during the year.
- All anticipated renewal commissions on life insurance policies sold in the year. If the agent-beneficiary cannot determine the exact amount of his anticipated renewals from such policies, as a last resort he should assume that they equal the amount of the original commission.
- Insurance service fees, persistency fees, and the like earned during the year.

- All renewal commissions received in the taxable year from policies sold in prior years while he was self-employed.
- All remuneration classified as earnings from other jobs, trades, or business.

Thus, renewal commissions on business in past years are not "earnings" for retirement test purposes when received by the agent-beneficiary if he was an **employee** when he sold the policies.

An employee-agent earns his commission on a life insurance policy in the month in which he performs the last act required to entitle him to the commission. The acts to be performed before entitlement to commissions are usually set out in the agent's contract with the company or can be determined from the company's regulations, rules, or practices. The agent should submit a copy of the contract or other evidence if there is any doubt about the last act required.

The month in which the company approves the policy is not the month in which the commission was earned unless it happens to coincide with the last act required of the agent; as, for instance, if later in that month the agent forwarded the first premium due on the approved policy and this qualified for his commission. Similarly, the month in which the agent delivered the policy and collected the initial premium is not the month in which the commission was earned if the agent qualified for his commission when the customer signed the policy application.

This same rule applies to converted policies. If the conversion of the life insurance policy resulted in new commissions, the commissions are earned in the month in which the agent performed the last act which qualified him for those new commissions. In the latter case, it is immaterial that the conversion was accomplished with the help of another agent through the insistence of the purchaser of the policy; some action (even if it is only his signature) was required of the selling agent in order for him to be entitled to the new rate of commissions.

If the life insurance agent is a **self-employed** person when he sells a policy, first-year and renewal commissions are treated as earnings for purposes of social security taxes for the taxable year in which they are **received**. When he sells a policy, he will report in the year of sale only the first-year commission received on the policy in that year. Renewal commissions on such a policy will be treated as earnings for purposes of social security taxes in the year when received. Renewal commissions received in a year after the year of entitlement to social security benefits are not included as earnings for purposes of the retirement test if they were the result of services rendered in or prior to the initial month of entitlement.

A self-employed agent includes the following in figuring his total earnings for a particular taxable year for purposes of the retirement test:

- Original commissions received during the year.
- Renewal commissions received during the year from policies sold while he was a self-employed agent if the policies were sold after his initial month of entitlement to social security benefits, but not for such policies sold in or before such initial month. Further, he will exclude all renewal commissions received from policies sold in prior years while he was an employee. Also, he will exclude anticipated renewal commissions on policies sold during the current year while he was self-employed.
- All net earnings from self-employment derived during the year in the form of insurance service fees, persistency fees, etc.
- All remuneration classified as earnings from other jobs, trades, or businesses.
- Any net loss from other self-employment during the year.

| Are Self-Employed Earnings Subject to Social Security Retirement Test? | | |
| --- | --- | --- |
| | Commissions Received In | |
| Time of Sale | Year of First Entitlement* | Years After Year of First Entitlement* |
| Prior to Year of First Entitlement | Yes | No |
| In Year of First Entitlement | | |
| (1) Sold in months through month of First Entitlement | Yes | No |
| (2) Sold in months after month of First Entitlement | Yes | Yes |
| After Year of First Entitlement | Yes | Yes |

*Entitlement means (a) being eligible by virtue of age and insured status (i.e., having the required number of Quarters of Coverage) and (b) having filed a claim for benefits.

The receipt of renewal commissions in the initial year of retirement on policies sold by a self-employed agent will not necessarily result in a loss of benefits even though in 1992 they exceed $10,200 ($7,440 if under age 65) for the taxable year. The reason is that such "self-employment" earnings cannot be charged against benefits for any month in the initial year of retirement in which the agent-beneficiary does not render any substantial services in self-employment. Even large amounts of renewal commissions will not cause loss of any benefits if the agent-beneficiary renders no substantial services in self-employment during the taxable year in which he receives the commissions.

Generally, repeat commissions paid on **casualty insurance policies** (e.g., accident and health) differ from renewal commissions in the life insurance field; this is true even though the repeat commissions are sometimes called "renewal" commissions. Each repeat commission is in fact for a policy written for a new and different term.

Ordinarily, the rate of commission on these repeats is the same regardless of how many times the insurance is extended for a new term. In life insurance renewals, on the other hand, there is a limit on the number of years for which renewal commissions are paid on the same life insurance policy. Regardless of the amount of work done by an agent when a casualty insurance policy is extended, the commission paid is for the new term only; it is not additional compensation for the original term of the policy. For these reasons, repeat commissions from accident and health policies are, normally, earned in the month in which the policy is extended. Thus, they are wages for the month and year if the agent then was an employee; if the agent then was self-employed, they may be included as earnings from self-employment for the year in which they are received.

# MEDICARE

## I-1. What is Medicare?

Medicare is a federal health insurance program for persons 65 or older, persons of any age with permanent kidney failure, and certain disabled persons. It is run by the Health Care Financing Administration of the U.S. Department of Health and Human Services. Social Security Administration offices across the country take applications for Medicare and provide general information about the program.

One part of the program consists of a Basic Hospital Insurance Benefits plan (Part A). This part of the program covers institutional care, including inpatient hospital care, skilled nursing home care, home health care, and, under certain circumstances, hospice care. Part A is financed for the most part by Social Security taxes.

Another part of the program consists of a voluntary Supplementary Medical Insurance Plan. Supplementary Medical Insurance covers physician's services, outpatient hospital care, physical therapy, ambulance trips, medical equipment, prosthesis, and a number of other services not covered under the Hospital Plan. It is largely financed through monthly premiums paid by those who enroll and contributions from the federal government. The government's share of the cost far exceeds that paid by those enrolled.

New benefits for catastrophic health problems were introduced in 1989 after Congress passed the Medicare Catastrophic Coverage Act of 1988 (MCCA), but the Act was repealed by the Medicare Catastrophic Coverage Repeal Act of 1989. MCCA expanded coverage for inpatient hospital care, skilled nursing facility care, hospice care and home health care. It also provided coverage for all prescription drugs by 1991 and for home intravenous drug therapy, mammography screening and respite care. Congress repealed MCCA after Medicare-eligible persons protested against the supplemental premium that some would have been required to pay to finance catastrophic coverage. The maximum premium payable, based on 1989 federal income taxes, would have been $800 for a single taxpayer or $1,600 for a married couple filing a joint tax return.

## BASIC HOSPITAL INSURANCE PLAN

### I-2. What persons are eligible for benefits under the basic hospital insurance plan?

All persons age 65 and over who are entitled to monthly social security cash benefits (or would be entitled except that an application for cash benefits has not been filed), or monthly cash benefits under railroad retirement programs (whether retired or not) are eligible for benefits.

Persons age 65 and over can receive Medicare benefits even if they continue to work. Enrollment in the program while working will not affect the amount of future social security benefits.

A dependent or survivor of a person entitled to hospital insurance benefits, or a dependent of a person under age 65 who is entitled to retirement or disability benefits, is also eligible for hospital benefits if such dependent or survivor is at least 65 years old. For example, a woman age 65 or over who is entitled to a spouse's or widow's social security benefit is eligible for benefits under the Basic Hospital Plan.

A social security disability beneficiary is covered under Medicare after entitlement to disability benefits for 24 months or more. Those covered include disabled workers at any age, disabled widows and widowers age 50 or over, beneficiaries age 18 or older who receive benefits because of disability beginning before age 22, and disabled qualified railroad retirement annuitants.

A person who becomes reentitled to disability benefits within five years after the end of a previous period of entitlement (within seven years in the case of disabled widows or widowers and disabled children) is automatically eligible for Medicare coverage without having to wait another 24 months. However, and further, if the previous period of disability ends after February 20, 1988, he is covered under Medicare without again having to meet the 24 month waiting period requirement, regardless of not meeting the five year (or seven year) requirement if his current impairment is the same as (or directly related to) that in the previous period of disability.

Coverage will continue for 24 months after an individual is no longer entitled to receive disability payments because he has returned to work, provided he was considered disabled on or after December 10, 1980, and the disabling condition continues.

### End-Stage Renal Disease

Insured workers (and their dependents) with end-stage renal disease who require renal dialysis or a kidney transplant are deemed disabled for Medicare coverage purposes even if they are working. Coverage can begin with the first day of the third month after the month dialysis treatments begin. This three-month waiting period is waived if the individual participates in a self-care dialysis training course during the waiting period. Medicare coverage based on transplant begins with the month of the transplant or with either of the two preceding months if the patient was hospitalized during either of those months for procedures preliminary to transplant. If entitlement could be based on more than one of the factors the earliest date is used.

Beginning July 1, 1991, coverage is provided under Medicare for the self-administration of erythropoietin for home renal dialysis patients.

During a period of up to the first 18 months of entitlement, Medicare benefits are secondary to benefits payable under an employer's health benefit plan for individuals entitled to Medicare solely on the basis of end-stage renal disease. During this period, if an employer plan pays less than the provider's charges, then Medicare may supplement the plan's payments.

### Government Employees

Federal employees who were not covered under social security (e.g., temporary workers have been covered since 1951) began paying the portion of social security tax that is creditable for Medicare Hospital Insurance purposes in 1983. Those covered under social security, such as virtually all hired after 1983, pay the Hospital Insurance tax as well as the OASDI tax. A transitional provision provides credit for retroactive hospital quarters of coverage for federal employees who were employed before 1983 and also on January 1, 1983.

State and local government employees hired after March 31, 1986, are covered under Medicare coverage and tax provisions. A person who was performing substantial and regular service for a state or local government before April 1, 1986 is not covered provided he was a bona fide employee on March 31, 1986, and the employment relationship was not entered into in order to meet the requirements for exemptions from coverage.

State or local government employees whose employment is terminated after March 31, 1986, are covered under Medicare if they are later rehired.

Beginning after June 30, 1991, state and local government workers who are not covered by a retirement system in conjunction with their employment, and who are not already subject to the Medicare Hospital Insurance tax, are also automatically covered and must pay such taxes. A retirement system is defined as a pension, annuity, retirement, or similar fund or system established by a state or by a political subdivision of a state.

Individuals are not automatically covered under Medicare if employed by a state or local government:

1. to relieve them of unemployment;
2. in a hospital, home, or institution where they are inmates or patients;
3. on a temporary basis because of an emergency such as a storm, earthquake, flood, fire or snow;
4. if the individuals qualify as interns, student nurses or other student employees of District of Columbia government hospitals, unless the individuals are medical or dental interns or medical or dental residents in training.

State governments may voluntarily enter into agreements to extend Medicare coverage to employees not covered under the rules above.

### Medicare as Secondary Payor

Employers must offer employees age 65 or older the same health benefits offered to younger employees. Medicare will become the secondary payor for these employees age 65 or older. (This requirement does not apply to employers with less than 20 employees.) Medicare benefits are also secondary to benefits payable under employer health benefit plans for spouses age 65 or older of employed individuals of any age. Regulations issued by the Health Care Financing Administration on October 11, 1985, state that Medicare payment is secondary even if the employer health plan expressly stipulates that its benefits are secondary to Medicare. The regulations also include the federal government in the definition of an employer to which the secondary payment provisions apply.

An employee may reject the employer's plan and retain Medicare as the primary payor, but regulations prevent employers from offering a health plan or option designed to induce the employee to reject the employer's plan and retain Medicare as primary payor.

For persons who are not eligible for social security or railroad retirement benefits, see I-3 and I-6.

Medicare is also the secondary payor (1) when medical care can be paid for under any liability policy (including automobile policies), (2) in the first 18 months for end-stage renal disease under age 65 when private group health insurance provides coverage, and (3) when a disability beneficiary (under age 65) is covered under an employer plan as a current employee (or family member of an employee) for employers with at least 100 employees (effective only in 1987 through September 1995).

### I-3. Can a person age 65 or over qualify for hospital benefits even though he cannot qualify for Social Security or Railroad Retirement benefits?

Most persons age 65 or over and otherwise ineligible for hospital insurance may enroll voluntarily and pay a monthly premium if they are also enrolled for Supplementary Medical Insurance. (See I-6 and I-21).

Most persons who reached age 65 before 1968 are eligible to enroll for hospital insurance for which no premiums need be paid even if they have no coverage under social security. Also eligible for enrollment under this transitional provision are persons age 65 and over with specified amounts of earnings credits less than that required for cash benefit eligibility.

Not eligible under the transitional provision are retired federal employees covered by the Federal Employees' Health Benefits Act of 1959, non-residents of the U.S., or aliens admitted for permanent residence unless they have five consecutive years of residence and the required covered quarters.

### I-4. How is the basic hospital insurance plan financed?

By a separate Hospital Insurance Tax imposed upon employers, employees and self-employed persons. The tax must be paid by every individual, regardless of age, who is subject to the regular social security tax or to the railroad retirement tax. It must also be paid by all permanent federal employees and by all state and local government employees (1) hired after March 1986, or (2) not covered by a state retirement system in conjunction with their employment (beginning July 2, 1991).

The maximum earnings base (the maximum amount of annual earnings subject to tax) is $130,200 in 1992. (The maximum earnings

base for Old-Age, Survivors, and Disability Insurance (OASDI) taxes is $55,500 in 1992.) (See C-2 and C-15). For 1992, the rates of the
Hospital Insurance Tax are 1.45% for employees and employers and
2.90% for self-employed persons, resulting in maximum Hospital Insurance Tax (on $130,200 income) of $1,887.90 for employees and employers and $3,775.80 for self-employed persons.

### Hospital Insurance Tax

| Year | Max. Wage Base | Rate for Employer & Employee | Rate for Self-Employed Person | Max. Tax on Employer & Employee | Max. Tax on Self-Employed Person |
|------|------|------|------|------|------|
| 1992 | $130,200 | 1.45% | 2.90% | $1,887.90 | $3,775.80 |

There is a special federal (and generally following through to state)
income tax deduction of 50% of the OASDI/Hospital Insurance self-
employment tax. This income tax deduction, which is taken directly against net self-employment income, is designed to treat the self-
employed in much the same manner as employees and employers
are treated for social security and income tax purposes under present
law.

### I-5. Is the basic hospital benefits plan a compulsory program?

Yes. Every person who works in employment or self-employment
covered by the Social Security Act, or in employment covered by the
Railroad Retirement Act, must pay the hospital insurance tax and
will be eligible for hospital insurance benefits if fully insured when
he reaches age 65, receives disability benefits for more than 24
months, or has end-stage renal disease.

### I-6. Is there any way that an individual not eligible for the hospital insurance plan can be enrolled?

Yes. An individual who: (1) has attained age 65; (2) is enrolled in
the supplementary medical benefits plan (see I-21 through I-28); (3)
is a resident of the U.S. and is either (a) a citizen or (b) an alien lawfully admitted for permanent residence who has resided in the U.S.
continuously for five years; and (4) is not otherwise entitled to
benefits, is eligible to enroll. The monthly premium is $192 a month
for the 12-month period beginning January 1, 1992.

The premium for an individual who enrolls after the close of the
initial enrollment period or who reenrolls is $192 a month increased
by 10% if there were at least 12 months of delayed enrollment, regardless of how late the individual enrolls. This limitation on the amount
of the increased premium for late enrollment does not apply to premiums paid before July 1986.

The increased-premium paying period is limited to twice the number of years an individual delayed enrolling. The premium then reverts to the standard monthly premium in effect at that time.

### I-7. In general, what benefits are provided under the basic hospital insurance plan?

Over and above the "deductibles" and "coinsurance" amounts which must be paid by the patient, the following services are covered:

(1) *Inpatient hospital care* for up to 90 days in each "benefit period." The patient pays a deductible of $652 for the first 60 days and coinsurance of $163 a day for each additional day up to a maximum of 30 days. In addition, each person has a non-renewable "reserve" of 60 additional hospital days with coinsurance of $326 a day, which can only be used once during a lifetime.

(2) *Posthospital extended care in a skilled nursing facility* for up to 100 days in each "benefit period." The patient pays nothing for the first 20 days. After 20 days the patient pays coinsurance of $81.50 a day for each additional day up to a maximum of 80 days.

(3) An unlimited number of *home health services*. The patient pays nothing toward home health services.

(4) *Hospice care* for terminally ill patients (See I-10).

### I-8. Specifically, what inpatient hospital services are paid for under the basic hospital insurance plan?

Except for the deductible amount which must be paid by the patient, Medicare helps pay for inpatient hospital services for up to 90 days in each "benefit period." Medicare will also pay (except for a coinsurance amount) for 60 additional hospital days over each person's lifetime (applies to disabled beneficiaries at any age; others after age 65).

The patient must pay a deductible of $652 for the first 60 days in each benefit period. If he stays longer than 60 days during a benefit period, he must pay coinsurance of $163 a day for each additional day up to a maximum of 30 days. Thus, a 90-day stay would cost the patient $5,542. After 90 days the patient pays the full bill unless he can draw upon his lifetime reserve of 60 days. He must pay coinsurance of $326 a day for these 60 additional lifetime reserve days.

The coinsurance amount is based on the inpatient hospital deductible in effect when services are furnished, rather than on the deductible in effect at the beginning of the beneficiary's spell of illness (benefit period).

The 90-day benefit period starts again with each spell of illness. A "benefit period" begins the day a patient is admitted to a hospital. It ends when the patient has been in neither a hospital nor a facility primarily furnishing skilled nursing or rehabilitative services for 60 straight days. There is no limit on the number of 90-day benefit periods a person can have in his lifetime (except in the case of hospitalization for mental illness—see I-11). However, his lifetime reserve of 60 days is not renewable.

In 1989, the patient paid a deductible of $560 for the first period of continuous hospitalization beginning in a calendar year. Inpatient hospital care was covered for an unlimited number of hospital days of covered services. This expanded coverage, for 1989 only, was repealed by the Medicare Catastrophic Coverage Repeal Act of 1989.

### Specifically, the following inpatient services are covered:

- Bed and board in a semi-private room (two to four beds). Medicare will pay the cost of a private room only if it is required for medical reasons. If the patient requests a private room, Medicare will pay the cost of semi-private accommodations; the patient must pay the extra charge for the private room.

- Nursing services provided by or under the supervision of licensed nursing personnel (other than the services of a private duty nurse or attendant).

- Services of the hospital's medical social workers.

- Use of regular hospital equipment, supplies and appliances, such as oxygen tents, wheel chairs and crutches.

- Drugs and biologicals ordinarily furnished by the hospital.

- Diagnostic or therapeutic items and services ordinarily furnished by the hospital or by others (including clinical psychologists, as defined by the Health Care Financing Administration), under arrangements made with the hospital.

- Operating room costs, including hospital costs for anesthesia services.

- Services of interns and residents in training under an approved teaching program.

- Blood transfusions, after the first three pints. The patient must pay for the first three pints of blood unless he secures donors or the hospital received the blood at no charge other than a processing charge. Medicare pays blood processing charges beginning with the first pint. The term "blood" includes packed red blood cells as well as whole blood. If the blood deductible is satisfied under Part B of Medicare, it will reduce the blood deductible requirements under the Basic Hospital Insurance Plan (Part A).

- X-rays and other radiology services, including radiation therapy, billed by the hospital.
- Lab tests.
- Cost of special care units, such as an intensive care unit, coronary care unit, etc.
- Rehabilitation services, such as physical therapy, occupational therapy, and speech pathology services.
- Appliances (such as pacemakers, colostomy fittings, and artificial limbs) which are permanently installed while in the hospital.

**The basic hospital plan does *not* pay for:**

- The services of physicians and surgeons, including the services of pathologists, radiologists, anesthesiologists, and physiatrists. (Nor does Part A of Medicare pay for the services of a physician, resident physician or intern—except those provided by an intern or resident in training under an approved teaching program.)
- Services of a private duty nurse or attendant.
- Items supplied at the patient's request, such as television rental or telephone.

### I-9. What is a Health Maintenance Organization?

A Health Maintenance Organization (HMO) is a form of prepayment group practice providing service to its enrollees either directly or under arrangements with hospitals, skilled nursing facilities, or other health care suppliers. Generally, services include those covered under *both* the basic hospital insurance plan and the voluntary supplementary medical benefits plan, and are available to all Medicare beneficiaries in the area served by the HMO.

Qualified HMO's are paid on an estimated per capita basis. Such payments are made only to established HMOs, which are those: (1) with a minimum enrollment of 25,000, not more than half of whom are age 65 or older; and (2) which have been in operation for at least two years. Exception to the size requirement is provided for HMOs in small communities or sparsely populated areas (5,000 members and three years of operation).

HMOs which do not meet the requirements for fully qualified HMOs can contract for Medicare participation and be paid on a reasonable cost basis for their services.

The Department of Health and Human Services designates a single 30-day period each year in which all HMOs in an area participating in Medicare must have an open enrollment period. During this 30-day period, HMOs must accept Medicare beneficiaries up to the limits of their capacity.

An individual may disenroll from an HMO effective on the first day of the calendar month following the date on which he requested disenrollment. Under previous law, disenrollment could not be effective until the first day of the second month following the date on which the individual requested disenrollment.

HMOs must provide assurances to the Health Care Financing Administration that if they cease to provide items and services for which they have contracted, they will provide or arrange for supplemental coverage of Medicare benefits relating to a preexisting condition.

## I-10. How is hospice care covered under the Basic Hospital Plan?

The Tax Equity and Fiscal Responsibility Act of 1982 authorized coverage under the Basic Hospital Plan for hospice care for terminally ill beneficiaries with a life expectancy of six months or less. Benefits covered include nursing care, medical social services, homemaker-home health aid services, short-term inpatient care, outpatient drugs for pain relief, counseling and physical or occupational therapy or speech-language pathology.

The benefit period consists of two 90-day periods and one 30-day period.

The hospice benefit may be extended beyond the 210-day limit if the beneficiary is recertified as terminally ill by the medical director or the physician member of the interdisciplinary group of the hospice program.

The amount paid by Medicare is equal to the reasonable costs of providing hospice care or based on other tests of reasonableness as prescribed by regulations. No payment may be made for bereavement counseling, and no reimbursement may be made for other counseling services (including nutritional and dietary counseling) as separate services.

Prescription drugs for symptom management and pain relief are covered, whether in or out of a hospice, with coinsurance of 5% of reasonable cost (but not more than $5 per prescription). Respite care as an inpatient in a hospice (to give a period of relief to the family providing home care for the patient, available for no more than 5 consecutive days) is covered with coinsurance of 5% (but not to exceed, in the aggregate in a spell of respite care ((which ends after 14 consecutive days when the hospice care option is not in effect)), the amount of the Medicare initial deductible).

Persons must be certified as terminally ill within two days after hospice care is initiated. However, beginning January 1, 1990, if verbal certification is provided within two days, certification may occur within eight days after care is initiated.

**I-11. Are inpatient hospital benefits provided for care in a psychiatric hospital?**

Yes, but benefits for psychiatric hospital care are subject to a lifetime limit of 190 days. Furthermore, if the patient is already in a mental hospital when he becomes eligible for Medicare, the time he has spent there in the 150-day period before becoming eligible will be counted against the maximum of 150 days available in such cases (including any later period of such hospitalization when he has not been out of a mental hospital for at least 60 consecutive days between hospitalizations). However, this latter limitation does not apply to inpatient service in a general hospital for other than psychiatric care.

**I-12. What special provisions apply to care in a Christian Science sanatorium?**

Benefits are payable for services provided by a Christian Science sanatorium operated or certified by the First Church of Christ Scientist in Boston. In general, these institutions can participate in the plan as a hospital and the regular coverages and exclusions relating to inpatient hospital care apply. Thus, the patient pays a $652 deductible for the first 60 days, and coinsurance of $163 a day for the next 30 days (plus $326 a day for the 60 lifetime reserve days). A Christian Science sanatorium may also be paid as a skilled nursing facility. However, extended care benefits will be paid for only 30 days in a calendar year (instead of the usual 100 days), and the patient must pay the coinsurance amount ($81.50 a day) for each day of service (instead of for each day after the 20th day).

**I-13. Must a doctor certify that hospitalization is required?**

Initial certification is no longer required except for inpatient psychiatric hospital services and inpatient tuberculosis hospital services. For prolonged hospital stays, however, certification by a doctor will be required as often, and with such supporting material, as will be stipulated in the regulations under the law.

**I-14. What must a hospital or Health Maintenance Organization do to qualify for Medicare payments?**

It must meet certain standards and must enter into a Medicare agreement with the Federal government. However, provision is made for paying nonparticipating hospitals in cases of emergency.

**I-15. What provisions are made under the hospital insurance plan for posthospital care in a skilled nursing facility or other such facility?**

Except for a coinsurance amount payable by the patient after the first 20 days, the Basic Hospital Plan will pay the reasonable cost of posthospital care in a skilled nursing facility for up to 100 days in a benefit period. The following items and services are covered:

- Bed and board in semi-private accommodations (two to four bed room).
- Nursing care provided by, or under the supervision of, a registered nurse (but not private-duty nursing).
- Drugs, biologicals, supplies and appliances for use in the facility.
- Medical services of interns and residents in training under an approved teaching program of a hospital.
- Other diagnostic or therapeutic services provided by a hospital with which the facility has a transfer agreement.
- Such other health services as are generally provided by a skilled nursing facility.

The patient pays nothing for the first 20 days of covered service in each spell of illness; after 20 days, he pays coinsurance for each additional day, up to a maximum of 80 days. For a patient in the skilled nursing facility in 1992, the coinsurance is $81.50 a day. Thus, a 100-day stay during 1992 will cost the patient $6,520.

There is no lifetime limit on the amount of skilled nursing facility care provided under the Basic Hospital Plan. Except for the coinsurance (which must be paid after the first 20 days in each spell of illness), the Plan will pay the cost of 100 days' post-hospital care in each benefit period, regardless of how many benefit periods the person may have. After 100 days of coverage the patient must pay the full cost of skilled nursing facility care.

In order to qualify for extended care benefits, the patient must have been hospitalized for at least three days, and must have been admitted to the facility within 30 days after his discharge from the hospital.

Legislation enacted in 1982 permits skilled nursing facility coverage without regard to the three-day prior hospital stay requirement if there is no increase in cost to the program involved, and the acute care nature of the benefit is not altered. Persons covered without a prior hospital stay may be subject to limitations in the scope of or extent of services. The Department of Health and Human Services will decide when to lift the three-day prior hospital stay requirement but has not done so yet (and is not likely to do so).

Payment will be made for skilled nursing care only if the following conditions are met:

(1) The beneficiary must file a written request for payment (another person may sign the request if it is impracticable for the patient to sign).

(2) A physician must certify that the patient needs skilled nursing care on an in-patient basis, and that the care is needed for the condition for which the patient was hospitalized (or for a condition which arose while he was receiving care for the original condition). Recertification is required for extended stays.

(3) The facility must be "participating" under the Medicare law.

### I-16. What is a qualified skilled nursing facility?

A skilled nursing facility may be a skilled nursing home, or a distinct part of an institution, such as a ward or wing of a hospital, or a section of a facility another part of which is an old-age home. Not all nursing homes will qualify; those which offer only custodial care are excluded. The facility must be primarily engaged in providing skilled nursing care or rehabilitation services. At least one registered nurse must be employed full-time and adequate nursing service (which may include practical nurses) must be provided at all times. Every patient must be under the supervision of a doctor, and a doctor must always be available for emergency care. Generally, the facility must be certified by the state. It also must have a written agreement with a hospital that is participating in the Medicare program for the transfer of patients.

An institution which is primarily for the care and treatment of mental diseases or tuberculosis is not a skilled nursing facility.

### I-17. What post-hospital home health services are provided under the basic hospital insurance plan?

The Basic Hospital Plan covers the cost of an unlimited number of home health visits made on an "intermittent" basis under a plan of treatment established by a physician. "Intermittent" is defined as no more than 5 days a week.

A home health agency is a public or private agency that specializes in giving skilled nursing services and other therapeutic services, such as physical therapy, in the home.

The Basic Hospital Plan can pay for home health visits if all four of the following conditions are met:

1. The care provided includes part-time skilled nursing care, physical therapy, or speech therapy.

2. The person is confined at home,

3. A doctor determines the need for home health care and sets up a home health plan for the person, and

4. The home health agency providing services is participating in Medicare.

Generally, a doctor may not perform this function (number 3 above) for a patient of any agency in which the doctor has a significant ownership interest or a significant financial or contractual relationship. However, a doctor who has a financial interest in an agency which is a sole community health agency may carry out certification and plan of care functions for patients served by the agency.

**The Basic Hospital Insurance Plan will pay for these services:**

• Part-time skilled nursing care.

• Physical therapy.

• Speech therapy.

If a person needs part-time skilled nursing care, physical therapy, or speech therapy, Medicare also pays for:

• Part-time services of home health aide.

• Medical social services.

• Medical supplies and equipment provided by the agency.

• Occupational therapy.

The patient pays nothing for home health visits, except he must pay a 20 percent coinsurance amount for durable medical equipment provided by home health agencies (except for the purchase of certain used items—for which the coinsurance is waived). Durable medical equipment includes iron lungs, oxygen tents, hospital beds and wheelchairs.

Medicare does not cover home care services furnished primarily to assist people in meeting personal, family, and domestic needs. These non-covered services include general household services, preparing meals, shopping, or assisting in bathing, dressing, or other personal needs.

While the patient must be homebound to be eligible for benefits, payment will be made for services furnished at a hospital, skilled nursing facility, or rehabilitation center if the patient's condition requires the use of equipment that ordinarily cannot be taken to the patient's home. However, Medicare will not pay the patient's transportation costs.

A patient is considered "confined to his home" if he has a condition, due to an illness or injury, that restricts his ability to leave home except with the assistance of another person or the aid of a supportive device (such as crutches, a cane, a wheelchair, or a walker), or if the patient has a condition such that leaving home is medically contraindicated. While a patient does not have to be bedridden to be considered "confined to his home", the condition should be such that there exists a normal inability to leave home, that leaving home requires a considerable and taxing effort, and that absences from home are infrequent or of relatively short duration, or are attributable to the need to receive medical treatment.

### I-18. Does the hospital insurance plan pay any of the cost of outpatient hospital services?

No, outpatient diagnostic services are covered under the Supplementary Medical Insurance Plan (see I-26).

### I-19. Will the amounts to be paid by patients as deductible and coinsurance remain the same in future years?

No. The $652 initial deductible for inpatient hospital care for 1992 is based on the 1966-68 figure of $40 and increases in average per diem inpatient hospital cost since 1966 (and also some legislative changes) and, beginning with the 1987 determination, on increases in average national hospital costs, based on a hospital-cost market basket index. The daily coinsurance amounts are based on this per diem rate. The daily coinsurance for inpatient hospital care for the 61st to 90th days in a benefit period is 1/4 of the initial deductible ($163). The daily coinsurance for post-hospital extended care after 20 days is 1/8 of this initial deductible ($81.50). The lifetime reserve days' coinsurance is 1/2 of the initial deductible ($326).

### I-20. Does a person have to be in financial need to receive the basic hospital plan benefits?

No, benefits are payable to rich and poor alike.

## SUPPLEMENTARY MEDICAL INSURANCE PLAN

### I-21. Who is eligible for benefits under the supplementary medical benefits plan?

All persons entitled to Medicare hospital insurance may enroll in the Supplementary Medical Benefits Plan. Social Security and Railroad Retirement beneficiaries, age 65 or over, are, therefore, automatically eligible. However, any other person age 65 or over may enroll provided only that he is a resident of the United States and is either (a) a citizen or (b) a lawfully admitted alien who has resided in the United States continuously for at least five years at the time of enrollment.

### I-22. How does a person enroll in the supplementary medical plan?

Those who are receiving social security or railroad retirement benefits will be enrolled automatically at the time they become entitled to hospital insurance unless they elect not to be covered for supplementary medical insurance by signing a form which will be sent to them. Others may enroll at their nearest social security office.

A person's initial enrollment period is a seven-month period beginning on the first day of the third month before the month he attains age 65. For example, if the person's 65th birthday is April 10, 1992, his initial enrollment period begins January 1, 1992 and ends July 31, 1992.

If a person decides not to enroll in the initial enrollment period, he may enroll during a special enrollment period beginning with the first day of the first month in which he is no longer enrolled in a group health plan by reason of employment and ending seven months later.

In order to obtain coverage at the earliest possible date, a person must enroll before the beginning of the month in which he will reach age 65. For a person who enrolls during his initial enrollment period, the effective date of coverage is as follows:

(a) If he enrolls before the month in which he reaches age 65, coverage will commence the first day of the month in which he reaches age 65.

(b) If he enrolls during the month in which he reaches age 65, coverage will commence the first day of the following month.

(c) If he enrolls in the month after the month in which he reaches age 65, coverage will commence the first day of the second month after the month of enrollment.

(d) If he enrolls more than one month (but at least within three months) after the month in which he reaches age 65, coverage will commence the first day of the third month following the month of enrollment.

A 7-month special enrollment period is provided if Medicare has been the secondary payor of benefits for individuals age 65 and older who are covered under an employer group health plan because of current employment. The special enrollment period generally begins with the month in which coverage under the private plan ended. Medical insurance will begin with the month after coverage under the private plan ends, if the individual enrolls in such month; or with the month after enrollment, if the individual enrolls during the balance of the special enrollment period.

### I-23. What if you decline to enroll during the automatic enrollment period?

Anyone who declines to enroll during his initial enrollment period may enroll during a general enrollment period. There are general enrollment periods each year from January 1st through March 31st. Coverage begins with the following July.

The premium will be higher for a person who fails to enroll within 12 months, or who drops out of the plan and later reenrolls. His monthly premium will be increased by 10% for each full 12 months during which he could have been, but was not, enrolled (see I-24).

If you decline to enroll (or terminate enrollment) at a time when Medicare is secondary payer to your employer group health plan, the months in which you are covered under the employer group health plan (based on current employment) and the basic hospital insurance part will not be counted as months during which you could have been but were not enrolled in supplementary medical insurance for the purpose of determining if your premium amount should be increased above the basic rate.

### I-24. How is the supplementary medical benefits program financed?

This program is voluntary and is financed through premiums paid by the people who enroll and through funds from the federal government. Each person who enrolls must pay a basic monthly premium of $31.80 per month through December 31, 1992, and the federal government will pay about three times as much as a matching amount from the general revenues. The premium rates are established by law for 1992-95. (See table on next page.) Thereafter, premium rates (and government contributions) may be increased from time to time if program costs rise. In September of each year (beginning in 1995), the government will announce the premiums for the 12-month period starting the following January.

As to the premium rate after 1995, should no social security cost-of-living adjustment take place, the monthly premium will not be increased for that year. In the case of an individual who has the Part B premium deducted from his social security check, if the amount of the cost-of-living adjustment is less than the amount of the increase in the premium, the premium increase will be reduced so as to avoid a reduction in the individual's net social security check.

The monthly premium for each individual enrolled in the supplementary medical insurance plan will be $36.60 in 1993, $41.40 in 1994, and $46.10 in 1995.

The premium rate for a person who enrolls after the first period when enrollment is open to him, or who reenrolls after terminating his coverage, will be increased by 10% for each full 12 months he stayed out of the program.

These monthly premiums are, of course, in addition to the "deductible" and "coinsurance" amounts which must be paid by the patient (see I-27).

## Basic Monthly Premium
## Supplementary Medical Insurance Plan

| Year | Monthly Premium |
|------|-----------------|
| 1992 | $31.80 |
| 1993 | 36.60 |
| 1994 | 41.40 |
| 1995 | 46.10 |

## Catastrophic Coverage Premium

In addition to the "regular" monthly Supplementary Medical Insurance Plan premium, each person enrolled in the Supplementary Medical Insurance Plan in 1989 paid an additional flat-rate premium of $4 (except for persons who were not covered under the Hospital Insurance Plan, who paid nothing in 1989, but would have paid much larger additional flat-rate premiums in 1990 and after than other persons).

Catastrophic coverage benefits after 1989 and the catastrophic coverage premium were repealed by the Medicare Catastrophic Coverage Repeal Act of 1989.

### I-25. How are premiums paid for under the supplementary plan?

Persons covered will have the premiums deducted from their social security benefits. Persons who are not receiving social security benefits will pay the premiums directly to the government.

### I-26. What benefits are provided under the supplementary medical plan?

Under the supplementary medical plan, Medicare usually pays 80% of the approved charges for doctors' services and the cost of other services that are covered under the medical insurance plan after the patient pays the first $100 of such covered services in each calendar year. The following fees and services are covered by this portion of Medicare.

- Doctors' services wherever furnished in the United States. This includes the cost of house calls, office visits, and doctors' services in a hospital or other institution. It includes the fees of physicians, surgeons, pathologists, radiologists, anesthesiologists, physiatrists, and osteopaths.

- Services of clinical psychologists are covered if they would otherwise be covered if furnished by a physician (or as an incident to a physician's service).

- Services by chiropractors with respect to treatment of subluxation of the spine by means of manual manipulation are covered.

- Fees of podiatrists, including fees for the treatment of plantar warts, but not for routine foot care, are covered. The cost of treatment for debridement of mycotic toenails (i.e., the care of toenails with a fungal infection) is not included if performed more frequently than once every 60 days. Exceptions are authorized if medical necessity is documented by the billing physician.

- The cost of routine physicals, most vaccine shots, examinations for eyeglasses and hearing aids is not covered. But the cost of diagnosis and treatment of eye and ear ailments is covered. Also covered is an optometrist's treatment of aphakia.

- Plastic surgery for purely cosmetic reasons is excluded; but plastic surgery for repair of an accidental injury, an impaired limb or a malformed part of the body is covered.

- Charges imposed by an immediate relative (e.g., a doctor who is a son/daughter or brother/sister of the patient) are not covered.

- Radiological or pathological services furnished by a physician to a hospital inpatient are covered.

- The cost of blood clotting factors and supplies necessary for the self-administration of the clotting factor.

- Immuno-suppressive drugs used in the first year of transplantation.

- Outpatient physical therapy and speech pathology services received as part of a patient's treatment in a doctor's office or as an outpatient of a participating hospital, skilled nursing facility, or home health agency; or approved clinic, rehabilitative agency, or public health agency, if the services are furnished under a plan established by a physician or physical therapist. A physician is required to review all plans of care. A podiatrist (when acting within the scope of his practice) is a physician for purposes of establishing a plan for outpatient physical therapy. A dentist and podiatrist are also within the definition of a physician for purposes of outpatient ambulatory surgery in a physician's office. Services of independent physical therapists is limited to a maximum of $750 in approved charges in any one year. Services of independent occupational therapists are covered up to a maximum of $750 in approved charges for such services in a calendar year.

- Services and supplies relating to a physician's services and hospital services rendered to outpatients; this includes drugs and biologicals which cannot be self-administered.

- A physician who includes charges for independent clinical laboratory services in his bill is entitled to the lesser of (1) the approved charge of the laboratory, or (2) the amount actually charged by the physician. The physician's charge can include a small fee for handling the specimen.

- Dentists' bills for jaw or facial bone surgery, whether required because of accident or disease, are covered. Also covered are hospital stays warranted by the severity of the noncovered dental procedure, and services provided by dentists which would be covered when provided by a physician. However, bills for ordinary dental care are not covered.

- The cost of psychiatric treatment outside a hospital for mental, psychoneurotic or personality disorders is covered, but with 50% coinsurance instead of the usual 20% (except that the latter applies when services are provided on a hospital-outpatient basis if, in the absence of treatment outside a hospital, hospitalization would have been required).

- An unlimited number of home health services each calendar year. This would include the same services as described in I-17. A doctor must certify to the need for the home visits. These home visits are covered under the basic hospital plan unless the person only has supplementary medical insurance coverage (and then under that program).

- Radiation therapy with X-ray, radium or radioactive isotopes.

- Surgical dressings, splints, casts and other devices for reduction of fractures and dislocations; rental or purchase of durable medical equipment, such as iron lungs, oxygen tents, hospital beds and wheel chairs, for use in the patient's home; prosthetic devices, such as artificial heart valves or synthetic arteries, designed to replace part or all of an internal organ (but not false teeth, hearing aids, or eye-glasses); braces, artificial limbs, artificial eyes (but not orthopedic shoes).

- Ambulance service if the patient's condition does not permit the use of other methods of transportation.

- Comprehensive outpatient rehabilitation facility service performed by a doctor or other qualified professionals in a qualified facility. Therapy and supplies are covered.

- Antigens prepared by one doctor and sent to another for administration to the patient.

- The cost of pneumococcal vaccine.

- The cost of hepatitis B vaccine for high and intermediate risk individuals when it is administered in a hospital or renal dialysis facility.

- The Department of Health and Human Services is implementing a policy under which a liver transplant is not considered an experimental procedure for Medicare beneficiaries solely because an individual is over 18 years of age. A liver transplant will be covered when reasonably and medically necessary.

- Certified nurse-midwife services. Coverage is not limited to services provided during the maternity cycle.

- Partial hospitalization services incident to a physician's services. Partial hospitalization services are items and services prescribed by a physician and provided in a program under the supervision of a physician pursuant to an individualized written plan of treatment.

- Screening pap smears for early detection of cervical cancer. Coverage is provided for screening pap smears, but only once every three years, except in cases where the Health Care Financing Administration has established shorter time periods for testing women at high risk of developing cervical cancer.

- Screening mammography, beginning January 1, 1991. Screening mammography is defined as a radiologic procedure provided to a woman for the early detection of breast cancer, including a physician's interpretation of the results of the procedure. No payment will be made for screening mammography for women under age 35. Payment will be made for only one screening mammography for women over 34 but under 40. For women over 39 but under 50, payment will be made annually (provided eleven months elapse after the last screening) for those at high risk of developing breast cancer, or biennially (provided 23 months elapse after the last screening) for those not at high risk of developing breast cancer. For women over 49 but under 65, payment will be made annually (provided 11 months elapse after the last screening). For women over 64, payment will be made biennially (provided 23 months elapse after the last screening).

- The cost of an injectable drug approved for the treatment of a bone fracture related to post-menopausal osteoporosis under the following conditions: (1) the patient's attending physician certifies that the patient is unable to learn the skills needed to self-administer or is physically or mentally incapable of self-administering the drug, and (2) the patient meets the requirements for Medicare coverage of home health services. This benefit began on January 1, 1991.

- One pair of eyeglasses following cataract surgery, beginning January 1, 1991.

- Services of nurse practitioners and clinical nurse specialists in rural areas for the services that nurse practitioners and clinical nurse specialists are authorized to perform under state law and regulations, beginning January 1, 1991.

**I-27. What portion of the cost must be borne by the patient?**

The patient pays the first $100 of covered expenses incurred in each calendar year. Medicare pays 80% of the balance of the approved charges (50% generally for out-of-hospital psychiatric services) over the $100 deductible. However, there is no cost-sharing for most home health services, pneumococcal vaccine, outpatient clinical diagnostic laboratory tests performed by hospitals and independent laboratories which are Medicare-certified and by physicians who accept assignment, and costs of second opinions for certain surgical procedures when Medicare requires such opinions.

## GENERAL

**I-28. Is there any over-all limit to the benefits a person can receive under Medicare?**

Under the basic hospital plan, benefits begin anew each "benefit period." In addition, there are no dollar limits under the supplementary medical plan except for psychiatric care and independent physical and occupational therapy. Under the basic plan, care in a psychiatric hospital is subject to a lifetime limit of 190 days (see I-11). (The time a patient has spent in a hospital for psychiatric care immediately prior to becoming eligible for Medicare counts against the special 150-day limit in the first hospitalization period, but not against the 190-day life-time limit.) Under the supplementary plan, coverage of psychiatric treatment outside a hospital is subject to an annual benefit limit of $1,100 and services of independent physical therapists are reimbursable to no more than $750 per calendar year (as also applies to the services of independent occupational therapists).

Medicare may limit benefit payments for services for which other third party insurance programs (e.g., workers' compensation, auto or liability insurance, and employer health plans) may ultimately be liable. The Spending Reduction Act of 1984 establishes the statutory right of Medicare to (1) bring an action against any entity which would be responsible for payment with respect to such item or service; (2) bring an action against any entity (including any physician or provider) which has been paid with respect to such item or service; or (3) join or intervene in an action against a third party.

**I-29. What are some of the medical items and services *not covered* by Medicare?**

(1) Private rooms in a hospital or nursing home—(unless required for medical reasons)—see I-8; (2) private nursing; (3) routine physical check-ups, eyeglasses (except after cataract surgery), hearing aids (and examinations for same); (4) most immunizing vaccines; (5) ordinary dental care and dentures; (6) orthopedic shoes; (7) cosmetic plastic surgery (but see I-27); (8) custodial care; (9) services required as a result of war; (10) services covered by workers' compensation; (11) acupuncture; (12) drugs and medicines the patient buys with or without a doctor's prescription.

### I-30. Is the wife of a 65-year-old Social Security beneficiary entitled to Medicare if she is under age 65?

No, no one is entitled to Medicare who is not eligible as a result of being either age 65 or disabled. (See I-2.)

### I-31. Who makes the payments under Medicare?

The government has appointed organizations engaged in the health insurance field (mainly insurance companies or Blue Cross and Blue Shield) to act as contractors in administering the plan. Using federal guidelines, a contractor determines the approved charges and makes payments, either directly or by way of reimbursement, to participants and suppliers of services.

### I-32. Who receives the payments from Medicare?

Hospitals, skilled nursing facilities, and home health agencies are paid directly by the contractors. However, a hospital may collect deductibles and coinsurance amounts directly from the patient. Payment of a doctor's fees (or charges of another individual supplier of services) may be handled in either of two ways. The patient may submit an itemized bill (receipted or unpaid) to the contractor and receive payment (or the doctor may do this for the patient). Or, with the doctor's approval, the patient may assign his right to payment to the doctor or other supplier of services (and such doctor or other supplier agrees to limit the charges to what Medicare determines). This is called the "assignment" method.

Under the first method, the patient will receive 80% of what the contractor determines is an approved charge for the services after the $75 deductible—regardless of the actual charge. If the doctor or other suppliers of services accepts an assignment, his combined charge to Medicare and the patient cannot exceed what the contractor determines is an approved charge for his services.

The Spending Reduction Act of 1984 permits benefits to be paid to a health benefits plan, provided the beneficiary agrees and the physician or other supplier accepts the plan's payment as payment in full. This indirect payment procedure is available to group, as well as non-group, employments and non-employment health benefits plans such as employers, unions and insurance companies.

### I-33. What is Medicare's approved charge"?

The "approved charge" or allowable charge used by the Medicare contractor is always the *lowest* of the following three options:

1. The doctor's *actual* charge, or

2. The doctor's *customary* charge (i.e., the charge that he most frequently makes for a given service), or

3. The *prevailing* charge (i.e., a charge which is no higher than the customary charges of 75% of the doctors in a specified area). Annual increases in the amount of the prevailing charge in a locality are limited to an amount justified by the economic index.

### I-34. Can a person choose his own doctor or hospital?

Generally, the patient is free to choose his own doctor or other supplier of services. However, except for hospital care in emergency cases, Medicare will pay only to "qualified" hospitals, extended care facilities and home health agencies.

Use of a foreign hospital by a U.S. resident is authorized when such hospital is closer to his residence or more accessible than the nearest United States hospital. But such hospitals must be approved. Medicare also authorizes payment for emergency care in a foreign hospital when the emergency occurred in the United States or in transit between Alaska and other continental states. Necessary physicians' services in connection with such foreign hospitalization are authorized under the supplementary medical benefits plan.

## TABLE OF MEDICARE BENEFITS
### Effective after January 1, 1992

### MEDICARE BASIC PLAN: HOSPITAL INSURANCE-- COVERED SERVICES PER BENEFIT PERIOD (1)

| Service | Benefit | Medicare Pays | A Person Pays** |
|---|---|---|---|
| HOSPITALIZATION Semiprivate room and board, general nursing and miscellaneous hospital services and supplies | First 60 days | All but $652 | $652 |
| | 61st to 90th day | All but $163 a day | $163 a day |
| | 91st to 150th day* | All but $326 a day | $326 a day |
| | Beyond 150 days | Nothing | All costs |
| POST-HOSPITAL SKILLED NURSING FACILITY CARE... In a facility approved by Medicare. A person must have been in a hospital for at least 3 days and enter the facility within 30 days after hospital discharge. (2) | First 20 days | 100% of approved amount | Nothing |
| | Additional 80 days | All but $81.50 a day | $81.50 a day |
| | Beyond 100 days | Nothing | All costs |
| HOME HEALTH CARE | Unlimited as medically necessary | Full cost | Nothing |
| HOSPICE CARE | Two 90-day periods and and one 30-day period (and possible extentions) | All but limited costs for outstanding drugs and inpatient respite care | Limited cost sharing for out-patient drugs and inpatient respite care |
| BLOOD | Blood | All but first 3 pints | For first 3 pints |

\* 60 Reserve days may be used only once, days used are not renewable.
\*\* These figures are for 1992 and are subject to change each year.
(1) A Benefit Period begins on the first day a person receives service as an inpatient in a hospital and ends after he has been out of hospital or skilled nursing facility for 60 days in a row.
(2) Medicare and private insurance will not pay for most nursing home care. A person pays for custodial care and most care in a nursing home.

### MEDICARE SUPPLEMENTARY PLAN: MEDICAL INSURANCE-- COVERED SERVICES PER CALENDAR YEAR

| Service | Benefit | Medicare Pays | A Person Pays |
|---|---|---|---|
| MEDICAL EXPENSE Physician's services, inpatient and outpatient medical services and supplies, physical and speech therapy, ambulance, etc. | Medicare pays for medical expenses in or out of the hospital. Some insurance policies pay less (or nothing) for hospital outpatient medical services in a doctor's office. | 80% of approved amount (after $100 deductible), with some exceptions (when no cost-sharing) | $100 deductible* plus 20% of balance of approved amount (plus any charge above ap-proved amount)** |
| HOME HEALTH CARE | Unlimited as medically necessary | Full cost | Nothing |
| OUTPATIENT HOSPITAL CARE | Unlimited as medically necessary | 80% of approved amount (after $100 deductible) | Subject to deductible plus 20% of balance of approved amount |
| BLOOD | Blood | 80% of approved amount (after first 3 pints) | For first 3 pints plus 20% of balance of approved amounts |

\* Once a person has $100 of expense for covered services in 1992, the deductible does not apply to any further covered services received for the rest of the year.
\*\* A person pays for charges higher than the amount approved by Medicare unless the doctor or supplier agrees to accept Medicare's approved amount as the total charge for services rendered.

# SOCIAL SECURITY TAXES

### J-1. What are the Social Security tax rates for employers and employees?

The tax rate is the same for both the employer and the employee. Every employer who employs one or more persons and every employee in covered employment is subject to the tax imposed under the Federal Insurance Contributions Act (FICA).

The social security tax consists of two taxes: the OASDI tax (the tax for old-age, survivors and disability insurance) and the Hospital Insurance (HI) tax (for the hospital part of Medicare).

For 1992, there are two maximum wage bases (the maximum amount of annual wage subject to the tax). The maximum wage base for the OASDI tax is $55,500. The maximum wage base for the Hospital Insurance (HI) tax is $130,200. Wages in excess of these amounts are not taxable.

For employees and employers in 1992, the rate of the OASDI tax is 6.20%, and the rate of the HI tax is 1.45%. Thus, the maximum OASDI tax for an employee in 1992 (with maximum earnings of $55,500) is $3,441.00. The maximum HI tax for an employee in 1992 (with maximum earnings of $130,200) is $1,887.90.

| SOCIAL SECURITY TAX ON EMPLOYEES AND EMPLOYERS | | | | |
| --- | --- | --- | --- | --- |
| Year | % Rate (OASDI) | Max. Wage Base | Max. Tax (each) | Max. Tax (both) |
| 1992 | 6.20 | $55,500 | $3,441.00 | $6,882.00 |

| MEDICARE TAX ON EMPLOYEES AND EMPLOYERS | | | | |
| --- | --- | --- | --- | --- |
| Year | % Rate (HI) | Max. Wage Base | Max. Tax (each) | Max. Tax (both) |
| 1992 | 1.45 | $130,200 | $1,887.90 | $3,775.80 |

The maximum wage bases and maximum taxes are subject to automatic adjustment in 1993 and after based on changes in wage levels.

**J-2. If an employee works for two employers during the year and more than the maximum tax is paid on his wages, will the overpayment be refunded to the employee and his employers?**

Each employer is required to withhold the employee's tax, and to pay the employer's tax, on wages up to the maximum earnings base for the year. Consequently, if an employee works for more than one employer during the year, the taxes paid may exceed the maximum payable for the year. In this case, the employee is entitled to a refund of his overpayment, or the overpayment will be credited to his income tax for the year. His employers, however, are not entitled to any refund or credit; each employer is liable for tax on his wages up to the maximum earnings base.

However, a group of corporations concurrently employing an individual will be considered a single employer if one of the group serves as a common paymaster for the entire group. This will result in such corporations having to pay no more in social security taxes than a single employer pays.

**J-3. Does an employer get an income tax deduction for his Social Security tax payments?**

Yes, the employer's social security tax is deductible as a business expense, but only if wages upon which taxes are paid are also deductible.

**J-4. Must Social Security taxes be paid on cash tips?**

Yes, an employee must pay Social Security taxes on cash tips of $20 or more a month from one employer. Such tips will be treated as wages for social security and income tax withholding purposes and must be reported. Cash tips of less than $20 a month are not reported.

The employee is required to report his tips to his employer within 10 days following the month in which the tips equal or exceed $20.

The employer must pay the usual employer tax on such tips.

Prior to 1988, an employer generally did not have to pay the tax on any tips to employees.

The employer must withhold income tax and deduct the employee social security and hospital insurance tax on tips reported to him. The withholding is to be made from any wages (other than tips) which are under the employer's control. Employers may deduct the tax due on tips during a calendar quarter on an estimated basis and adjust the amount deducted from wages paid to the employee either during the calendar quarter or within 30 days thereafter. If these wages are not sufficient to cover the employee tax due, the employee may (but is not required to) furnish the employer with additional funds to cover the tax.

The employee is directly responsible for paying any portion of the employee tax which the employer cannot collect from wages or from funds furnished by the employee. The employer is required to give statements to both the employee and the Internal Revenue Service showing the difference between the amount of the employee tax due and the amount collected by the employer.

### J-5. How does an individual report Social Security taxes on domestic help?

If an individual pays a domestic at least $50 in a calendar quarter, he must report the wages for social security purposes even though he has only the one employee. Ordinarily, the wages should be reported on Form 942. This is a special, simplified form, printed on the back of a return envelope. (A person who has business employees may report the wages of household employees on the same form he uses for other employees—Form 941.) The name, address, and social security number of the employee must be given, along with the amount of wages paid.

The tax (including both the employee and the employer tax), must be paid with the return. The return for the first quarter (January, February and March) is due on or before April 30; for the 2nd quarter, July 31; for the 3rd quarter, October 31; and for the last quarter, January 31st of the following year.

The employer should deduct the employee tax from each payment of cash wages to the employee if the employer expects to pay the employee at least $50 in the quarter. If the employer wishes to pay the employee tax without deducting it from the employee's wages, he or she may do so. The payment of the employee's tax will not constitute additional wages to the employee.

The employer does not withhold income tax on a household worker's wages. The household worker files an estimated tax return and pays his own income tax.

### J-6. What is the rate of Social Security tax for a self-employed person?

The tax on self-employed persons is imposed under the Self-Employment Contributions Act.

The self-employment tax consists of two taxes: the OASDI tax (the tax for old-age, survivors and disability insurance) and the Hospital Insurance (HI) tax (for the hospital insurance part of Medicare).

For 1992, there are two maximum wage bases (the maximum amount of net earnings subject to the tax). The maximum wage base for the OASDI tax is $55,500. The maximum wage base for the Hospital Insurance (HI) tax is $130,200. Net earnings in excess of these amounts are not taxable.

For 1992, the rate of the OASDI tax is 12.40%, and the rate of the HI tax is 2.90%. Thus, the maximum OASDI tax for a self-employed person in 1992 (with maximum earnings of $55,500) is $6,882.00. The maximum HI tax for a self-employed person in 1992 (with maximum earnings of $130,200) is $3,775.80.

There is a special federal (and generally following through to state) income tax deduction of 50% of the social security self-employment tax. This income tax deduction is designed to treat the self-employed in much the same manner as employees and employers are treated for Social Security and income tax purposes under present law.

### SOCIAL SECURITY TAX ON SELF-EMPLOYED PERSONS*

| Year | % Rate (OASDI) | Max. Earnings Base | Max. Tax |
|------|------|------|------|
| 1992 | 12.40 | $55,500 | $6,882.00 |

*There is a special income tax deduction of 50% of the self-employment tax.

### MEDICARE TAX ON SELF-EMPLOYED PERSONS*

| Year | % Rate (HI) | Max. Earnings Base | Max.Tax |
|------|------|------|------|
| 1992 | 2.90 | $130,200 | $3,775.80 |

*There is a special income tax deduction of 50% of the self-employment tax.

The maximum earnings bases and maximum taxes are subject to automatic adjustment in 1993 and after based on changes in wage levels.

(If a self-employed person reports his earnings on a fiscal year basis, the tax rate to be used is the one that applies to the calendar year in which the fiscal year began.)

**J-7. If a self-employed person also receives wages as an employee, what portion of his income is subject to tax as self-employment income?**

Only the difference between the maximum earnings base for the year and his wages received as an employee is subject to tax as self-employment income.

*Example (1).* Mr. Butts, an attorney, is employed as a part-time instructor for a law school; his salary is $20,000 a year. During 1992, Mr. Butts earned an additional $40,000 from his private practice, which counts as $36,940 for Social Security purposes (i.e., 92.35% of $40,000). Only $35,500 of his net earnings from self-employment is subject to the OASDI self-employment tax ($55,500 – $20,000). Note, however, that all of Mr. Butts' wages and $36,940 of his self-employment income are subject to the HI self-employment tax because the maximum earnings base for the HI tax is $130,200.

No self-employment tax is due unless net earnings from self-employment are at least $434 for the taxable year (because of the 92.35% factor). Nevertheless, in some cases, the amount of income subject to self-employment tax may be less than $400.

*Example (2).* Assume the same facts as in Example (1), except that Mr. Butts' salary as a law instructor is $55,300. Mr. Butts' net earnings from self-employment after application of the 92.35% factor ($36,940) exceed $400 and, hence, must be reported. However, only $200 is subject to the OASDI self-employment tax ($55,500 – $55,300 = $200), but the entire $36,940 is subject to the HI tax.

**J-8. Must a Social Security beneficiary who works pay Social Security taxes?**

Yes, even though he is receiving social security benefits, he must pay taxes at the same rate as other individuals.

*Example.* In 1992, Mr. Anderson, age 73, receives $500 a month in Social Security retirement benefits; he also works as an employee and earns $10,000 for the year. Mr. Anderson must pay $765 in social security taxes for 1992.

**J-9. How does a life insurance agent pay Social Security taxes on first-year and renewal commissions?**

If the agent is an *employee* when the policy is sold, both first-year and renewal commissions are *wages* at the time they are paid. (For status of a life insurance agent as an employee, see B-11.) Consequently, they are subject to the employer-employee tax in the year they are received by him. It does not matter whether, at the time of payment, the agent is an employee or a self-employed person. If the agent is a self-employed individual when the policy is sold, first-year and renewal commissions are treated as net earnings from self-employment in the year they are received.

Renewal commissions paid to the estate (or other beneficiary) of a deceased life insurance agent in a year after death are not subject to the employer-employee tax. Renewal commissions paid to a disabled life insurance agent after 1972 are not subject to the social security tax if he became entitled to disability insurance benefits before the year in which the renewal commission is paid and did not work for the employer during the period for which the payment is made. The renewal commissions of a self-employed agent do not constitute net earnings from self-employment to his widow(er) (they were not derived from a trade or business carried on by the widow(er)).

### J-10. Must the self-employment tax be included in a person's estimated tax return?

Yes.

### J-11. What is the federal income tax deduction for medical expense insurance premiums?

No premiums other than those for medical expense insurance will qualify for the deduction. If the taxpayer itemizes deductions, he may deduct the full amount of the medical expense insurance premiums subject to the 7.5% of adjusted gross income limit. The monthly premium for the voluntary medical plan under Medicare is treated as a medical expense insurance premium for this purpose.

### J-12. Are unemployment insurance benefits taxable?

All unemployment benefits received are fully taxable. They no longer qualify for a limited exclusion.

# SURVIVOR BENEFIT PLAN

### K-1. Is there a relationship between Social Security and the Survivor Benefit Plan for retired military personnel?

Yes. The Survivor Benefit Plan provides for a reduction in plan benefits for certain beneficiaries also eligible for social security benefits. Those beneficiaries are widows and widowers age 62.

### K-2. In general, how does the Survivor Benefit Plan work?

The plan provides survivor benefits for eligible widows, widowers and dependent children of retired military personnel. It applies to a person who is married or has a dependent child when he becomes entitled to retired pay *unless* he elects not to participate. The retired pay of a participant is reduced from the full pay he would otherwise receive.

### K-3. What is the amount of the survivor benefit?

It is determined from what the retiree designates as his *base amount*. The base amount may be either his full retirement pay, which would produce the maximum survivor benefits, or some lesser amount, but not less than $300 per month. In most instances, the survivor benefit is 55% of the base amount.

### K-4. Since mothers and fathers of dependent children and widow(er)s are entitled to Social Security benefits, are their survivor benefits reduced?

Yes, but not necessarily on a matching basis. Under the Survivor Benefit Plan, the calculation is made as if the serviceman had lived to age 65, whether or not he did. Also, only earnings after 1956 are counted. This means that, for calculation purposes, following retirement there would be a period of years of no earnings under social security (military retirement pay is not subject to social security taxes). The AIME which would be calculated would be considerably lower than the AIME the retiree would have at the time of his death, assuming he died before age 65. As a result, the reduction for social security benefits would be less than the amount actually being received by the beneficiary.

## K-5. Is the retiree's military retirement pay reduced to pay for the survivor benefit?

Yes. The formula for the reduction is 2-1/2% of the first $300 ($7.50) plus 10% of the remainder of the base amount.

# FILING FOR BENEFITS

## GENERAL INFORMATION

**L-1. Basically, what procedure should be followed to determine if a person is eligible for social security benefits?**

An individual eligible for benefits should not delay more than six months before contacting his social security office because the law in almost all cases does not permit the payment of monthly benefits retroactively for a period longer than six months.

Payment of monthly benefits retroactively for a period of 12 months is permitted for worker's disability benefits, widow(er)'s benefits based on disability, and spouse's and child's benefits based on the earnings record of a worker entitled to disability benefits.

In general, retroactive benefits cannot be paid if doing so would cause a reduction in future benefits (i.e., it would effectively mean that an individual would be filing for "early retirement," in which case an actuarial reduction in benefits is required). For example, if a retroactive application for retirement benefits were to cause a retiree's initial entitlement month to fall before the individual reached age 65, no retroactive benefits could be paid for the months prior to age 65. However, there are exceptions to this rule which permit payment of retroactive benefits even though it causes an actuarial reduction in benefits.

Beginning with applications for benefits filed on or after January 1, 1991, the following two categories of individuals eligible for actuarially reduced benefits are no longer eligible for retroactive benefits: (1) individuals who have dependents who would be entitled to unreduced benefits during the retroactive period (e.g., a retiree under age 65 who has a spouse age 65 or over), and (2) individuals who have pre-retirement earnings over the amount allowed under the social security retirement test that could be charged off against benefits for months prior to the month of application, thus permitting an early retiree to receive benefits for months prior to actual retirement.

A person cannot receive more than one full monthly benefit. If eligible for more than one monthly benefit, the amount payable will be equal to the largest one for which the person is eligible.

Each application form clearly shows the extent to which it may be used as an application for benefits. For example, the applications for the lump-sum death payment or for monthly benefits (other than disability benefits) may be applications for all benefits that a claimant may be entitled to on any social security account. The scope of any application may, however, be expanded or restricted as the claimant desires if appropriate remarks are added in writing on the application form. The Social Security Administration will use the application to make an *initial determination* regarding the amount of benefits, if any.

When the application for benefits has been approved, the U.S. Treasury mails a check to the applicant. The benefit *for* a month is paid *in* the next month. Monthly benefit payments to a husband and wife who are entitled to benefits on the same social security account and are living at the same address are usually combined into one check made out to them jointly. However, individual checks will be sent if either prefers to have a separate check. Benefit payments to children in one family unit are usually combined in one check. Where the children are members of different households, separate checks will be issued to each family group.

Benefit notices from the Social Security Administration must: (1) use clear and simple language, (2) include the local office telephone number and address (in notices generated by local social security offices), and (3) include the address and telephone number of the social security office serving the recipient (in notices generated by central offices of the Social Security Administration).

### L-2. When should a person file for retirement benefits?

A person should get in touch with the nearest social security district office two or three months before retirement (age 62 or later). The district office will provide the information needed to decide whether or not to file an application for retirement benefits at that time. Beginning in 1991, because of the rules regarding retroactive benefits, a person should consider filing for benefits on January 1 of the year that he attains age 65.

If a worker does not file an application, he should contact the social security office again (1) one or two months before retirement, (2) as soon as the worker knows he or she will neither earn more than the monthly exempt amount in wages nor render substantial services in self-employment in one or more months of the year, or (3) two or three months before the worker's 65th birthday, even if still working.

### L-3. At what time should the survivors of a deceased worker file for survivor's benefits?

An application should be filed immediately in the month of death by or for *each* person who is entitled to a benefit as a survivor of a deceased worker.

An application for the lump-sum death payment must be filed within the two-year period after the worker's death, unless the applicant is the widow (or widower) of the deceased and she (or he) was entitled to spouse's benefits when the insured person died. In the latter case, no application for the lump-sum is required.

### L-4. When should a person file an application for disability benefits?

An application for the establishment of a period of disability may be filed before the first day that the period can begin. In such circumstances, the application will be valid if the person actually becomes eligible for the period of disability at some time before a final decision on his application is made.

When a person applies for monthly disability benefits, he simultaneously applies for a "disability freeze."

### L-5. When should a person file an application for the lump-sum death payment?

An application must be filed within a two-year period by the person eligible for the lump sum unless the eligible person is the widow(er) of the deceased worker, and was entitled to spouse's benefits for the month before the month in which the worker died. In the later case, no application for the lump sum is required.

An application filed after the two-year period will be deemed to have been filed within the two-year period if there is good cause for a failure to file the application in time.

### PROOF REQUIRED

### L-6. What proofs are required before survivors' and retirement benefits can be paid?

Social security survivors' and retirement benefits cannot be paid until satisfactory proofs have been furnished of (a) the death of a covered person, (b) ages of the retired person and of each other person entitled to a benefit, and (c) the relationship of each beneficiary to the deceased or retired person upon whose wage base benefits are payable.

### L-7. What is an acceptable proof of death?

Acceptable proofs of death are easy to get in every part of the U.S. today: certified copy of the city or county vital statistics record, certificate of the attending physician, of the hospital where death occurred, and of the funeral director.

### L-8. What are the best forms of proof of a deceased person's age and family relationship?

Satisfactory proof of a deceased person's age may occasionally be difficult to obtain; and a long delay and great effort may be required to gather acceptable proofs of the ages and family relationships of living persons—especially older people and people who were born in countries other than the U.S.

The best forms of proof of age, in approximate order of preference, are as follows:

1. Birth certificate or copy of official public record.
2. Baptismal certificate or copy of church or other religious record.
3. Certified copy of hospital birth record.
4. (Old) family Bible record.
5. Naturalization, immigration, military, passport and similar official government records.

A person should obtain, and file among his valuable papers, the most acceptable form of proof of the ages and relationships of all members of his family. This will save time, effort and money later when social security benefits become payable. Numbers 1-3 above should be established before age 5 to be considered of highest value.

The best forms of proof of family relationships are as follows:

1. Adoption papers if any.
2. Marriage certificates or transcript of license record.
3. Certified copy of church record.
4. Affidavit of the minister, rabbi, priest or civil officer who performed the wedding ceremony.
5. Affidavits of two witnesses to the marriage ceremony.
6. Children's birth certificates showing names and ages of parents.

## RIGHT TO APPEAL

### L-9. Is there a review procedure available if a person is disappointed with the Social Security Administration's initial determination regarding benefits?

Yes, if a person requests a reconsideration of the initial determination. The request for reconsideration must be made by letter or on a special form (available at social security offices) within 60 days after the date the notice of the initial determination is received. The date of receipt of such notice is presumed to be five days after the date listed on the notice.

The reconsideration process is an independent review of the case by the Social Security Administration. It is based on evidence submitted for the initial determination plus any additional information that is provided. A reconsideration is made by a member of a different staff from the one that made the initial determination and who is specially trained in the handling of reconsiderations.

When a person can demonstrate that he failed to appeal an adverse decision because of reliance on incorrect, incomplete, or misleading information provided by the Social Security Administration, his failure to appeal may not serve as the basis for denial of a second application for any social security benefit. This protection applies to both initial denials and reconsiderations. The Social Security Administration is required to include in all notices of denial a clear, simple description on the effect of reapplying for benefits rather than filing an appeal.

### L-10. Is it possible to appeal the reconsideration determination?

Yes, if a person asks for a hearing. However, if the claim was regarding the amount of hospital insurance benefits, the amount in question must be $100 or more. Carriers review complaints about the amount of medical insurance benefits.

A person may also be able to use the expedited appeals procedure if he has no dispute with the findings of fact of the reconsideration determination beyond a contention that a section of the applicable statute is unconstitutional. (For further details, see L-14.)

A hearing is conducted by an administrative law judge of the Office of Hearings and Appeals. A person may represent himself or be represented by a lawyer or any other individual. If a person does not wish to appear at the hearing, he may request that the case be reviewed based on the evidence on file. Any additional evidence should be submitted with the request for a hearing or soon after.

The hearing is usually held within 75 miles of a person's home or normal business travel area. A person will be notified of the date and place of the hearing at least 10 days in advance.

At times, the administrative law judge will examine the evidence and certify a case to the Appeals Council with a recommended decision. (See L-13.)

### L-11. How is a hearing request made?

A request for a hearing is made by filling out Form HA-501, "Request for Hearing," or by writing a letter to the nearest social security office, a presiding officer, or with the Appeals Council. The request for a hearing must be made within 60 days after the date that the notice of the reconsidered decision is received and must include: (1) the name and social security number of the individual; (2) the reason for disagreeing with the reconsidered or revised determination; (3) a statement of additional evidence which will be submitted; and (4) the name and address of the individual's representative, if any. The 60 day time limit can be extended if there is a good reason.

A beneficiary of disability benefits has the option of having his benefits continued through the hearing stage of appeal. If the earlier unfavorable determinations are upheld by the administrative law judge, the benefits are subject to recovery by the Social Security Administration. (If an appeal is made in good faith, recovery may be waived.) Medicare eligibility is also continued, but Medicare benefits are not subject to recovery.

### L-12. What will a hearing cost?

There is no charge for a hearing. Of course, if a person is represented by a lawyer, he must pay that fee. A person must pay for all travel expenses also unless the hearing is held more than 75 miles from his or her home. If this happens, he will be reimbursed for reasonable travel expenses.

### L-13. If a person disagrees with the hearing decision, may he ask for a review?

Yes, within 60 days from the receipt of the notice of the hearing decision. A review of the hearing by the Appeals Council of the Office of Hearings and Appeals may be requested on a special form (available at any social security office) or by writing the nearest social security district office, a presiding officer or the Appeals Council.

The Appeals Council will review a hearing decision or dismissal where: (1) there appears to be an abuse of discretion by the administrative law judge; (2) there is an error of law; (3) the presiding officer's action, findings, or conclusions are not supported by substantial evidence; or (4) there is a broad policy of procedural issue which may affect the general public interest.

The Appeals Council will notify the person as to whether or not it will review the case. If the Council decides to review the case, the claimant may request an appearance before the Appeals Council (either personally or through a representative), for the presentation of oral arguments. If the Appeals Council determines that a significant question of law or policy is presented, or that oral arguments would be beneficial in rendering a proper decision, the request will be granted. The claimant may also file written briefs in support of his claim. The Appeals Council will notify the claimant of its action in the case.

If an administrative law judge makes a decision in favor of a person in a disability case on or after November 10, 1988, and the Appeals Council does not render a final decision within 110 days, interim disability benefits are provided to the person. (Delays in excess of 20 days caused by or on behalf of the claimant do not count in determining the 110-day period.) These benefits begin with the month before the month in which the 110-day period expires, and are not considered overpayments if the final decision is adverse, unless the benefits are fraudulently obtained.

### L-14. May a person file a civil action in the U.S. District Court?

Yes, if he disagrees with the decision of the Appeals Council or if the Appeals Council has denied his request for a review of the hearing decision. To file a civil action regarding the amount of hospital insurance benefits, however, the amount in question must be $1,000 or more. The Social Security Act does not provide for court review of a determination concerning the amount of benefits payable under the Medical Insurance Plan.

A person has 60 days from the receipt of the notice of the Appeals Council's decision (or its denial of a request for review) to file a civil action. This time limit may be extended by the Appeals Council for good reason.

The Court's jurisdiction is limited to rendering a decision on the record and the Social Security Administration's findings of fact are binding on the Court, if supported by substantial evidence.

A person may be able to advance directly from a reconsideration determination to the U.S. District Court by filing a claim contending that the applicable statute of the Social Security Act is unconstitutional. This procedure, known as expedited appeals process, is allowable when: (1) the individual has presented his or her claim at the reconsideration level; (2) the only issue is the constitutionality of the statutory requirement; (3) the claim is neither invalid or cognizable under a different section of the Act; and (4) the amount in controversy is $1,000 or more.

In order to reach the U.S. District Court after a reconsideration determination, the Social Security Administration must determine that the claim raises a constitutional question and is appropriate for treatment under the expedited appeals procedure. After this is done, the Social Security Administration and the individual must sign an agreement that identifies the constitutional issue involved and explains the final reconsideration determination.

A person must file for expedited judicial review within 60 days after the date of receipt of notice of the reconsideration determination. An extension of time is available if good cause is established for not filing on time.

Should the Social Security Administration determine that a claim is not appropriate for expedited judicial review before the U.S. District Court, its decision is final and not subject to administrative or judicial review. It is required, however, to notify the person filing the claim of its decision, and to treat the person's request as a request for a reconsideration, a hearing, or an Appeals Council review (whichever is appropriate).

Note, however, that in 1977 the Supreme Court held that the Social Security Act does not permit a person to have subject-matter jurisdiction to the U.S. District Courts to review a decision of the Social Security Administration not to reopen a previously adjudicated claim for social security benefits. The Court found that unless the claim was based on a constitutional challenge, the Act did not authorize judicial review to reopen a final decision on disability benefits after the 60 day limit for a review by civil action had terminated (*Califano v. Sanders*).

# BENEFITS FOR FEDERAL GOVERNMENT EMPLOYEES

## INTRODUCTION

### M-1. What are the two retirement systems for federal employees?

There are nearly two million full-time civilian federal employees. About 2.4 million Americans currently receive some form of benefits under the retirement systems for federal employees.

There are two retirement systems for federal employees: the Civil Service Retirement System (CSRS) and the Federal Employees' Retirement System (FERS).

The CSRS, created in 1920, was the only retirement system for federal employees until the FERS became public law in 1986. FERS created a new federal retirement program coordinated with Social Security retirement benefits for federal employees hired after 1983. Federal employees in FERS are automatically covered by Social Security and must pay Social Security taxes, while federal employees who remain in CSRS are exempt from Social Security taxes. FERS also provides a guaranteed basic annuity and a tax-deferred savings plan similar to a Section 401(k) retirement plan.

## FEDERAL EMPLOYEES' RETIREMENT SYSTEM

### M-2. Who is covered under the Federal Employees' Retirement System?

The Federal Employees' Retirement System (FERS) is a three-tier retirement system for federal workers who began work with the government after 1983. In addition, a number of federal employees hired before 1984 elected to transfer from the Civil Service Retirement System (CSRS) to FERS during a 1987 transfer period.

### M-3. Who is eligible for FERS benefits?

Unreduced retirement benefits are provided at age 60 with 20 or more years of service, at age 62 with five or more years of service, and at "minimum retirement age" with 30 years of service. The minimum retirement age is currently 55.

The "minimum retirement age" for employees with 30 or more years of service is gradually increasing. Until the year 2003, an employee with 30 years of service may retire at age 55. Beginning in the year 2003, the minimum retirement age increases by two months every year until year 2009. Thus, at 2009 the employee must be age 56 to retire with 30 or more years of service. Age 56 continues to be the minimum retirement age until 2020. Beginning in the year 2021, the minimum retirement age again increases by two-month increments until the year 2027. The minimum retirement age for employees with 30 or more years of service is 57 in the year 2027 and after. The minimum retirement age for reduced benefits is also being gradually increased from 55 to 57. An employee must have at least 10 years of service to be eligible for reduced retirement benefits. For an employee retiring with less than 30 years of service, a reduction of 5 percent per year for each year under age 62 is imposed. Thus, benefits for an employee retiring at age 55 are reduced 35%.

An employee can leave government employment prior to the date that he is eligible for a retirement benefit and still be eligible for a Basic Annuity at a later date. If the employee has five years of creditable service and does not withdraw contributions when he terminates government service, he may receive a deferred, unreduced annuity when he attains age 62 with at least five years of civil service employment; age 60 with at least 20 years of service; or at minimum retirement age (currently age 55) with at least 30 years of service.

An employee is entitled to a Basic Annuity at age 50 with 20 years of service or at any age after completing 25 years of service, if: (1) his retirement is involuntary (except by removal by cause for misconduct or delinquency) and he did not decline a reasonable offer for a position which is not lower than two grades below his present position; or (2) his retirement is voluntary because his agency is undergoing a major reduction in employees, reorganization, or a transfer of function in which a number of employees are separated or downgraded.

## Basic Annuity

### M-4. What is the Basic Annuity?

The Basic Annuity is the second tier of benefits under FERS. Social Security is the first tier of benefits. Social Security includes retirement, disability and survivor benefits, and health insurance benefits under Medicare. The Basic Annuity provides retirement, disability and survivor benefits in addition to those provided by Social Security. The Basic Annuity guarantees a specific monthly retirement payment based on the employee's age, length of creditable service, and "high-3" years' average salary. An employee must have five years of creditable service and be subject to FERS at separation in order to be eligible for a Basic Annuity.

### M-5. How much must an employee contribute to the Basic Annuity?

An employee contributes 0.8% of his basic pay to the Basic Annuity. Certain FERS members pay an additional 0.5% to the Basic Annuity. These members include firefighters, law enforcement personnel, air traffic controllers, members of Congress and Congressional employees. Basic pay does not include bonuses, overtime pay, military pay, holiday pay, cash awards or special allowances given in addition to basic pay. The federal government makes a contribution to the Basic Annuity plan pursuant to formula.

### M-6. What annuities are available to a retiring employee?

The following annuities are available to a retiring federal employee:

- an annuity with no survivor benefit.

- a lump-sum credit of the employee's contributions (excluding interest) with a reduced annuity.

- an annuity to the employee for life, with a survivor annuity payable for the life of the surviving spouse.

- a lump-sum credit of the employee's contributions (excluding interest) with a reduced annuity which is further reduced to provide a survivor benefit.

- a reduced annuity with a survivor benefit to a person with an insurable interest, provided the employee is in good health.

Note, however, that an employee cannot elect against providing survivor benefits to his spouse unless his spouse consents to the election in writing.

### M-7. What is the amount of the Basic Annuity?

The amount of the Basic Annuity depends on the employee's years of service and highest three-year ("high-3") average salary. It also depends on whether an annuity supplement is added into the Basic Annuity formula.

For employees under age 62, or age 62 or older with less than 20 years of FERS service, the formula, not including the supplement where applicable, is:

- 1.0 percent × "high-3" average salary x length of service

For employees age 62 or older with at least 20 years of FERS service, the formula is:

- 1.1 percent × "high-3" average salary x length of service

(No annuity supplement is payable if the employee is age 62 or older.)

For law enforcement officers, firefighters, air traffic controllers, employees of Congress, foreign service employees, and certain CIA employees, the formula is:

(1) 1.7 percent × "high-3" average salary × years of service up to 20 years, plus

(2) 1.0 percent × "high-3" average salary × years of service over 20 years, plus

(3) the annuity supplement, where applicable.

All periods of creditable service are totaled to determine length of service. Years and months of creditable service (extra days are dropped) are then used in the annuity computation formula.

"High-3" average salary is the highest pay obtainable by averaging an employee's rates of basic pay in effect over any 3 consecutive years of service. The 3 years need not be continuous, but they must consist of consecutive periods of service. In other words, two or more separate periods of employment which follow each other can be joined to make up the 3 consecutive years.

*Example.* Steve Johnston retires at age 65 after 30 years of civil service employment. His "High-3" average salary is $31,000 ($30,000 + $31,000 + $32,000 ÷ 3 = $31,000. His FERS benefit is computed as follows:

(1) 1.1% × $31,000 = $341

(2) $341 × 30 years of service = $10,230 Basic Annuity.

## M-8. How is the Basic Annuity adjusted for cost-of-living increases?

The Basic Annuity for employees age 62 or older is adjusted for cost-of-living increases pursuant to the following schedule:

(1) Where the change in the Consumer Price Index for All Urban Wage Earners and Clerical Workers (CPI) for the year is less than 2.0%, the annuity is increased by the full amount of the CPI increase.

(2) Where the change in the CPI for the year is at least 2.0% but is not more than 3.0%, the annuity is increased by 2.0%.

(3)  Where the change in the CPI for the year is more than 3.0%, the annuity is increased by the CPI less one percent. For example, if the CPI increases 4.5%, the Basic Annuity will increase 3.5%.

The cost-of-living increase for 1992 is 2.7%. The increase is effective December 1 for any year that a cost-of-living adjustment is necessitated.

## M-9. What is the Annuity Supplement?

An Annuity Supplement is added to the Basic Annuity as a substitute for Social Security when the employee is receiving the Basic Annuity and is under age 62. It is equal to the estimated amount of Social Security benefits that the employee would be eligible to receive at age 62 based on civil service employment earnings. The Supplement ends when the employee first becomes eligible for a Social Security retirement benefit (age 62).

The Supplement is payable to: (1) employees who retire after the minimum retirement age (currently age 55) with 30 years of service; (2) employees who retire at age 60 with 20 years of service; and (3) employees who retire involuntarily and have reached minimum retirement age (currently age 55).

The Supplement is not subject to cost-of-living increases, and is reduced for excess earnings after retirement in much the same way that Social Security benefits are reduced for excess earnings. In 1992, the Supplement is reduced by $1 for every $2 that the beneficiary earns over $7,440.

## Survivor Benefits

## M-10. What survivors' benefits are payable under FERS?

Survivor benefits are paid upon the death of an employee or retired civil service employee. Benefits are paid on a monthly basis or in a lump-sum to eligible survivors. The spouse, former spouse and dependent children of a deceased employee may be entitled to a survivor annuity.

A spouse may be entitled to a "post-retirement survivor benefit." The annuity of a married employee who retires is reduced by 10% to provide a survivor annuity for his spouse, unless the employee and his spouse both waive the survivor annuity. A surviving spouse is entitled to 50% of the employee's unreduced annuity increased by cost-of-living benefit adjustments.

The surviving spouse: (1) must have been married to the employee for at least nine months; or (2) must be the parent of a child of the marriage at the time of death, or (3) the death of the retired employee must have been accidental.

If the survivor is under age 60 and Social Security survivor benefits are *not* payable, benefits are the lesser of: (1) current CSRS survivor benefits; or (2) 50% (25% if elected) of accrued annuity plus a Social Security "equivalent." When Social Security survivor benefits are payable, FERS pays 50% (25% if elected) of the deceased retiree's annuity.

If the employee was unmarried at the time of retirement and then married after retirement, he may elect a reduced annuity with a survivor benefit for his spouse. Such an election must take place within two years after the marriage.

If the spouse dies before the retired employee, and the retired employee remarries, the new spouse is eligible to receive the same survivor benefits as the former spouse. The retired employee must elect to take a reduced annuity with a survivor benefit for his new spouse.

A retired employee and spouse who have elected against a survivor benefit can change their election within 18 months. The retired employee must pay the full cost of providing the survivor annuity if an election is made during this second election period.

There is also a survivor benefit for the spouse of an employee who dies prior to retirement. The surviving spouse is entitled to: (1) a guaranteed amount of $18,601.94 in 1992, plus 50% of the employee's final salary or, if higher, his "high-3" average. In addition, if the deceased employee completed 10 or more years of service, the surviving spouse is entitled to an annuity equal to 50% of the unreduced annuity the employee would have been entitled to had he reached retirement age. Survivor benefits are subject to cost-of-living adjustments.

The $18,601.94 payment can be in a lump-sum or in monthly installments.

The surviving spouse: (1) must have been married to the employee for at least nine months, or (2) must be the parent of a child of the marriage, or (3) the death of the employee must have been accidental. The deceased employee must also have at least 18 months of creditable service while subject to FERS.

### M-11. Is the former spouse of a deceased employee entitled to a survivor benefit?

The former spouse of a deceased employee may be entitled to a survivor benefit if he or she: (1) was married to the deceased employee for at least nine months; (2) has not remarried prior to age 55; and (3) a court order or court-approved property settlement agreement provides for payment of a survivor annuity to the former spouse.

The survivor annuity is payable to a former spouse when: (1) the deceased employee has at least 18 months of creditable service under FERS; or (2) the deceased former employee has title to a deferred annuity and has 10 years of service.

A former spouse who does not meet the requirements listed above may still be entitled to an annuity if the retiree, at the time of retirement, elected to provided the former spouse with a survivor annuity.

The amount of the survivor annuity for a former spouse is the same as that for a spouse, except that the Guaranteed Amount ($18,601.94) is not payable unless payment is required under a court order or agreement.

### M-12. Is there a survivor benefit for the children of a deceased employee?

If a retiree or an employee has 18 months of creditable service under FERS before he dies, his dependent children are entitled to monthly annuities reduced by the amount of any Social Security survivor benefits they receive. The annuity begins on the day after the death and ends on the last day of the month before the one in which the child dies, marries, reaches age 18, or if over 18, becomes capable of self-support. The annuity of a child who is a student ends on the last day of the month before he: (1) marries; (2) dies; (3) ceases to be a student; or (4) attains the age of 22. If a student drops out of school or his annuity is terminated, it can be restored if he later returns to school and is still under age 22 and unmarried.

The amount of the benefit depends on whether the child is eligible to receive Social Security benefits and whether the deceased worker's spouse is still living.

If the retiree or employee is survived by a spouse or the child has a living parent, each eligible child is entitled to receive an annuity in 1992 equal to the lessor of:

(1) 60 percent of the employee's "high-3" average pay, divided by the number of qualified children.

(2) $882 per month, divided by the number of qualified children.

(3) $294 per month.

If the retiree or employee is *not* survived by a spouse or the child has *no* living parent, each eligible child is entitled to receive an annuity in 1992 equal to the lessor of:

(1) 75 percent of the employee's "high-3" average pay, divided by the number of qualified children.

(2) $1,056 per month, divided by the number of qualified children.

(3) $352 per month.

## M-13. Is a person with an insurable interest in a retiree or employee eligible for a survivor benefit?

A retiree or employee can designate that a survivor annuity be paid to a person with an insurable interest in the life of the retiree or employee. The benefit is equal to 50% of the retiree's benefit, but is reduced depending on the difference in the age of the person with the insurable interest and the age of the retiring employee.

If the age difference is 30 years or more, the annuity is reduced 40%; if the age difference is 25 to 29 years, the reduction is 35%; if the age difference is 20 to 24 years, the reduction is 30%; if the age difference is 15 to 19 years, the reduction is 25%; if the age difference is 10 to 14 years, the reduction is 20%; if the age difference is 5 to 9 years, the reduction is 15%; if the age difference is less than 5 years, the reduction is 10%.

## M-14. When is a lump-sum survivor benefit paid?

A lump-sum survivor benefit is payable immediately after the death of an employee if the employee: (1) has *less* than 18 months of creditable service; or (2) leaves *no* widow(er), former spouse or children who are eligible for a survivor annuity.

The lump-sum survivor benefit is the amount paid into the Civil Service Retirement and Disability Fund by the employee. It also includes accrued interest.

The employee, former employee or annuitant has the right to name the lump-sum survivor benefit beneficiary. If no beneficiary is named, the lump-sum is payable to the widow(er); if there is no widow(er), it is paid to his living children in equal shares; if no children, it is paid to his parents; if no parents, it is paid to the executor or administrator of his estate; if none of the above, it is paid to the next of kin under the laws of the state where the deceased was domiciled.

### Disability Benefits

## M-15. What disability benefits are paid under FERS?

Disability benefits are payable to an employee with 18 months of creditable service who, because of injury or disease, can no longer perform his job in a useful and efficient manner. The beneficiary is entitled to a benefit equal to 60% of his "high-3" average pay during the first year of disability, reduced dollar for dollar by any Social Security disability benefit. After the first year, the beneficiary is entitled to 40% of his "high-3" average pay, reduced by 60% of the Social Security disability benefit. The benefit is further adjusted at age 62 to equal the *lessor* of: (1) a retirement benefit computed as if he had worked during his years of disability; or (2) the disability benefit he would receive after the benefit is offset by any Social Security disability benefit. Disability benefits are adjusted after the first year of disability by the increase in the Consumer Price Index for All Urban Wage Earners and Clerical Workers (CPI). Where the change in the CPI for the year is less than 2.0%, the benefit is increased by the full amount of the CPI increase. Where the change in the CPI for the year is at least 2.0% but is not more than 3.0%, the benefit is increased by 2%. Where the change in the CPI for the year is more than 3.0%, the benefit is increased by the CPI less one percent. Periodic medical examinations are required until the beneficiary reaches age 60.

## Thrift Savings Plan

### M-16. What is the Thrift Savings Plan for FERS employees?

The Thrift Plan creates a kind of third tier of benefits under FERS. A thrift plan account is set up automatically for every employee covered under FERS.

The government contributes 1 percent of pay to an account for each employee even if the employee declines to contribute to the plan. In addition, the government matches employee contributions as follows:

(1) Contributions up to the first 3 percent of pay, dollar for dollar;

(2) Contributions that are more than 3 percent but not more than 5 percent of pay, 50 cents per dollar.

A FERS employee may contribute up to 10 percent of his salary towards the Thrift Plan.

Contributions, and earnings on contributions, are not subject to federal income taxation until distributed to the employee at retirement. In addition, contributions reduce the employee's gross income for federal income tax purposes. (Contributions are subject to Social Security taxes, however.)

Contributions can be directed by employees to three investment funds:

(1) Government securities fund (G Fund);

(2) Fixed-income fund (F Fund);

(3) Stock index fund (C Fund).

All government contributions through 1992 must be held in the government securities fund (G Fund). FERS employees may elect to invest any portion of their current account balances and/or future contributions in the G Fund, F Fund or C Fund. Participants may make four interfund transfers in any calendar year, subject to a one-transfer per month limit.

Thrift Plan payments may be made in the following manner:

(1) At retirement or disability, if eligible for a Basic Annuity, the payment may be made as an immediate or deferred annuity, a lump-sum payment, a fixed-term payment, or by transfer to an IRA or other qualified pension plan.

(2) At death, funds in the Thrift Plan are paid to eligible survivors or to beneficiaries as specified by FERS.

(3) At termination of employment, if eligible for a deferred Basic Annuity, the payment may be made as an immediate or deferred annuity, a transfer to an IRA or other qualified pension plan, or over a fixed term after the employee retires with a Basic Annuity.

(4) At termination of employment, if not eligible for a deferred Basic Annuity, the payment must be transferred to an IRA or qualified pension plan.

## M-17. Can members of the Civil Service Retirement System take advantage of the Thrift Plan?

Yes, but there are two differences:

(1) The government does not contribute to the employee's plan, no matter how much the employee contributes.

(2) CSRS employees may contribute no more than 5% of base pay to the Thrift Plan.

### CIVIL SERVICE RETIREMENT SYSTEM

## M-18. Which federal employees are covered under the Civil Service Retirement System?

The Civil Service Retirement System (CSRS) covers employees of the U.S. government and the District of Columbia who were hired before January 1, 1984, unless coverage is specifically excluded by law.

Among the exclusions from CSRS coverage are employees who are subject to another federal retirement system. Employees subject to the Federal Employees' Retirement System (FERS) are excluded from participation in CSRS.

CSRS coverage for pre-1984 employees is automatic for all federal employees except those who are employed by Congress. Congressional employees must have elected coverage.

### M-19. Who is eligible for a CSRS retirement annuity?

An employee must meet two requirements in order to be eligible for a CSRS retirement annuity. First, the employee must complete at least five years of civilian service with the government. Second, the employee, unless retiring on account of total disability, must have been employed under the CSRS for at least one year out of the last two years before separation from service.

The total service of an employee or member of Congress is measured in full years and months. Anything less than a full month is not counted. An employee's service is credited from the date of original employment to the date of separation. No credit is allowed for a period of separation from service in excess of three calendar days.

An employee is allowed credit for periods of military service if performed prior to the date of separation from his civilian position.

### M-20. How are CSRS benefits paid for?

CSRS benefits are funded by deductions from the basic pay of covered employees, matching contributions from their employing agencies, and by payments from the General Treasury for the balance of the cost of the system. Under the current law, the employee and the employing agency *each* contribute:

- 8.0% of basic pay for Members of Congress,
- 7.5% of basic pay for Congressional employees, law enforcement officers and firefighters, and
- 7.0% of basic pay for other employees.

The portion of compensation withheld and contributed to the retirement and disability fund is includable in the employee's gross income in the same taxable year in which it would have been included if it had been paid to the employee directly. No refund is allowed for taxes attributable to mandatory contributions from the employee's salary to the Civil Service Retirement Fund.

## M-21. Who is entitled to an immediate annuity?

An immediate annuity begins no later than one month after separation from the service. This includes an annuity for an employee who retires optionally — for age, for disability, or due to involuntary separation from the service. It does not include an annuity for a separated employee who is entitled to a deferred retirement annuity at a future date.

An employee who is separated from the service is entitled to an annuity:

(1) at age 55 with 30 years of service,

(2) at age 60 with 20 years of service,

(3) at age 62 with 5 years of service,

(4) at age 50 with 20 years of service as a law enforcement officer or firefighter, or a combination of such service totaling at least 20 years.

An employee whose separation is involuntary, except for removal for cause on charges of misconduct or delinquency, is entitled to a reduced annuity after 25 years of service or after age 50 and 20 years of service. However, no annuity is payable if the employee has declined a reasonable offer of another position in the employee's agency for which the employee is qualified, which is not lower than two grades (pay levels) below the employee's grade, and which is within the employee's commuting area.

Also entitled to this reduced annuity is an employee who, while serving in a geographic area designated by the Office of Personnel Management, is voluntarily separated during a period in which: (1) the agency in which the employee is serving is undergoing a major reorganization, a major reduction in force, or a major transfer of function, and (2) a significant percentage of employees serving in this agency will be separated or subject to an immediate reduction in the rate of basic pay.

Such early retirements must be approved by the Office of Personnel Management. The annuities are reduced by 2 percent for each year the employee is under age 55.

## M-22. Are there alternative forms of CSRS retirement annuities?

Yes, an employee may, at the time of retirement, elect the following alternative forms of annuities:

(1) payment of an annuity to the employee for life,

(2) payment of an annuity to the employee for life, with a survivor annuity payable for the life of a surviving spouse,

(3) payment of an annuity to the employee for life, with benefit to a named person having an insurable interest,

(4) election of lump-sum credit option and reduced monthly annuity.

### M-23. What is an annuity for life?

The annuitant has a right to receive monthly payments during his lifetime unless he is convicted of certain offenses against the United States. Upon the annuitant's death, any accrued annuity that remains unpaid will be paid to: (1) the deceased annuitant's executor or administrator, or (2) if there is no executor or administrator, to the decedent's next of kin under state law, after 30 days have passed from the date of death.

### M-24. What are the features of an annuity with a survivor benefit?

An annuity with survivor benefit entitles the survivor to an annuity equal to 55% of the annuity amount prior to reduction for the election of the survivor benefit. An annuity for a married employee will automatically include an annuity for a surviving spouse unless the employee and spouse waive the spouse's annuity in writing. The written waiver requirement can be overcome only in instances where the employee's spouse cannot be located or where other exceptional circumstances are present.

Generally, the survivor benefit is paid until the survivor dies or remarries. However, remarriage of a widow or widower who is at least age 55 does not terminate the survivor annuity. Where the survivor annuity is terminated because the survivor had remarried prior to reaching age 55, the annuity may be restored if the remarriage is dissolved by death, annulment, or divorce.

Where the spouse properly consents, an employee may elect to reduce that portion of the annuity that is to be treated as a survivor annuity.

The portion of the employee's annuity treated as a survivor annuity will be reduced according to formula. The reduction is 2.5% of the first $3,600 chosen as a base, plus 10% of any amount over $3,600. For example, if the employee chooses $4,800 as a base, the reduction in the annual annuity would be 2.5% of the first $3,600 ($90 a year), plus 10% of the $1,200 balance ($120 a year), making a total reduction of $210 ($90 + $120) a year.

If marriage is terminated after retirement by the divorce, annulment or death of the spouse named as beneficiary, the retiree may elect to have the annuity recomputed and payment at the single-life unreduced rate will be made for each full month the employee is not married. Should the employee remarry, he has two years from the date of remarriage to notify the Office of Personnel Management in writing that he wants the annuity reduced again to provide a survivor annuity for the new spouse.

If a retired employee dies, absent a waiver of benefits by the survivor, the surviving spouse will receive 55% of the yearly annuity which the deceased employee had earned at the time of death. This earned annuity is computed in the same manner as if the deceased employee had retired, but with no reduction for being under age 55, and no increase for voluntary contributions.

The surviving spouse's annuity begins on the day after the employee's death and terminates on the last day of the month before the surviving spouse dies or remarries before age 55.

### M-25. How does an annuity with benefit to a named person having an insurable interest work?

If the employee is in good health at retirement, he may elect an Annuity With Benefit to Named Person Having an Insurable Interest. A disabled dependent relative or former spouse is considered as having an insurable interest. An employee electing this annuity will have his annuity reduced by a percentage amount as follows:

| Age of Named Person In Relation to Retiring Employee's Age | Reduction in Annuity of Retiring Employee |
|---|---|
| Older, same age, or less than 5 years younger | 10% |
| 5 but less than 10 years younger | 15% |
| 10 but less than 15 years younger | 20% |
| 15 but less than 20 years younger | 25% |
| 20 but less than 25 years younger | 30% |
| 25 but less than 30 years younger | 35% |
| 30 or more years younger | 40% |

Upon the employee's death after retirement, the named beneficiary will receive an annuity equal to 55% of the employee's reduced annuity rate. The survivor's annuity begins on the day after the retired employee's death and terminates on the last day of the month before the survivor dies. However, if the person named as having an insurable interest dies before the employee, the employee's annuity will be restored to life rate upon written request.

### M-26. Is there a lump-sum credit option upon retirement under CSRS?

An employee who is covered under CSRS (as well as FERS) may elect a lump-sum payout option upon retirement. Generally, this option consists of: (1) a payout, in two installments of equal amounts, of an amount equal to the employee's CSRS or FERS contributions, and (2) a reduced annuity.

Note, however, that the Budget Reconciliation Act of 1990 suspended the lump-sum annuity option for most federal employees for five years, beginning December 1, 1990.

### M-27. How is the reduced annuity computed?

You need to know the amount of the member's contributions into the plan. You will also need to compute the member's regular annuity. To determine the amount of monthly reduction of the annuity, the computation is as follows:

- LS/PV = monthly reduction in annuity
- where LS equals the lump-sum credit and PV equals the present value factor of the annuity

The present value factors of CSRS and FERS appear below.

To obtain the amount of the reduced monthly annuity, subtract the monthly reduction figure obtained above from the amount of the regular (unreduced) monthly annuity.

*Example.* Mr. Placke, a member of the CSRS, is 64 at the time he retires from government service. His contributions to CSRS total $25,000. His present value factor (from the table) is 169.9. Using the formula below, $25,000 ÷ 169.9 = $147.14. Mr. Placke's monthly annuity would therefore be reduced by $147.14.

# REDUCED ANNUITY TABLES

## CSRS

| Age at Retirement | Factor | Age at Retirement | Factor |
|---|---|---|---|
| | Present Value Factors | | |
| 40 | 317.4 | 66 | 157.5 |
| 41 | 312.1 | 67 | 152.2 |
| 42 | 306.7 | 68 | 146.5 |
| 43 | 301.3 | 69 | 140.7 |
| 44 | 295.6 | 70 | 135.5 |
| 45 | 288.5 | 71 | 129.7 |
| 46 | 280.8 | 72 | 124.9 |
| 47 | 271.7 | 73 | 119.5 |
| 48 | 264.3 | 74 | 114.2 |
| 49 | 258.3 | 75 | 108.1 |
| 50 | 251.3 | 76 | 103.9 |
| 51 | 245.1 | 77 | 99.6 |
| 52 | 239.9 | 78 | 93.9 |
| 53 | 234.2 | 79 | 87.9 |
| 54 | 228.5 | 80 | 82.5 |
| 55 | 222.2 | 81 | 78.0 |
| 56 | 216.2 | 82 | 74.2 |
| 57 | 210.5 | 83 | 70.8 |
| 58 | 204.9 | 84 | 67.7 |
| 59 | 199.0 | 85 | 64.8 |
| 60 | 194.1 | 86 | 61.2 |
| 61 | 189.5 | 87 | 57.7 |
| 62 | 182.3 | 88 | 54.3 |
| 63 | 176.4 | 89 | 51.0 |
| 64 | 169.9 | 90 | 48.0 |
| 65 | 163.6 | | |

# FERS

*Present Value Factors for Most Employees*

| Age at Retirement | Present Value Factor | Age at Retirement | Present Value Factor |
|---|---|---|---|
| 40 | 170.0 | 61 | 168.4 |
| 41 | 169.8 | 62 | 166.1 |
| 42 | 169.6 | 63 | 160.9 |
| 43 | 169.3 | 64 | 155.5 |
| 44 | 168.7 | 65 | 150.2 |
| 45 | 167.7 | 66 | 145.3 |
| 46 | 166.3 | 67 | 140.6 |
| 47 | 164.8 | 68 | 135.7 |
| 48 | 164.0 | 69 | 130.9 |
| 49 | 163.4 | 70 | 126.0 |
| 50 | 162.8 | 71 | 121.4 |
| 51 | 162.8 | 72 | 116.9 |
| 52 | 162.8 | 73 | 112.1 |
| 53 | 162.8 | 74 | 107.0 |
| 54 | 162.8 | 75 | 102.3 |
| 55 | 162.8 | 76 | 98.5 |
| 56 | 163.0 | 77 | 93.9 |
| 57 | 163.6 | 78 | 88.6 |
| 58 | 164.2 | 79 | 83.3 |
| 59 | 165.3 | 80 | 78.8 |
| 60 | 167.2 | | |

## Computing The CSRS Annuity

### M-28. How is the amount of the CSRS annuity determined?

The amount of an annuity depends primarily on the employee's length of service and "high-3" average pay. These two factors are used in a formula to determine the basic annuity which may then be reduced or increased for various reasons.

The "high-3" average pay is the highest pay obtainable by averaging the rates of basic pay in effect during any three consecutive years of service, with each rate weighted by the time it was in effect. The three years need not be continuous, but they must consist of consecutive periods of service. Thus, two or more separate periods of employment which follow each other may be joined to make up the three consecutive years of service on which the "high-3" average pay is based. The pay rates for each period of employment are weighted on an annual basis.

*Example.* Mr. Stegman's final three years of government service included pay rates of:

$$
\begin{array}{llll}
\text{6 months at \$14,500} & - & \tfrac{1}{2}\text{ year} & \times \text{\$14,500} = \text{\$ } 7{,}250 \\
\text{18 months at \$15,000} & - & 1\tfrac{1}{2}\text{ years} & \times \text{\$15,000} = \phantom{0}22{,}500 \\
\text{12 months at \$15,500} & - & 1\text{ year} & \times \text{\$15,500} = \phantom{0}15{,}500 \\
\end{array}
$$

Mr. Stegman's average pay is computed as:     $45,250

$$
\frac{\$45{,}250}{3} = \$15{,}083 = (\text{Average Pay})
$$

A three-part formula is used to determine the basic annuity.

- *Step I*. 1.5% × Average Pay × number of years of service up to 5 years, plus

- *Step II*. 1.75% × Average Pay × number of years of service over 5 and up to 10 years, plus

- *Step III*. 2.0% × Average Pay × number of years of service over 10.

Note that for employees with over 10 years of service, all three parts apply. For those with less than 10 years of service, only parts 1 and 2 apply.

*Example.* Mr. Martin retires from civil service employment with 30 years of service. The three consecutive years of service with the highest rates of basic pay were his last three years before retirement.

$$
\begin{array}{lr}
\text{Rate of pay during 28th year of service} & \$14{,}500 \\
\text{Rate of pay during 29th year of service} & 15{,}000 \\
\text{Rate of pay during 30th year of service} & 15{,}500 \\
\hline
& \$45{,}000 \text{ (total)}
\end{array}
$$

$$
\frac{\$45{,}000}{3} = \$15{,}000 = (\text{Average Pay})
$$

The general formula, using Mr. Martin's $15,000 average pay and 30 years of service, is applied as follows:

$$
\begin{array}{llllll}
1. & 1\tfrac{1}{2}\% & \times \text{\$15,000} & \times & 5 \text{ years} = & \$1{,}125.00 \\
2. & 1\tfrac{3}{4}\% & \times \text{\$15,000} & \times & 5 \text{ years} = & 1{,}312.50 \\
3. & 2\% & \times \text{\$15,000} & \times & 20 \text{ years} = & 6{,}000.00 \\
\hline
& & & & \text{Basic Annuity} & \$8{,}437.50
\end{array}
$$

The employee's basic annuity may not exceed 80% of his average pay. If the formula produces an amount exceeding the 80% maximum, it must be reduced to an amount which equals 80% of the average pay.

### M-29. What is the substitute computation method?

A substitute computation method is provided as an alternative for employees with a "high-3" of under $5,000. Instead of taking the 1.5%, 1.75%, and 2% of the "high-3" average pay, the employee may substitute 1% of the "high-3" average pay plus $25 for all parts of the general formula. If the "high-3" average pay is between $2,500 and $3,333, substitute the 1% plus $25 for the 1.5% and 1.75% in the first and second parts of the general formula. If the "high-3" average pay is between $3,334 and $4,999, substitute the 1% plus $25 for the 1.5% in the first part of the general formula.

### M-30. How is the benefit determined for disability retirement?

An employee under age 60 who retires on account of total disability will receive no less than the guaranteed minimum annuity which is the *lessor* of:

(1)  40% of the employee's "high-3" average pay, or

(2)  the amount obtained under the general formula after adding to years of actual service the number of years he is under age 60 on the date of separation.

An employee must have completed at least five years of government service in order to be eligible for disability benefits. The provision for a minimum disability annuity does not apply to employees over age 60. The disability annuity rate for an employee over age 60 is always computed by using actual service in the general formula.

### M-31. Can an employee obtain a larger retirement annuity by making voluntary contributions?

An employee can obtain a larger retirement annuity by making voluntary contributions, in multiples of $25, to purchase an additional annuity. Total voluntary contributions may not exceed 10% of the employee's total basic pay.

Voluntary contributions are interest-bearing. They earned 3% through 1984, and thereafter at varying annual rates determined by formula. Voluntary contributions earned 8.125% in 1992. Each $100 in the account provides an additional annuity in the amount of $7, plus 20 cents for each full year the employee is over age 55 at retirement.

## Death Benefits

### M-32. Is there a death benefit under the CSRS?

Death benefits are of two kinds: survivor annuities and lump-sum payments. Survivor annuities are payable to an employee's surviving spouse and children upon the death of the employee. A lump-sum benefit is payable upon the death of the employee if there is no spouse or dependent children entitled to an annuity, or, if one is payable, after the right of the last person entitled thereto has been terminated.

While not formally called a "death benefit", where the employee has retired, annuities are payable to the surviving spouse (unless the spouse had waived survivor benefit entitlement) and, where applicable, payable to a named person with an insurable interest.

## Annuity Eligibility Requirements

### M-33. Who is eligible for a survivor annuity?

*Employee's Spouse.* In order for the surviving spouse to qualify for a survivor annuity:

(1) The spouse must have been married to the employee for at least nine months before death, or

(2) The spouse must be the parent of the deceased's child born of the marriage.

However, these requirements are waived where: (1) the employee dies as a result of an accident, or (2) the employee had previously married and subsequently divorced the surviving spouse, and the aggregate time married is at least nine months.

*Employee's Child.* Generally, for a deceased employee's child to qualify for the survivor annuity, the child must be unmarried, under 18 years of age, and a dependent of the employee. The following rules also apply:

(1) An adopted child is considered to be the employee's child.

(2) A stepchild is considered to be the employee's child even if the child did not live with the deceased employee. An illegitimate child, however, must prove he was dependent upon the deceased employee.

(3) An illegitimate child is considered to be the employee's child even if the child did not live with the deceased employee. An

illegitimate child, however, must prove he was dependent upon the deceased employee.

(4) A child who lived with the employee and for whom the employee had filed an adoption petition is considered to be the employee's child, but only where the surviving spouse did in fact adopt the child following the employee's death.

Notwithstanding the age requirement above, each of the following persons is considered to be a child for purposes of the survivorship annuity:

(1) An unmarried dependent child, regardless of age, who is incapable of self-support because of a mental or physical disability incurred before age 18.

(2) An unmarried dependent child between 18 and 22 who is a "student" (pursuing a full-time course of study or training in residence in a high school, trade school, college, university, or comparable recognized educational institution.

## Computing The Survivor Annuity

### M-34. How do you compute the survivor annuity?

If an employee dies after completing at least 18 months of civilian service, there is a guaranteed minimum survivor annuity based upon the employee's average pay over the total civilian service. The annuity, however, is at least 55 percent of the smaller of: (1) 40% of the deceased employee's "high-3" average pay, or (2) the regular computation obtained after increasing service by the period of time between the date of death and the date the employee would have become age 60.

This guaranteed minimum does not apply if 55% of the employee's earned annuity produces a higher benefit than the guaranteed minimum. Also, since active service cannot be projected beyond age 60 in any case, the guaranteed minimum does not apply where the employee dies after reaching age 60.

Where an employee is survived by a spouse and is survived by children who qualify for survivor benefits, each surviving child is entitled to a benefit equal to whichever of the following amounts is the least: (1) 60% of the employee's high-3 average pay, divided by the number of qualified children, (2) $882 per month, divided by the number of qualified children, or (3) $294 per month.

When an employee leaves no surviving spouse but leaves children who qualify for survivor benefits, each child will be paid the least of: (1) 75% of the employee's high-3 average pay, divided by the number of qualified children, (2) $1,056 per month, divided by the number of qualified children, or (3) $352 per month.

A child's annuity begins on the day after the employee or annuitant dies and continues until the last day of the month before the child marries, dies or reaches age 18, except in the following cases:

(1) For a child age 18 or over who is incapable of self-support because of disability which began before age 18, payments stop at the end of the month before the child becomes capable of self-support, marries or dies.

(2) The annuity of a student age 18 or over stops at the end of the month before the child ceases to be a student, reaches age 22, marries, or dies, whichever occurs first.

## Lump-Sum Death Benefit

### M-35. When does the lump-sum death benefit become payable?

The lump-sum death benefit becomes payable to the estate of the proper party where the employee dies:

(1) without a survivor, or

(2) with a survivor, but the survivor's right to an annuity terminates before a claim for a survivor annuity has been filed.

The lump-sum benefit consists of the amount paid into the Civil Service Retirement and Disability Fund by the employee, plus any accrued interest.

If all rights to a CSRS annuity cease before the total annuity paid equals the lump-sum credit, the difference between the lump-sum credit and the total annuity paid becomes payable to the estate of the proper party. Thus, if an employee leaves a spouse or children who are eligible for a survivor annuity, a lump-sum death benefit may be payable after all survivors' annuities have been paid. The lump-sum benefit would consist of that portion of the employee's lump-sum credit which has not been exhausted by the annuity payments to survivors.

## Annuity Payments

### M-36. How are annuity payments made?

Annuities are paid by monthly check. The Office of Personnel Management authorizes the payment, and the Treasury Department issues the check. After the initial check, each regular check is dated the first workday of the month after the month for which the annuity is due. For example, the annuity payment for the month of April will be made by a check dated May 1.

An employee annuity begins on the first day of the month after: (1) separation from the service, or (2) pay ceases and the service and age requirements for entitlement to an annuity are met. Any other annuity payable begins on the first day of the month after the occurrence of the event on which payment is based.

## Disability Retirement

### M-37. When is an annuity payable for disability retirement?

An immediate annuity is payable to an employee for disability retirement when each of the following conditions are met:

(1) The employee has completed five years of civilian service.

(2) The employee has become totally disabled for useful and efficient service in the position occupied, or the duties of a similar position at the same grade or level.

A claim for disability retirement must be filed with the Office of Personnel Management before separation from the service or within one year thereafter. The one-year requirement may be waived in cases of incompetency.

The annuity payable will be the earned annuity based on the high-3 average salary, the years of actual service, and the three-part formula (see M-28), but not less than: (1) 40% of the high-3 average salary, or (2) the amount computed under the general formula after adding to years of actual service the number of years he is under age 60 on the date of separation.

Unless the disability is permanent in nature, an employee receiving a disability retirement annuity must be medically examined annually until age 60. The Government pays for the examination.

Upon recovery before reaching age 60, the annuity is continued temporarily (not to exceed one year) to give the individual an opportunity to find a position. If reemployed in Government service within the year, the annuity stops on reemployment. If the individual is not reemployed, the annuity stops at the expiration of the 180 day period.

## Cost-of-Living Adjustments

### M-38. Is there a cost-of-living adjustment to CSRS annuities?

Annuities for retirees and survivors are subject to a cost-of-living adjustment in December of each year. The increases are reflected in the annuity payment received the following month. The percentage of the cost-of-living increase each year is determined by the average price index for the third quarter of each year over the third quarter average of the Consumer Price Index for Urban Wage Earners and Clerical Workers of the previous year. Annuitants received an increase of 3.7% in the most recent COLA (December 1991).

## Refund Of Contributions

### M-39. Is there a refund of contributions if an employee leaves government service?

Yes, an employee who leaves government service or transfers to government work under another retirement system, may withdraw his retirement lump-sum credit (contributions plus any interest payable) so long as the employee: (1) is separated from the job for at least 31 consecutive days, (2) is transferred to a position that is not subject to CSRS or FERS and remains in that position for at least 31 consecutive days, (3) files an application for a refund of retirement deductions, (4) is not reemployed in a position subject to CSRS or FERS at the time the application is filed, *and* (5) will not become eligible to receive an annuity within 31 days after filing the application.

# BENEFITS FOR SERVICEMEN AND VETERANS

## MILITARY RETIREMENT

**N-1. In general, who is entitled to military retirement benefits?**

Members of the armed forces may retire after a certain amount of active service. Monthly retirement pay is based on a percentage of base pay of the highest rank held, as well as number of years of service.

Members who become disabled while in service may be placed on either temporary or permanent disability retirement, depending on the degree and length of disability, and also on whether they satisfy certain other conditions of eligibility.

Reservists are entitled to receive retirement benefits if they meet certain eligibility requirements.

**N-2. What retirement benefits are available for those who first became members before August 1, 1986?**

An immediate annuity is available to a service member who completes 20 years of service. No benefit is available to a service member who does not complete 20 years of service.

The retirement annuity is based in part on the servicemen's retirement "pay base", as well as the date on which the individual became a member of the uniformed service.

For those becoming members of a uniformed service for the first time *on or before September 7, 1980*, the retired pay base equals the servicemen's final monthly basic pay to which he was entitled the day before retirement.

For persons becoming members of a uniformed service for the first time *after September 7, 1980*, the monthly retired pay base is one thirty-sixth of the total amount of the monthly basic pay which the member received for the highest thirty-six months (whether or not consecutive) of active duty.

In order to compute the monthly retirement benefit, the monthly retired pay base is multiplied by an amount equaling 2.5% for each year of service up to a maximum of thirty years. The benefits range from 50% at 20 years of service to 75% at 30 or more years of service.

Retired pay is adjusted annually by the increase in the cost-of-living as measured by the Consumer Price Index for All Urban Wage Earners and Clerical Workers (CPI).

The uniformed services retirement system is noncontributory. However, the service member contributes, while on active duty, to the Social Security system and, thereby, earns eligibility for a Social Security retirement benefit.

### N-3. Describe retirement benefits for those who first become members on or after August 1, 1986?

Under the Military Retirement Reform Act of 1986, anyone who becomes a member of a uniformed service on or after August 1, 1986 is subject to a new retirement system.

The average monthly basic pay for the highest three years of pay during service becomes the pay base for members. This is known as "high-3". The multiplier, or percentage, for each year of service which is multiplied by the pay base, remains unchanged at 2.5% for each year of service. The maximum number of years creditable toward retirement is 30 — or 75% of pay base.

Under this system, where the member has retired and has completed fewer than 30 years of service, the percent reached above is reduced by 1 percentage point for each year between 30 years and the number of years completed.

This means that a 20-year retiree will receive 40% of the pay base, as opposed to 50% under the system for those who became members before August 1, 1986. A 30-year retiree, however, will receive the full 75% of the pay base, the same as under the old system.

| Years of Service | Multiplier | |
|---|---|---|
| | Before 62 | After 62 |
| 20 | 40.0 | 50.0 |
| 21 | 43.5 | 52.5 |
| 22 | 47.0 | 55.0 |
| 23 | 50.5 | 57.5 |
| 24 | 54.0 | 60.0 |
| 25 | 57.5 | 62.5 |
| 26 | 61.0 | 65.0 |
| 27 | 64.5 | 67.5 |
| 28 | 68.0 | 70.0 |
| 29 | 71.5 | 72.5 |
| 30 | 75.0 | 75.0 |

Cost-of-living adjustments to retirement benefits are guaranteed in years of inflation. Annual benefit increases will equal the increase in the Consumer Price Index (CPI), less 1 percentage point. This formula is known as "CPI Minus 1."

There is a one-time recomputation of retirement pay at age 62 in recognition of the fact that at about age 62 military retirement pay becomes the primary source of retirement income for career military personnel. At the point when a retiree reaches age 62, retirement pay is recomputed as if the 1 percentage point penalty for retirement at less than 30 years of service had not been applied. Additionally, at the same time, the retirement pay is increased to the level it would have reached if cost-of-living adjustments had been made under the full CPI rather than the"CPI Minus 1" formula.

In short, at age 62, the level of military retirement pay is restored to the level at which it would have been under the law for military members who entered the service prior to August 1, 1986. Note, however, that all cost-of-living adjustments after age 62 are under the "CPI Minus 1" formula. Thus, military retirees will lose 1 percent to inflation each year after age 62.

A military member retiring after 30 years of service will receive 75% of basic pay both before and after age 62. His retirement pay will be affected only by the change in the cost-of-living adjustment formula.

### Survivor Annuity

### N-4. What is the Survivor Benefit Plan?

The Survivor Benefit Plan provides survivor benefits for eligible widows, widowers and dependent children of eligible military personnel. Benefits are essentially the same as those provided federal government employees.

Those eligible to participate in the Survivor Benefit Plan (SBP) must be: (1) entitled to retired or retainer pay, or (2) eligible for retired pay but for the fact that they are under 60 years of age. The standard annuity is paid to those entitled to retired or retainer pay. The reserve-component annuity is paid to those who are eligible but under age 60. If a person entitled to retired or retainer pay is married or has a dependent child, he is automatically covered by the SBP *with maximum coverage* unless he elects lessor coverage or declines participation before the first day he becomes eligible for the retired or retainer pay. Unmarried service personnel who have no dependent children may elect a survivor annuity in favor of someone who has an insurable interest in their life. Retired pay is, of course, reduced for Plan participants.

A retiree who has a spouse and a child (or children) at retirement may elect survivor benefits for the *spouse only* or for the *child (or children) only*. Absent some election, coverage for both the spouse and child (or children) is automatic. The spouse must concur in: (1) an election not to participate in the plan, (2) an election to provide the spouse with an annuity at less than the maximum level, and (3) an election to provide an annuity for a dependent child but not the spouse.

An election not to participate in the Plan by a person eligible for retired pay is irrevocable unless revoked before the date on which the person first becomes entitled to that pay. An election by a person under age 60 not to participate in the Plan becomes irrevocable if not revoked by the end of the 90-day period beginning on the date he receives notification that he has completed the required years of service.

### N-5. Who is eligible to receive Survivor Benefit Plan benefits?

The Survivor Benefit Plan provides a monthly annuity payment effective the first day after the death of the retiree. The annuity is paid to one of the following:

- The eligible surviving widow or widower;
- The surviving dependent children in equal shares, if the eligible widow or widower or eligible former spouse is dead, dies, or otherwise becomes ineligible;
- The dependent children in equal shares if the retiree elected to provide an annuity for dependent children but not for the spouse or former spouse; or
- The former spouse under certain conditions.

The following criteria apply for the purposes of determining eligible beneficiaries:

- A *widow* is the surviving wife of a person who, if not married to the retiree at the time he became eligible for retired pay, was married to him for at least one year immediately before his death, or is the mother of issue by that marriage.
- A *widower* is the surviving husband of a retiree who, if not married to the person at the time she became eligible for retired pay, was married to her for at least one year immediately before her death, or is the father of issue by that marriage.

- A *former spouse* is the surviving former husband or wife of a person who is eligible to participate in the Plan.

- A *dependent child* is a person who is: (1) unmarried, (2) under 18 years of age; or at least 18, but under 22 years of age, and pursuing a full-time course of study or training in a high school, vocational school or college; or incapable of self-support because of a mental or physical incapability existing before age 18 or incurred on or after that birthday, but before age 22, while pursuing such a full-time course of study or training, (3) the child of a retiring participant, including an adopted child, a stepchild, foster child, or recognized natural child who lived with the retiree in a regular parent-child relationship.

- A *person with an insurable interest* is any person who has a bona fide financial interest in the continued life of the retiree. The relationship of the person to the retiree normally does not extend beyond the mother, father, brother, sister or single child of the retiree.

The annuity payable to a surviving spouse of the retiree is paid for life, except that if the annuitant remarries before age 55, the remarriage terminates the annuity. If the remarriage is terminated by death, annulment or divorce, payment of the annuity is resumed upon the termination of the remarriage.

## N-6. What is the amount of the Survivor Benefit Plan annuity?

The amount of a Survivor Benefit Plan annuity payable to a widow, widower, former eligible spouse or dependent children is based on a figure known as the *base amount*. The base amount is: (1) the amount of monthly retired pay to which a retiree became entitled when first eligible or later became entitled to by being advanced on the retired list, performing active duty, or being transferred from the temporary disability retired list to the permanent disability retired list, or (2) any lesser amount designated by the retiree on or before the first day of eligibility for retired pay, but not less than $300.

A retiree who wants maximum survivor benefits for a spouse and children (at the cost of maximum reduction in retirement pay), will designate as the base amount on which survivor benefits are figured the full amount of retired pay. For a lower level of survivor benefits (in exchange for a smaller reduction in retirement pay), a base amount less than full retirement pay will be designated.

The following are categories of dependents and the rules for determining the amount of annuity payable:

(1) In the case of a standard annuity for a widow, widower or child, the monthly annuity is an amount equal to 55% of the base amount, if the beneficiary is under 62 years of age or is a dependent child when becoming entitled to the annuity. If the beneficiary (other than a dependent child) is 62 years of age or older when becoming entitled to the annuity, the monthly annuity is an amount equal to 35% of the base amount.

(2) In the case of a standard annuity for an ex-spouse or person with an insurable interest in the annuitant (other than a widow, widower or dependent child), the monthly annuity payable to the beneficiary is an amount equal to 55% of the retired pay of the person who elected to provide the annuity.

(3) An annuity is also payable to a surviving spouse of a member who dies on active duty after: (a) becoming eligible to receive retired pay, (b) qualifying for retired pay except that he has not applied for or been granted that pay, or (c) completing 20 years of active service but before he is eligible to retire as a commissioned officer because he has not completed 10 years of active commissioned service. An annuity is payable to the dependent child of the member if there is no surviving spouse of if the member's surviving spouse subsequently dies.

If a person receiving an annuity in (3) above is under 62 or is a dependent child when the member or former member dies, the monthly annuity is an amount equal to 55% of the retired pay to which the member or former member would have been entitled if the member or former member had been entitled to that pay based upon his years of active service when he died.

If a person receiving an annuity in (3) above (other than a dependent child) is 62 or older when the member or former member dies, the monthly annuity is an amount equal to 35% of the retired pay to which the member of former member would have been entitled if the member or former member had been entitled to that pay based upon his years of active service when he died.

### N-7. Are Survivor Benefit Plan annuities subject to cost-of-living increases?

Whenever retirees receive a cost-of-living increase in their retired pay, Survivor Benefit Plan annuities are increased at the same time by the same total percent. The percentage is applied to the monthly annuity payable before any reduction is made in consideration of the annuitant's eligibility for Dependency and Indemnity Compensation or Social Security survivor benefits.

### N-8. How does the Survivor Benefit Plan reduce the regular retirement annuity?

The Survivor Benefit Plan reduces the regular retirement annuity according to the following formulas:

Where the individual first becomes a member of the uniformed service before March 1, 1990, the reduction is the lesser of:

(1) an amount equal to 2.5% of the first $364 of the base amount of the annuity subject to the survivor benefit, plus 10% of the remainder, or

(2) an amount equal to 6.5% of the base amount of the annuity subject to the survivor benefit.

Where the individual first becomes a member of the uniformed service on or after March 1, 1990, the reduction for the Survivor Benefit Plan is a flat 6.5% of the base amount of the annuity.

"Base amount" does not include cost-of-living increases.


### Disability Retirement


### N-9. When is a servicemen entitled to retire on permanent disability?

When he has been called or ordered to active duty for a period of more than 30 days (excluding Ready Reserve training duty), and:

(1) He is unfit to perform his duties because he has incurred a physical disability while entitled to basic pay;

(2) The disability is of a permanent and stable nature based on commonly accepted medical principles;

(3) The disability is not due to intentional or willful neglect, and not incurred during a period of unauthorized absence; and

(4) One of the following applies: (a) the disability is rated at least 30% under the Department of Veterans Affairs disability rating schedule, or (b) the member has completed at least 20 years of service.

Where the member has not completed 20 years of service but has a disability of at least 30% as explained in (a) above, one of the following tests must additionally be satisfied:

(1) The disability must be incurred in the line of duty.

(2) The disability must be the proximate result of performing active duty.

(3) The member must have completed at least 8 years of service.

Where the active-duty or inactive training period is 30 days or less, a regular serviceman or reservist is entitled to permanent disability based on *injury* where the following conditions are met:

(1) He is unfit to perform his duties because he has incurred a physical disability while entitled to basic pay;

(2) The disability is of a permanent and stable nature based on commonly accepted medical principles;

(3) The disability is the proximate result of performing active duty or inactive training;

(4) The disability is not due to intentional misconduct or willful neglect, and not incurred during a period of unauthorized absence; and

(5) One of the following applies: (a) the disability is rated at least 30% under the Department of Veterans Affairs disability rating schedule, or (b) the member has completed at least 20 years of service.

### N-10. How is disability retirement pay determined?

Disability retirement pay is figured by either of two methods, at the retiree's option, up to a maximum of 75% of basic pay: (1) 2.5% of monthly basic pay multiplied by the number of years of active service, or (2) the percentage rating of disability.

A member who meets the requirements of temporary disability may be placed on temporary disability retirement for up to 5 years. Retired pay for temporary disability is no less than 50% of basic pay. A member will be permanently retired for physical disability if still disabled after 5 years.

### Social Security

### N-11. Are servicemen entitled to Social Security benefits in addition to military benefits?

Servicemen are entitled to Social Security retirement, disability and survivor benefits in addition to military benefits. Beginning in 1957, they are credited with an additional $300 for each calendar quarter when calculating their Average Indexed Monthly Earnings (AIMEs) for determining Social Security benefits. This is done as an allowance for the value of quarters and subsistence. For additional information, see SURVIVOR BENEFIT PLAN, SECTION K.

## Reservists' Retirement Pay

### N-12. Are Reservists entitled to retired pay?

To qualify for retired pay in the Reserves, a person must complete at least 20 years of "satisfactory Federal service" as a member of the armed forces. He meets this requirement for a year by earning at least 50 points in his anniversary year. Points are earned for both inactive duty and active duty. The branch of service will advise the reservist of point totals and the number of years of satisfactory federal service he has completed. The last eight qualifying years must have been spent in a Reserve unit. Entitlement to Reserve retired pay begins at age 60.

The Reserve point system is an element used in computing retirement pay. In totalling points, there is no limit to the number of active points that may be earned in a year, but no more than 60 inactive duty points may be counted for any one year.

### N-13. How is Reserve retired pay computed?

Generally, reserve retired pay is computed by:

(1) Dividing the reservist's cumulative active and inactive point total by 360 to convert the points into years of service;

(2) Taking the monthly basic pay rate for the member's grade and length of service at the time he becomes entitled to retired pay at age 60;

(3) Multiplying that rate by 2.5% × the years of service that are credited to him through the point conversion process (but not in excess of 30 years).

Where the reservist first became a member after September 7, 1980, instead of using his actual pay rate as described in (2) above, he uses an average of the basic monthly pay to which he would have been entitled had he been on active duty for the three years in which he was a member of an armed force.

### N-14. How does the Survivor Benefit Plan work for Reservists?

Generally, the Survivor Benefit Plan for Reservists follows the rules for the regular serviceman's Survivor Benefit Plan. With respect to the amount of reduction in retired pay of the reserve component annuity, the reduction, effective March 1, 1991, is the lessor of:

(1) an amount equal to 2.5% of the first $364 of the base amount of the annuity subject to the survivor benefit, plus 10% of the remainder, or

(2)   an amount equal to 6.5% of the base amount of the annuity
      subject to the survivor benefit.


# VETERANS

## Dependency And Indemnity Compensation

### N-15. What is Dependency and Indemnity Compensation?

Dependency and Indemnity Compensation (DIC) is the benefit program providing monthly payments to a surviving spouse, child or
parent of the veteran due to a *service-connected* death that occurs after 1956. (Where the death occurred prior to 1957, certain survivors
could have elected to take benefits under DIC.)

Generally, DIC is payable to survivors of servicemen or reservists
who died from: (1) disease or injury incurred or aggravated in line
of duty while on active or inactive duty training, or (2) disability com-
pensable under laws administered by the VA.

### N-16. Who is eligible for DIC benefits?

DIC benefits are payable to an eligible *surviving spouse* regardless of
the survivor's income or employment status. The survivor's death
or remarriage terminates the benefit. Benefit eligibility is not reestablished if survivor's remarriage is terminated by death or divorce.
A surviving spouse may receive DIC payments as well as Social Security survivor benefits.

The surviving spouse must have been married: (1) before expiration of 15 years after the end of the period of active duty, active duty
for training, or inactive training duty, in which the injury or disease
causing death was incurred or aggravated, or (2) for one or more
years, or (3) for any period of time if a child was born of or before
the marriage.

The surviving spouse's benefit is increased when the spouse has
children under age 18. Where there is no surviving spouse eligible
to receive DIC, children under 18 are eligible to receive DIC benefits.

The definition of *"child"* includes the veteran's legitimate child,
legally adopted child, stepchild who is a member of the veteran's
household or was a member at the time of the veteran's death, and
illegitimate child (provided a number of requirements are met).

DIC payments are made to children who are unmarried and who: (1) are under age 18, or (2) before attaining age 18, become permanently incapable of self-support, or (3) after attaining age 18 and until completion of education or training (but not after attaining age 23), are pursuing a course of instruction at an approved educational institution.

Eligibility of *parents* to receive DIC is measured by an annual income test rather than by dependency. A remarriage of a parent does not terminate the benefits. Parent's DIC benefits continues until death.

### N-17. How is the amount of the DIC benefit determined?

Monthly payments to a *surviving spouse* are made according to the veteran's pay grade at the time of death. If the veteran did not die in active service, the pay grade will be determined as of: (1) the time of last discharge or release from active duty, or (2) the time of discharge or release from any period of active duty for training or inactive duty training, if death results from service-connected disability incurred during such period. The discharge must have been other than dishonorable.

The monthly rate of DIC is increased by $186 if the surviving spouse is: (1) a patient in a nursing home, or (2) helpless and blind, or so nearly helpless and blind as to need the regular aid and attendance of another person.

The monthly rate of DIC will be increased by $90 if the surviving spouse is permanently housebound by reason of disability, and does not qualify for the aid and attendance allowance described above.

If a *child* is under age 18, and there is no surviving spouse entitled to DIC, DIC is paid in equal shares to the children of the deceased veteran at the following monthly rates: one child, $310; two children, $447; three children, $578; more than three children, $578 plus $114 for each child in excess of three.

If a child is 18 or over, and the child became permanently incapable of self-support while under 18 and eligible for DIC, the child's DIC is continued past age 18 and increased by $185 per month. If DIC is payable to a surviving spouse with a child, age 18 or older, who became permanently incapable of support while under 18, the VA will pay an additional sum of $310 for such child.

If DIC is payable to a spouse with a child, age 18 or over and under age 23, who is attending an approved educational institution, DIC is paid to the child, concurrently with the payment of DIC to the spouse, in the amount of $157 per month.

In addition to an annual limitation, the amount of DIC payable monthly to a *parent* depends upon whether there is only one parent; whether two surviving parents are or are not living together; and whether a parent has remarried and is living with a spouse.

The maximum monthly benefit payable to *one parent only* is $349. No DIC is payable if annual income exceeds $8,414. *Two parents not living together* are entitled to a maximum monthly benefit of $250 each. No DIC is paid to a parent whose annual income exceeds $8,414. *Two parents living together* (or remarried parents living with spouses, when both parents are alive) are entitled to a maximum monthly benefit of $235 each. No DIC is paid to a parent if total combined annual income exceeds $11,313. The monthly rate of DIC payable to a parent is increased by $186 if such parent is: (1) a patient in a nursing home, or (2) helpless or blind, or so nearly helpless and blind as to need or require the regular aid and attendance of another person.

### Disability Benefits — Service-Connected

### N-18. What benefits are available for service-connected disability?

There are three kinds of benefits for a service-connected disability: (1) compensation paid by VA, (2) severance pay, and (3) disability retirement pay. Disability retirement is discussed in SECTION M.

Monthly compensation is paid by the VA without regard to other income on the basis of average impairments of earning capacity in civilian employment. A person eligible for both disability retirement pay and this compensation may elect which to receive but cannot receive full benefits from both sources.

| Degree of Disability | Rate |
|---|---|
| 10% | $   83 |
| 20 | 157 |
| 30 | 240 |
| 40 | 342 |
| 50 | 487 |
| 60 | 614 |
| 70 | 776 |
| 80 | 897 |
| 90 | 1,010 |
| 100 | 1,680 |

The veteran must be disabled by injury or disease incurred in or or aggravated by active service in line of duty. Discharge or separation must be other than dishonorable, and the injury cannot have resulted from willful misconduct. Reservists disabled while on active training duty may qualify for compensation.

The monthly compensation amount depends on the veteran's degree of disability.

Any veteran entitled to monthly compensation whose disability is rated not less than 30% is entitled to additional compensation for dependents. The current rates listed below are based upon 100% disability. If the disability rating is at least 30% but less than 100%, the amount of dependent benefits will be approximately the same percent of these rates as the percent of disability rating.

The monthly compensation rates for dependents are as follows:

| Spouse and — | Amount |
|---|---|
| no children | $ 100 |
| 1 child | 169 |
| 2 children | 221 |
| 3 children | 273 |
| additional children, each | 52 |

| If no surviving spouse — | |
|---|---|
| 1 child | 69 |
| 2 children | 121 |
| 3 children | 173 |
| additional children, each | 52 |

| Dependent parent(s) | |
|---|---|
| each parent | 80 |

A child's benefit usually ends at age 18. However, each dependent child between ages 18 and 23 who is attending an approved school is eligible for $149 monthly if the veteran is totally disabled, and a proportionate amount if the veteran is partially disabled.

The spouse of a totally disabled veteran is entitled to $176 a month if: (1) a patient in a nursing home, or (2) helpless and blind, or so nearly helpless and blind as to need or require the regular aid and attendance of another person. The spouse of a veteran who is not totally disabled, but at least 30% disabled, is entitled to a proportionate monthly benefit.

These dependency allowances are not payable if the serviceman receives any other allowance for dependents under any other law with the exception of Social Security benefits. The higher of the two amounts may be elected but not both. Social Security benefits for total and permanent disability will not be reduced by the amount of any service-connected disability compensation received from the VA.

Service personnel are entitled to *disability severance pay* when separated from service for physical disability but are not eligible for disability retirement pay where: (1) the rated disability is less than 30%, or (2) length-of-service credits are insufficient.

Disability severance pay is a lump-sum equal to twice the monthly base and longevity pay multiplied by years of service, but not exceeding the amount of two years' basic pay, and is payable by the member's branch of service.

### Death Benefits — Service-Connected

**N-19. What other service-connected death benefits are available?**

The VA reimburses survivors up to $1,500 (or more, the the case of a federal employee who dies in the performance of duty) for the burial expenses of a veteran who dies as a result of service-connected disability or disabilities.

When a member of the armed forces dies while on active duty, active or inactive training duty, or while receiving hospital treatment for a service-connected ailment, his branch of service will provide for the disposition of his remains. Additional costs of transportation of the remains of the deceased may be allowed if the veteran died while hospitalized or residing in a VA facility, or while in transit, a VA's expense, to or from a hospital, domiciliary, or VA regional office.

Other allowances include burial in a national cemetery, American flag, and transportation from place of death to place of burial. The next of kin is also entitled to a headstone, or a headstone monetary allowance in the event the veteran purchased a headstone prior to death.

A lump-sum equal to six months basic pay, plus special incentive and hazard pay, is paid to the survivors of a serviceman who dies on active duty, active or inactive training duty, or within 120 days after separation from active duty if death is from a service-connected cause. The minimum payment is $800 and the maximum is $3,000. This death gratuity is paid by the branch of service of the deceased to the spouse, if living; otherwise to any children in equal shares; otherwise to parents, brothers or sisters as designated by the deceased.

Dependents of a serviceman may remain in government housing for 90 days without charge after the serviceman's death.

Survivors and dependents may also be eligible for the survivors and dependents educational assistance program. The purpose of this program is: (1) to enable children to obtain an education they might not otherwise have had an opportunity to obtain, and (2) to enable surviving spouses to prepare to support themselves and their families at a standard of living which the veteran, but for death or disability, could have expected to provide.

### Pension, Disability And Death Benefits
### Not Service-Connected

### N-20. When is a veteran eligible for non-service-connected pension, disability and death benefits?

Veterans with limited income who are discharged under conditions other than dishonorable may be eligible for: (1) an Improved Pension, (2) Section 306 pension, or (3) old law pension. The old law pension is for veterans who died before July 1, 1960.

The pension-eligible veteran must have:

(1) had 90 days active service during the Mexican border period, World War I, World War II, the Korean Conflict, or Viet Nam Era, or

(2) been discharged because of service-connected disability, or

(3) at the time of death been receiving (or entitled to receive) compensation or retirement pay based on a service-connected disability incurred during wartime.

### N-21. When is a surviving spouse and dependents eligible for non-service-connected pension, disability and death benefits?

A surviving spouse must have lived continuously with the veteran from the time of marriage until the veteran's death, except where there was a separation due to the misconduct of, or caused by, the veteran, without fault on the surviving spouse's part. The surviving spouse's valid remarriage or death permanently terminates the benefit. However, if the remarriage is annulled, or is terminated by death or divorce (unless divorced secured by fraud or collusion), the surviving spouse is not barred from receiving benefits.

The surviving spouse must have been married to the veteran: (1) for at least one year, or (2) for any period if a child was born either before or after the marriage. For Viet Nam Era veterans, the marriage must have taken place before May 8, 1985.

## N-22. Are children entitled to benefits?

Unmarried children and surviving spouses under 18 of a deceased veteran may be eligible for a pension. The pension is based on need. Regardless of the income limit, however, benefits will be denied a child or surviving spouse who owns capital which, in the VA's judgment, should be consumed for his or her support.

Unmarried children and surviving spouses over 18 may qualify for pension in their own right if they are: (1) permanently incapable of self-support since prior to age 18, or (2) under 23 and attending a VA-approved educational institution.

## N-23. What is the amount of the Improved Pension?

Under the "Improved Pension Program", which went into effect on January 1, 1979, the maximum annual rates payable (effective December 1, 1991) are as follows:

### Veterans and Dependents

Veteran without dependent spouse or child ................................. $7,397

Veteran with one dependent (spouse or child) .......................... $9,689

Veteran in need of regular aid and attendance
without dependents .................................................................. $11,832

Veteran in need of regular aid and attendance
with one dependent .................................................................. $14,124

Veteran permanently housebound without
dependents ................................................................................ $9,041

Veteran permanently housebound with one
dependent .................................................................................. $11,333

Two veterans married to one another, one of
which is in need of aid and attendance ................................ $14,124

Two veterans married to one another, both of
which are in need of aid and attendance ............................. $18,557

Two veterans married to one another, one of
which is housebound ................................................................ $11,333

Two veterans married to one another, both of
which are housebound ............................................................. $12,979

Two veterans married to one another, one
housebound and the other in need of aid
and attendance .......................................................................... $15,766

Mexican border period and
World War I veteran ............................................. add $1,673 to the
                                                                      applicable annual rate

Increase for each additional dependent child ........................... $1,258

### Spouse and Dependents

Surviving spouse without dependent children ............................ $4,957

Surviving spouse with one dependent child ................................. $6,494

Surviving spouse in need of regular aid and
    attendance without dependent child ...................................... $7,929

Surviving spouse in need of regular aid and
    attendance with one dependent child ..................................... $9,462

Surviving spouse permanently housebound
    without dependent child .......................................................... $6,061

Surviving spouse permanently housebound
    with one dependent child ........................................................ $7,594

Increase for each additional dependent child ............................. $1,258

Child not in custody of veteran's surviving
    spouse, or child if no living surviving spouse
    of the veteran ........................................................................... $1,258

Benefits are generally paid monthly and are reduced by the annual countable income of the claimant and any dependent of the claimant. Generally, all non-pension income is included for this purpose, but income paid for certain educational or medical expenses is excluded from the computation.

In addition, the pension may be denied or discontinued if the claimant's net worth is such that it is reasonable that some portion of the estate by used for his suuport. Additional pension for a child may be denied if the child's net worth is excessive.

Pensioners must provide income and net worth reports to the VA on an annual basis.

## N-24. What is the Section 306 Pension?

The veteran, his surviving spouse, and children who came on the pension rolls on or after July 1, 1960 but prior to January 1, 1979 may continue to receive a pension at the monthly rate in effect as of December 31, 1978. The pension will be paid so long as he remains permanently and totally disabled, there is no charge in dependency, and his income does not exceed the adjusted income limitation. The income limitation is Consumer Price Index (CPI) sensitive.

Pensions range from $5 to $197 monthly for veterans with no dependents and up to $222 per month for veterans with dependents. If the annual income of a veteran with no children exceeds $8,414, no pension is paid. Where there is one child and annual income exceeds $11,313, no pension is paid.

A surviving spouse with no minor children may receive up to $139 a month, but if annual income exceeds $8,414, no pension is paid. Where there is one child and annual income exceeds $11,313, no pension is paid.

Where there is no eligible surviving spouse, a child may receive $61 a month with $26 added fro each additional child and the total divided among them. A child is not entitled if the income, not counting his or her own earnings, exceeds $6,877.

### N-25. What is the Old Law Pension?

Eligible veterans, their suviving spouses and children of certain deceased veterans who died before July 1, 1960, may be entitled to an Old Law pension or death benefit. Where the veteran's surviving spouse or children are claiming Old Law death benefits, it must be shown that the veteran died of causes not due to service. The veteran must have served during World War I, World War II or the Korean conflict.

The monthly rates: Surviving spouse, no child — $50.40. Surviving spouse, one child — $63 (each additional child, $7.56). No surviving spouse, one child — $27.30. No surviving spouse, two children — $40.95. No surviving spouse, three children — $54.60 (each additional child, $7.56).

These pensions are not payable to a veteran or surviving spouse without children, or to an entitled child, if the claimant receives other income over $7,365 annually, or to a veteran or surviving spouse with child if his or her other income is in excess of $10,620.

# SOCIAL SECURITY TABLES

# TABLES

## Table 1 — Benefits as Percentage of PIA

RETIREMENT BENEFIT
    Starting at Normal Retirement Age
        (currently age 65) . . . . . . . . . . . . . .    PIA
    Starting age 62 or above (but below
        Normal Retirement Age) . . . . . . . . . .    PIA reduced

DISABILITY BENEFIT . . . . . . . . . . . . . . . . . .    PIA

SPOUSE'S BENEFIT (husband or wife
  of retired or disabled worker)
    Caring for child (under 16 or disabled)    50% of PIA
    Starting at Normal Retirement Age
        (currently age 65) . . . . . . . . . . . . . .    50% of PIA
    Starting age 62 or above (but below
        Normal Retirement Age) . . . . . . . . . .    50% of PIA
        reduced

CHILD'S BENEFIT
    Child of retired or disabled worker . . . .    50% of PIA
    Child of deceased worker . . . . . . . . . . .    75% of PIA

MOTHER'S OR FATHER'S BENEFIT (widow(er)
  caring for child under 16 or disabled) . . . .    75% of PIA

WIDOW(ER)'S BENEFIT (widow(er)
  not caring for child)
    Starting at Normal Retirement Age
        (currently age 65) . . . . . . . . . . . . . .    100% of PIA
    Starting age 60 or above (but below
        Normal Retirement Age) . . . . . . . . . .    100% of PIA
        reduced

DISABLED WIDOW(ER)'S BENEFIT
    Starting age 50-60 . . . . . . . . . . . . . . . .    71½% of PIA

PARENT'S BENEFIT (dependent parent of
  deceased worker)
    One dependent parent . . . . . . . . . . . . .    82½% of PIA
    Two dependent parents . . . . . . . . . . . . .    75% of PIA (each)

## TABLE 2
### QUARTERS OF COVERAGE REQUIRED TO BE FULLY INSURED FOR RETIREMENT BENEFITS

| Birth Year | Men | Women |
|---|---|---|
| 1892 or earlier | 6 | 6 |
| 1893 | 7 | 6 |
| 1894 | 8 | 6 |
| 1895 | 9 | 6 |
| 1896 | 10 | 7 |
| 1897 | 11 | 8 |
| 1898 | 12 | 9 |
| 1899 | 13 | 10 |
| 1900 | 14 | 11 |
| 1901 | 15 | 12 |
| 1902 | 16 | 13 |
| 1903 | 17 | 14 |
| 1904 | 18 | 15 |
| 1905 | 19 | 16 |
| 1906 | 20 | 17 |
| 1907 | 21 | 18 |
| 1908 | 22 | 19 |
| 1909 | 23 | 20 |
| 1910 | 24 | 21 |
| 1911 | 24 | 22 |
| 1912 | 24 | 23 |
| 1913 | 24 | 24 |
| 1914 | 25 | 25 |
| 1915 | 26 | 26 |
| 1916 | 27 | 27 |
| 1917 | 28 | 28 |
| 1918 | 29 | 29 |
| 1919 | 30 | 30 |
| 1920 | 31 | 31 |
| 1921 | 32 | 32 |
| 1922 | 33 | 33 |
| 1923 | 34 | 34 |
| 1924 | 35 | 35 |
| 1925 | 36 | 36 |
| 1926 | 37 | 37 |
| 1927 | 38 | 38 |
| 1928 | 39 | 39 |
| 1929 or after | 40 | 40 |

## TABLE 3
### YEARS IN WHICH PERSON REACHES AGE 21

| | |
|---|---|
| 1930 | 1951 |
| 1931 | 1952 |
| 1932 | 1953 |
| 1933 | 1954 |
| 1934 | 1955 |
| 1935 | 1956 |
| 1936 | 1957 |
| 1937 | 1958 |
| 1938 | 1959 |
| 1939 | 1960 |
| 1940 | 1961 |
| 1941 | 1962 |
| 1942 | 1963 |
| 1943 | 1964 |
| 1944 | 1965 |
| 1945 | 1966 |
| 1946 | 1967 |
| 1947 | 1968 |
| 1948 | 1969 |
| 1949 | 1970 |
| 1950 | 1971 |
| 1951 | 1972 |
| 1952 | 1973 |
| 1953 | 1974 |
| 1954 | 1975 |
| 1955 | 1976 |
| 1956 | 1977 |
| 1957 | 1978 |
| 1958 | 1979 |
| 1959 | 1980 |
| 1960 | 1981 |
| 1961 | 1982 |
| 1962 | 1983 |
| 1963 | 1984 |
| 1964 | 1985 |
| 1965 | 1986 |
| 1966 | 1987 |
| 1967 | 1988 |
| 1968 | 1989 |
| 1969 | 1990 |
| 1970 | 1991 |

## TABLE 4
### MINIMUM NUMBER OF QUARTERS OF COVERAGE NEEDED TO BE FULLY INSURED AT DEATH

| Birth Year | 1991 | 1992 | 1993 |
|---|---|---|---|
| 1929 or before | 40 | 41 | 42 |
| 1930 | 39 | 40 | 41 |
| 1931 | 38 | 39 | 40 |
| 1932 | 37 | 38 | 39 |
| 1933 | 36 | 37 | 38 |
| 1934 | 35 | 36 | 37 |
| 1935 | 34 | 35 | 36 |
| 1936 | 33 | 34 | 35 |
| 1937 | 32 | 33 | 34 |
| 1938 | 31 | 32 | 33 |
| 1939 | 30 | 31 | 32 |
| 1940 | 29 | 30 | 31 |
| 1941 | 28 | 29 | 30 |
| 1942 | 27 | 28 | 29 |
| 1943 | 26 | 27 | 28 |
| 1944 | 25 | 26 | 27 |
| 1945 | 24 | 25 | 26 |
| 1946 | 23 | 24 | 25 |
| 1947 | 22 | 23 | 24 |
| 1948 | 21 | 22 | 23 |
| 1949 | 20 | 21 | 22 |
| 1950 | 19 | 20 | 21 |
| 1951 | 18 | 19 | 20 |
| 1952 | 17 | 18 | 19 |
| 1953 | 16 | 17 | 18 |
| 1954 | 15 | 16 | 17 |
| 1955 | 14 | 15 | 16 |
| 1956 | 13 | 14 | 15 |
| 1957 | 12 | 13 | 14 |
| 1958 | 11 | 12 | 13 |
| 1959 | 10 | 11 | 12 |
| 1960 | 9 | 10 | 11 |

## TABLE 5
### NUMBER OF YEARS EARNINGS THAT MUST BE USE IN COMPUTING RETIREMENT BENEFITS
(less if person had an established period of disability)

| Birth Year | Computation Age | Year of Computation | No. of Years | No. of Divisor Months |
|---|---|---|---|---|
| 1915 | 62 | 1977 | 21 | 252 |
| 1916 | 62 | 1978 | 22 | 264 |
| 1917 | 62 | 1979 | 23 | 276 |
| 1918 | 62 | 1980 | 24 | 288 |
| 1919 | 62 | 1981 | 25 | 300 |
| 1920 | 62 | 1982 | 26 | 312 |
| 1921 | 62 | 1983 | 27 | 324 |
| 1922 | 62 | 1984 | 28 | 336 |
| 1923 | 62 | 1985 | 29 | 348 |
| 1924 | 62 | 1986 | 30 | 360 |
| 1925 | 62 | 1987 | 31 | 372 |
| 1926 | 62 | 1988 | 32 | 384 |
| 1927 | 62 | 1989 | 33 | 396 |
| 1928 | 62 | 1990 | 34 | 408 |
| 1929 | 62 | 1991 | 35 | 420 |
| 1930 or later | 62 | 1992 | 35 | 420 |

## TABLE 6 — INSURED STATUS NEEDED FOR SOCIAL SECURITY BENEFITS

The worker must be FULLY insured to provide monthly benefits for:
   ... Retired worker (at age 62 or over)
   ... Spouse of retired worker (at age 62 or over)
   ... Spouse of retired worker (at any age if caring for a child)
   ... Child of retired worker
   ... Widow(er) of worker (at age 60 or over)
   ... Disabled widow(er) of worker (at age 50 or over)
   ... Dependent parent of deceased worker

The worker may be either FULLY or CURRENTLY insured to provide monthly benefits for:
   ... Child of deceased worker
   ... Widow(er) of worker (at any age if caring for child)

A disabled worker must be FULLY insured and (a) if disability began at or after age 31, must have worked in covered employment 5 out of the last 10 years, or (b) if disability began before age 31, must have worked in covered employment 1/2 of the quarters between age 21 and onset of disability (but not less than 6), to provide benefits for:
   ... Disabled worker (at any age)
   ... Child of disabled worker
   ... Spouse of disabled worker (at age 62 or over)
   ... Spouse of disabled worker (at any age if caring for a child)

A worker who is either FULLY or CURRENTLY insured qualifies for the lump-sum death benefit if he is survived by (1) a spouse who was living with him at the time of his death, or (2) a dependent child or spouse eligible to receive social security benefits based on his earnings record.

## TABLE 7 — MAXIMUM AIME FOR RETIREMENT, SURVIVOR AND DISABILITY BENEFITS*

| Year of Birth | Normal Retirement Age | Death in 1992 | Disability in 1992 | Year of Birth | Normal Retirement Age | Death in 1992 | Disability in 1992 |
|---|---|---|---|---|---|---|---|
| 1930 | 3,208 | 3,060 | 2,985 | 1950 | 4,469 | 4,008 | 3,834 |
| 1931 | 3,280 | 3,091 | 3,014 | 1951 | 4,493 | 4,083 | 3,834 |
| 1932 | 3,352 | 3,122 | 3,044 | 1952 | 4,513 | 4,128 | 3,896 |
| 1933 | 3,425 | 3,154 | 3,075 | 1953 | 4,529 | 4,170 | 3,964 |
| 1934 | 3,492 | 3,183 | 3,101 | 1954 | 4,544 | 4,206 | 4,042 |
| 1935 | 3,564 | 3,219 | 3,134 | 1955 | 4,559 | 4,236 | 4,087 |
| 1936 | 3,634 | 3,257 | 3,170 | 1956 | 4,573 | 4,253 | 4,087 |
| 1937 | 3,703 | 3,299 | 3,209 | 1957 | 4,586 | 4,272 | 4,129 |
| 1938 | 3,771 | 3,338 | 3,245 | 1958 | 4,599 | 4,296 | 4,164 |
| 1939 | 3,840 | 3,383 | 3,289 | 1959 | 4,610 | 4,324 | 4,193 |
| 1940 | 3,909 | 3,430 | 3,333 | 1960 | 4,625 | 4,356 | 4,207 |
| 1941 | 3,975 | 3,481 | 3,380 | 1961 | 4,625 | 4,399 | 4,207 |
| 1942 | 4,040 | 3,535 | 3,431 | 1962 | 4,625 | 4,450 | 4,222 |
| 1943 | 4,163 | 3,591 | 3,486 | 1963 | 4,625 | 4,537 | 4,241 |
| 1944 | 4,213 | 3,650 | 3,541 | 1964 | 4,625 | 4,537 | 4,264 |
| 1945 | 4,263 | 3,710 | 3,601 | 1965 | 4,625 | 4,537 | 4,289 |
| 1946 | 4,312 | 3,774 | 3,601 | 1966 | 4,625 | 4,537 | 4,289 |
| 1947 | 4,360 | 3,825 | 3,662 | 1967 | 4,625 | 4,537 | 4,324 |
| 1948 | 4,408 | 3,880 | 3,727 | 1968 | 4,625 | 4,537 | 4,362 |
| 1949 | 4,440 | 3,941 | 3,778 | 1969 | 4,625 | 4,537 | 4,362 |

* Normal Retirement Age for unreduced benefits (PIA) is 65 at this time but increases by two months a year for workers reaching age 62 in 2000-2005; maintains age 66 for workers reaching age 62 in 2006-2016; increases by two months a year for workers reaching age 62 in 2017-2022; and maintains age 67 for workers reaching age 62 after 2022.

* AIME calculations assume worker earned current Social Security maximum earnings base ($55,500) in year of death, and assume worker earned current Social Security maximum earnings base up to, but not including, year of retirement or disability.

## TABLE 8 — MAXIMUM AIME FOR PHYSICIAN'S RETIREMENT AND DEATH BENEFITS

| Year of Birth | Normal Retirement Age | Death in 1992 | Year of Birth | Normal Retirement Age | Death in 1992 |
|---|---|---|---|---|---|
| 1927 | 2,364 | 2,505 | 1948 | 4,408 | 3,880 |
| 1928 | 2,520 | 2,520 | 1949 | 4,440 | 3,941 |
| 1929 | 2,658 | 2,525 | 1950 | 4,469 | 4,008 |
| 1930 | 2,889 | 2,624 | 1951 | 4,493 | 4,083 |
| 1931 | 3,021 | 2,702 | 1952 | 4,513 | 4,128 |
| 1932 | 3,153 | 2,784 | 1953 | 4,529 | 4,170 |
| 1933 | 3,285 | 2,871 | 1954 | 4,544 | 4,206 |
| 1934 | 3,417 | 2,963 | 1955 | 4,559 | 4,236 |
| 1935 | 3,549 | 3,062 | 1956 | 4,573 | 4,253 |
| 1936 | 3,630 | 3,168 | 1957 | 4,586 | 4,272 |
| 1937 | 3,702 | 3,281 | 1958 | 4,599 | 4,296 |
| 1938 | 3,771 | 3,335 | 1959 | 4,610 | 4,324 |
| 1939 | 3,840 | 3,383 | 1960 | 4,625 | 4,356 |
| 1940 | 3,909 | 3,430 | 1961 | 4,625 | 4,399 |
| 1941 | 3,975 | 3,481 | 1962 | 4,625 | 4,450 |
| 1942 | 4,040 | 3,535 | 1963 | 4,625 | 4,537 |
| 1943 | 4,163 | 3,591 | 1964 | 4,625 | 4,537 |
| 1944 | 4,213 | 3,650 | 1965 | 4,625 | 4,537 |
| 1945 | 4,263 | 3,710 | 1966 | 4,625 | 4,537 |
| 1946 | 4,312 | 3,774 | 1967 | 4,625 | 4,537 |
| 1947 | 4,360 | 3,825 | 1968 | 4,625 | 4,537 |

# TABLE 9—WORKER'S AND SPOUSE'S RETIREMENT BENEFITS*

| Average Indexed Monthly Earnings | Worker Age 65 (PIA) | Spouse Age 65 | Total Age 65 Benefit | Worker Age 62** | Spouse Age 62 | Total Age 62 Benefit | Worker 65 & Spouse 62 |
|---|---|---|---|---|---|---|---|
| $4,625 | $1,314 | $657 | $1,971 | $1,051 | $492 | $1,543 | $1,806 |
| 4,600 | 1,311 | 655 | 1,966 | 1,048 | 491 | 1,539 | 1,802 |
| 4,575 | 1,307 | 653 | 1,960 | 1,045 | 489 | 1,534 | 1,797 |
| 4,550 | 1,303 | 651 | 1,954 | 1,042 | 488 | 1,530 | 1,791 |
| 4,525 | 1,299 | 649 | 1,948 | 1,039 | 486 | 1,525 | 1,786 |
| 4,500 | 1,296 | 648 | 1,944 | 1,036 | 486 | 1,522 | 1,782 |
| 4,475 | 1,292 | 646 | 1,938 | 1,033 | 484 | 1,517 | 1,776 |
| 4,450 | 1,288 | 644 | 1,932 | 1,030 | 483 | 1,513 | 1,771 |
| 4,425 | 1,284 | 642 | 1,926 | 1,027 | 481 | 1,508 | 1,765 |
| 4,400 | 1,281 | 640 | 1,921 | 1,024 | 480 | 1,504 | 1,761 |
| 4,375 | 1,277 | 638 | 1,915 | 1,021 | 478 | 1,499 | 1,755 |
| 4,350 | 1,273 | 636 | 1,909 | 1,018 | 477 | 1,495 | 1,750 |
| 4,325 | 1,269 | 634 | 1,903 | 1,015 | 475 | 1,490 | 1,744 |
| 4,300 | 1,266 | 633 | 1,899 | 1,012 | 474 | 1,486 | 1,740 |
| 4,275 | 1,262 | 631 | 1,893 | 1,009 | 473 | 1,482 | 1,735 |
| 4,250 | 1,258 | 629 | 1,887 | 1,006 | 471 | 1,477 | 1,729 |
| 4,225 | 1,254 | 627 | 1,881 | 1,003 | 470 | 1,473 | 1,724 |
| 4,200 | 1,251 | 625 | 1,876 | 1,000 | 468 | 1,468 | 1,720 |
| 4,175 | 1,247 | 623 | 1,870 | 997 | 467 | 1,464 | 1,714 |
| 4,150 | 1,243 | 621 | 1,864 | 994 | 465 | 1,459 | 1,709 |
| 4,125 | 1,239 | 619 | 1,858 | 991 | 464 | 1,455 | 1,703 |
| 4,100 | 1,236 | 618 | 1,854 | 988 | 463 | 1,451 | 1,699 |
| 4,075 | 1,232 | 616 | 1,848 | 985 | 462 | 1,447 | 1,694 |
| 4,050 | 1,228 | 614 | 1,842 | 982 | 460 | 1,442 | 1,688 |
| 4,025 | 1,224 | 612 | 1,836 | 979 | 459 | 1,438 | 1,683 |
| 4,000 | 1,221 | 610 | 1,831 | 976 | 457 | 1,433 | 1,678 |
| 3,975 | 1,217 | 608 | 1,825 | 973 | 456 | 1,429 | 1,673 |
| 3,950 | 1,213 | 606 | 1,819 | 970 | 454 | 1,424 | 1,667 |
| 3,925 | 1,209 | 604 | 1,813 | 967 | 453 | 1,420 | 1,662 |
| 3,900 | 1,206 | 603 | 1,809 | 964 | 452 | 1,416 | 1,658 |
| 3,875 | 1,202 | 601 | 1,803 | 961 | 450 | 1,411 | 1,652 |
| 3,850 | 1,198 | 599 | 1,797 | 958 | 449 | 1,407 | 1,647 |
| 3,825 | 1,194 | 597 | 1,791 | 955 | 447 | 1,402 | 1,641 |
| 3,800 | 1,191 | 595 | 1,786 | 952 | 446 | 1,398 | 1,637 |
| 3,775 | 1,187 | 593 | 1,780 | 949 | 444 | 1,393 | 1,632 |
| 3,750 | 1,183 | 591 | 1,774 | 946 | 443 | 1,389 | 1,626 |
| 3,725 | 1,179 | 589 | 1,768 | 943 | 441 | 1,384 | 1,621 |
| 3,700 | 1,176 | 588 | 1,764 | 940 | 441 | 1,381 | 1,617 |
| 3,675 | 1,172 | 586 | 1,758 | 937 | 439 | 1,376 | 1,611 |
| 3,650 | 1,168 | 584 | 1,752 | 934 | 438 | 1,372 | 1,606 |
| 3,625 | 1,165 | 582 | 1,747 | 932 | 436 | 1,368 | 1,601 |
| 3,600 | 1,161 | 580 | 1,741 | 928 | 435 | 1,363 | 1,596 |
| 3,575 | 1,157 | 578 | 1,735 | 925 | 433 | 1,358 | 1,590 |
| 3,550 | 1,153 | 576 | 1,729 | 922 | 432 | 1,354 | 1,585 |
| 3,525 | 1,150 | 575 | 1,725 | 920 | 431 | 1,351 | 1,581 |
| 3,500 | 1,146 | 573 | 1,719 | 916 | 429 | 1,345 | 1,575 |
| 3,475 | 1,142 | 571 | 1,713 | 913 | 428 | 1,341 | 1,570 |
| 3,450 | 1,138 | 569 | 1,707 | 910 | 426 | 1,336 | 1,564 |

| Average Indexed Monthly Earnings | Worker Age 65 (PIA) | Spouse Age 65 | Total Age 65 Benefit | Worker Age 62** | Spouse Age 62 | Total Age 62 Benefit | Worker 65 & Spouse 62 |
|---|---|---|---|---|---|---|---|
| 3,425 | 1,135 | 567 | 1,702 | 908 | 425 | 1,333 | 1,560 |
| 3,400 | 1,131 | 565 | 1,696 | 904 | 423 | 1,327 | 1,555 |
| | | | | | | | |
| 3,375 | 1,127 | 563 | 1,690 | 901 | 422 | 1,323 | 1,549 |
| 3,350 | 1,123 | 561 | 1,684 | 898 | 420 | 1,318 | 1,544 |
| 3,325 | 1,120 | 560 | 1,680 | 896 | 420 | 1,316 | 1,540 |
| 3,300 | 1,116 | 558 | 1,674 | 892 | 418 | 1,310 | 1,534 |
| 3,275 | 1,112 | 556 | 1,668 | 889 | 417 | 1,306 | 1,529 |
| | | | | | | | |
| 3,250 | 1,108 | 554 | 1,662 | 886 | 415 | 1,301 | 1,523 |
| 3,225 | 1,105 | 552 | 1,657 | 884 | 414 | 1,298 | 1,519 |
| 3,200 | 1,101 | 550 | 1,651 | 880 | 412 | 1,292 | 1,513 |
| 3,175 | 1,097 | 548 | 1,645 | 877 | 411 | 1,288 | 1,508 |
| 3,150 | 1,093 | 546 | 1,639 | 874 | 409 | 1,283 | 1,502 |
| | | | | | | | |
| 3,125 | 1,090 | 545 | 1,635 | 872 | 408 | 1,280 | 1,498 |
| 3,100 | 1,086 | 543 | 1,629 | 868 | 407 | 1,275 | 1,493 |
| 3,075 | 1,082 | 541 | 1,623 | 865 | 405 | 1,270 | 1,487 |
| 3,050 | 1,078 | 539 | 1,617 | 862 | 404 | 1,266 | 1,482 |
| 3,025 | 1,075 | 537 | 1,612 | 860 | 402 | 1,262 | 1,478 |
| | | | | | | | |
| 3,000 | 1,071 | 535 | 1,606 | 856 | 401 | 1,257 | 1,472 |
| 2,975 | 1,067 | 533 | 1,600 | 853 | 399 | 1,252 | 1,467 |
| 2,950 | 1,063 | 531 | 1,594 | 850 | 398 | 1,248 | 1,461 |
| 2,925 | 1,060 | 530 | 1,590 | 848 | 397 | 1,245 | 1,457 |
| 2,900 | 1,056 | 528 | 1,584 | 844 | 396 | 1,240 | 1,452 |
| | | | | | | | |
| 2,875 | 1,052 | 526 | 1,578 | 841 | 394 | 1,235 | 1,446 |
| 2,850 | 1,048 | 524 | 1,572 | 838 | 393 | 1,231 | 1,441 |
| 2,825 | 1,045 | 522 | 1,567 | 836 | 391 | 1,227 | 1,436 |
| 2,800 | 1,041 | 520 | 1,561 | 832 | 390 | 1,222 | 1,431 |
| 2,775 | 1,037 | 518 | 1,555 | 829 | 388 | 1,217 | 1,425 |
| | | | | | | | |
| 2,750 | 1,033 | 516 | 1,549 | 826 | 387 | 1,213 | 1,420 |
| 2,725 | 1,030 | 515 | 1,545 | 824 | 386 | 1,210 | 1,416 |
| 2,700 | 1,026 | 513 | 1,539 | 820 | 384 | 1,204 | 1,410 |
| 2,675 | 1,022 | 512 | 1,533 | 817 | 384 | 1,201 | 1,405 |
| 2,650 | 1,018 | 509 | 1,527 | 814 | 381 | 1,195 | 1,399 |
| | | | | | | | |
| 2,625 | 1,015 | 507 | 1,522 | 812 | 380 | 1,192 | 1,395 |
| 2,600 | 1,011 | 505 | 1,516 | 808 | 378 | 1,186 | 1,390 |
| 2,575 | 1,007 | 503 | 1,510 | 805 | 377 | 1,182 | 1,384 |
| 2,550 | 1,003 | 501 | 1,504 | 802 | 375 | 1,177 | 1,379 |
| 2,525 | 1,000 | 500 | 1,500 | 800 | 375 | 1,175 | 1,375 |
| | | | | | | | |
| 2,500 | 996 | 498 | 1,494 | 796 | 373 | 1,169 | 1,369 |
| 2,475 | 992 | 496 | 1,488 | 793 | 372 | 1,165 | 1,364 |
| 2,450 | 988 | 494 | 1,482 | 790 | 370 | 1,160 | 1,358 |
| 2,425 | 985 | 492 | 1,477 | 788 | 369 | 1,157 | 1,354 |
| 2,400 | 981 | 490 | 1,471 | 784 | 367 | 1,151 | 1,348 |
| | | | | | | | |
| 2,375 | 977 | 488 | 1,465 | 781 | 366 | 1,147 | 1,343 |
| 2,350 | 973 | 486 | 1,459 | 778 | 364 | 1,142 | 1,337 |
| 2,325 | 968 | 484 | 1,452 | 774 | 363 | 1,137 | 1,331 |
| 2,300 | 960 | 480 | 1,440 | 768 | 360 | 1,128 | 1,320 |
| 2,275 | 952 | 476 | 1,428 | 761 | 357 | 1,118 | 1,309 |
| | | | | | | | |
| 2,250 | 944 | 472 | 1,416 | 755 | 354 | 1,109 | 1,298 |
| 2,225 | 936 | 468 | 1,404 | 748 | 351 | 1,099 | 1,287 |
| 2,200 | 928 | 464 | 1,392 | 742 | 348 | 1,090 | 1,276 |
| 2,175 | 920 | 460 | 1,380 | 736 | 345 | 1,081 | 1,265 |
| 2,150 | 912 | 456 | 1,368 | 729 | 342 | 1,071 | 1,254 |

| Average Indexed Monthly Earnings | Worker Age 65 (PIA) | Spouse Age 65 | Total Age 65 Benefit | Worker Age 62** | Spouse Age 62 | Total Age 62 Benefit | Worker 65 & Spouse 62 |
|---|---|---|---|---|---|---|---|
| 2,125 | 904 | 452 | 1,356 | 723 | 339 | 1,062 | 1,243 |
| 2,100 | 896 | 448 | 1,344 | 716 | 336 | 1,052 | 1,232 |
| 2,075 | 888 | 444 | 1,332 | 710 | 333 | 1,043 | 1,221 |
| 2,050 | 880 | 440 | 1,320 | 704 | 330 | 1,034 | 1,210 |
| 2,025 | 872 | 436 | 1,308 | 697 | 327 | 1,024 | 1,199 |
| 2,000 | 864 | 432 | 1,296 | 691 | 324 | 1,015 | 1,188 |
| 1,975 | 856 | 428 | 1,284 | 684 | 321 | 1,005 | 1,177 |
| 1,950 | 848 | 424 | 1,272 | 678 | 318 | 996 | 1,166 |
| 1,925 | 840 | 420 | 1,260 | 672 | 315 | 987 | 1,155 |
| 1,900 | 832 | 416 | 1,248 | 665 | 312 | 977 | 1,144 |
| 1,875 | 824 | 412 | 1,236 | 659 | 309 | 968 | 1,133 |
| 1,850 | 816 | 408 | 1,224 | 652 | 306 | 958 | 1,122 |
| 1,825 | 808 | 404 | 1,212 | 646 | 303 | 949 | 1,111 |
| 1,800 | 800 | 400 | 1,200 | 640 | 300 | 940 | 1,100 |
| 1,775 | 792 | 396 | 1,188 | 633 | 297 | 930 | 1,089 |
| 1,750 | 784 | 392 | 1,176 | 627 | 294 | 921 | 1,078 |
| 1,725 | 776 | 388 | 1,164 | 620 | 291 | 911 | 1,067 |
| 1,700 | 768 | 384 | 1,152 | 614 | 288 | 902 | 1,056 |
| 1,675 | 760 | 380 | 1,140 | 608 | 285 | 893 | 1,045 |
| 1,650 | 752 | 376 | 1,128 | 601 | 282 | 883 | 1,034 |
| 1,625 | 744 | 372 | 1,116 | 595 | 279 | 874 | 1,023 |
| 1,600 | 736 | 368 | 1,104 | 588 | 276 | 864 | 1,012 |
| 1,575 | 728 | 364 | 1,092 | 582 | 273 | 855 | 1,001 |
| 1,550 | 720 | 360 | 1,080 | 576 | 270 | 846 | 990 |
| 1,525 | 712 | 356 | 1,068 | 569 | 267 | 836 | 979 |
| 1,500 | 704 | 352 | 1,056 | 563 | 264 | 827 | 968 |
| 1,475 | 696 | 348 | 1,044 | 556 | 261 | 817 | 957 |
| 1,450 | 688 | 344 | 1,032 | 550 | 258 | 808 | 946 |
| 1,425 | 680 | 340 | 1,020 | 544 | 255 | 799 | 935 |
| 1,400 | 672 | 336 | 1,008 | 537 | 252 | 789 | 924 |
| 1,375 | 664 | 332 | 996 | 531 | 249 | 780 | 913 |
| 1,350 | 656 | 328 | 984 | 524 | 246 | 770 | 902 |
| 1,325 | 648 | 324 | 972 | 518 | 243 | 761 | 891 |
| 1,300 | 640 | 320 | 960 | 512 | 240 | 752 | 880 |
| 1,275 | 632 | 316 | 948 | 505 | 237 | 742 | 869 |
| 1,250 | 624 | 312 | 936 | 499 | 234 | 733 | 858 |
| 1,225 | 616 | 308 | 924 | 492 | 231 | 723 | 847 |
| 1,200 | 608 | 304 | 912 | 486 | 228 | 714 | 836 |
| 1,175 | 600 | 300 | 900 | 480 | 225 | 705 | 825 |
| 1,150 | 592 | 296 | 888 | 473 | 222 | 695 | 814 |
| 1,125 | 584 | 292 | 876 | 467 | 219 | 686 | 803 |
| 1,100 | 576 | 288 | 864 | 460 | 216 | 676 | 792 |
| 1,075 | 568 | 284 | 852 | 454 | 213 | 667 | 781 |
| 1,050 | 560 | 280 | 840 | 448 | 210 | 658 | 770 |
| 1,025 | 552 | 276 | 828 | 441 | 207 | 648 | 759 |
| 1,000 | 544 | 272 | 816 | 435 | 204 | 639 | 748 |
| 975 | 536 | 268 | 804 | 428 | 201 | 629 | 737 |
| 950 | 528 | 264 | 792 | 422 | 198 | 620 | 721 |
| 925 | 520 | 260 | 780 | 416 | 195 | 611 | 715 |
| 900 | 512 | 256 | 768 | 409 | 192 | 601 | 704 |

| Average Indexed Monthly Earnings | Worker Age 65 (PIA) | Spouse Age 65 | Total Age 65 Benefit | Worker Age 62** | Spouse Age 62 | Total Age 62 Benefit | Worker 65 & Spouse 62 |
|---|---|---|---|---|---|---|---|
| 875 | 504 | 252 | 756 | 403 | 189 | 592 | 693 |
| 850 | 496 | 248 | 744 | 396 | 186 | 582 | 682 |
| 825 | 488 | 244 | 732 | 390 | 183 | 573 | 671 |
| 800 | 480 | 240 | 720 | 384 | 180 | 564 | 660 |
| 775 | 472 | 236 | 708 | 377 | 177 | 554 | 649 |
| 750 | 464 | 232 | 696 | 371 | 174 | 545 | 638 |
| 725 | 456 | 228 | 684 | 364 | 171 | 535 | 627 |
| 700 | 448 | 224 | 672 | 358 | 168 | 526 | 616 |
| 675 | 440 | 220 | 660 | 352 | 165 | 517 | 605 |
| 650 | 432 | 216 | 648 | 345 | 162 | 507 | 594 |

* The retirement age when unreduced benefits are available—now 65— will be increased to age 67 in gradual steps starting in the year 2000. If you were born in 1943-1954, your retirement age for full benefits is 66. If you were born in 1955-1959, your retirement age for full benefits is you 66th birthday plus two months for every year you were born after 1954. If you were born in 1960 and after, your retirement age for full benefits is 67.

** Benefits listed are 80% of the corresponding PIA, but age 62 benefits are reduced further if worker is born in 1938 or after. Ex.: Benefit is 75% of PIA for workers born in 1943-1954 and 70% of PIA for workers born in 1960 and after.

## TABLE 10—SURVIVOR'S BENEFITS

| Average Indexed Monthly Earnings | Worker's PIA | Surviving Spouse & 1 Child; or 2 Children | Surviving Spouse & 2 Children or 3 Children | One Child (No Mother) | Widow or Widower Age 60 | Widow or Widower Age 65 | Each of Two Parents | Sole Parent | Maximum Family Benefits |
|---|---|---|---|---|---|---|---|---|---|
| $4,625 | $1,314 | $1,971 | $2,299 | $985 | $939 | $1,314 | $985 | $1,084 | $2,299 |
| 4,600 | 1,311 | 1,966 | 2,293 | 983 | 937 | 1,311 | 983 | 1,081 | 2,293 |
| 4,575 | 1,307 | 1,960 | 2,286 | 980 | 934 | 1,307 | 980 | 1,078 | 2,286 |
| 4,550 | 1,303 | 1,954 | 2,279 | 977 | 931 | 1,303 | 977 | 1,074 | 2,279 |
| 4,525 | 1,299 | 1,948 | 2,272 | 974 | 928 | 1,299 | 974 | 1,071 | 2,272 |
| 4,500 | 1,296 | 1,944 | 2,267 | 972 | 926 | 1,296 | 972 | 1,069 | 2,267 |
| 4,475 | 1,292 | 1,938 | 2,260 | 969 | 923 | 1,292 | 969 | 1,065 | 2,260 |
| 4,450 | 1,288 | 1,932 | 2,253 | 966 | 920 | 1,288 | 966 | 1,062 | 2,253 |
| 4,425 | 1,284 | 1,926 | 2,246 | 963 | 918 | 1,284 | 963 | 1,059 | 2,246 |
| 4,400 | 1,281 | 1,921 | 2,241 | 960 | 915 | 1,281 | 960 | 1,056 | 2,241 |
| 4,375 | 1,277 | 1,915 | 2,234 | 957 | 913 | 1,277 | 957 | 1,053 | 2,234 |
| 4,350 | 1,273 | 1,909 | 2,227 | 954 | 910 | 1,273 | 954 | 1,050 | 2,227 |
| 4,325 | 1,269 | 1,903 | 2,220 | 951 | 907 | 1,269 | 951 | 1,046 | 2,220 |
| 4,300 | 1,266 | 1,899 | 2,215 | 949 | 905 | 1,266 | 949 | 1,044 | 2,215 |
| 4,275 | 1,262 | 1,893 | 2,208 | 946 | 902 | 1,262 | 946 | 1,041 | 2,208 |
| 4,250 | 1,258 | 1,887 | 2,201 | 943 | 899 | 1,258 | 943 | 1,037 | 2,201 |
| 4,225 | 1,254 | 1,881 | 2,194 | 940 | 896 | 1,254 | 940 | 1,034 | 2,194 |
| 4,200 | 1,251 | 1,876 | 2,188 | 938 | 894 | 1,251 | 938 | 1,032 | 2,188 |
| 4,175 | 1,247 | 1,870 | 2,181 | 935 | 891 | 1,247 | 935 | 1,028 | 2,181 |
| 4,150 | 1,243 | 1,864 | 2,174 | 932 | 888 | 1,243 | 932 | 1,025 | 2,174 |
| 4,125 | 1,239 | 1,858 | 2,167 | 929 | 885 | 1,239 | 929 | 1,022 | 2,167 |
| 4,100 | 1,236 | 1,854 | 2,162 | 927 | 883 | 1,236 | 927 | 1,019 | 2,162 |
| 4,075 | 1,232 | 1,848 | 2,155 | 924 | 880 | 1,232 | 924 | 1,016 | 2,155 |
| 4,050 | 1,228 | 1,842 | 2,148 | 921 | 878 | 1,228 | 921 | 1,013 | 2,148 |
| 4,025 | 1,224 | 1,836 | 2,141 | 918 | 875 | 1,224 | 918 | 1,009 | 2,141 |
| 4,000 | 1,221 | 1,831 | 2,136 | 915 | 873 | 1,221 | 915 | 1,007 | 2,136 |
| 3,975 | 1,217 | 1,825 | 2,129 | 912 | 870 | 1,217 | 912 | 1,004 | 2,129 |
| 3,950 | 1,213 | 1,819 | 2,122 | 909 | 867 | 1,213 | 909 | 1,000 | 2,122 |
| 3,925 | 1,209 | 1,813 | 2,115 | 906 | 864 | 1,209 | 906 | 997 | 2,115 |
| 3,900 | 1,206 | 1,809 | 2,110 | 904 | 862 | 1,206 | 904 | 994 | 2,110 |
| 3,875 | 1,202 | 1,803 | 2,103 | 901 | 859 | 1,202 | 901 | 991 | 2,103 |
| 3,850 | 1,198 | 1,797 | 2,096 | 898 | 856 | 1,198 | 898 | 988 | 2,096 |
| 3,825 | 1,194 | 1,791 | 2,089 | 895 | 853 | 1,194 | 895 | 985 | 2,089 |
| 3,800 | 1,191 | 1,786 | 2,083 | 893 | 851 | 1,191 | 893 | 982 | 2,083 |
| 3,775 | 1,187 | 1,780 | 2,076 | 890 | 848 | 1,187 | 890 | 979 | 2,076 |
| 3,750 | 1,183 | 1,774 | 2,069 | 887 | 845 | 1,183 | 887 | 975 | 2,069 |
| 3,725 | 1,179 | 1,768 | 2,062 | 884 | 842 | 1,179 | 884 | 972 | 2,062 |
| 3,700 | 1,176 | 1,764 | 2,057 | 882 | 840 | 1,176 | 882 | 970 | 2,057 |
| 3,675 | 1,172 | 1,758 | 2,050 | 879 | 837 | 1,172 | 879 | 966 | 2,050 |
| 3,650 | 1,168 | 1,752 | 2,043 | 876 | 835 | 1,168 | 876 | 963 | 2,043 |
| 3,625 | 1,165 | 1,747 | 2,038 | 873 | 832 | 1,165 | 873 | 961 | 2,038 |
| 3,600 | 1,161 | 1,741 | 2,031 | 870 | 830 | 1,161 | 870 | 957 | 2,031 |
| 3,575 | 1,157 | 1,735 | 2,024 | 867 | 827 | 1,157 | 867 | 954 | 2,024 |
| 3,550 | 1,153 | 1,729 | 2,017 | 864 | 824 | 1,153 | 864 | 951 | 2,017 |
| 3,525 | 1,150 | 1,725 | 2,012 | 862 | 822 | 1,150 | 862 | 948 | 2,012 |
| 3,500 | 1,146 | 1,719 | 2,005 | 859 | 819 | 1,146 | 859 | 945 | 2,005 |
| 3,475 | 1,142 | 1,713 | 1,998 | 856 | 816 | 1,142 | 856 | 942 | 1,998 |
| 3,450 | 1,138 | 1,707 | 1,991 | 853 | 813 | 1,138 | 853 | 938 | 1,991 |
| 3,425 | 1,135 | 1,702 | 1,985 | 851 | 811 | 1,135 | 851 | 936 | 1,985 |
| 3,400 | 1,131 | 1,696 | 1,978 | 848 | 808 | 1,131 | 848 | 933 | 1,978 |

| Average Indexed Monthly Earnings | Worker's PIA | Surviving Spouse & 1 Child; or 2 Children | Surviving Spouse & 2 Children or 3 Children | One Child (No Mother) | Widow or Widower Age 60 | Widow or Widower Age 65 | Each of Two Parents | Sole Parent | Maximum Family Benefits |
|---|---|---|---|---|---|---|---|---|---|
| 3,375 | 1,127 | 1,690 | 1,971 | 845 | 805 | 1,127 | 845 | 929 | 1,971 |
| 3,350 | 1,123 | 1,684 | 1,964 | 842 | 802 | 1,123 | 842 | 926 | 1,964 |
| 3,325 | 1,120 | 1,680 | 1,959 | 840 | 800 | 1,120 | 840 | 924 | 1,959 |
| 3,300 | 1,116 | 1,674 | 1,952 | 837 | 797 | 1,116 | 837 | 920 | 1,952 |
| 3,275 | 1,112 | 1,668 | 1,945 | 834 | 795 | 1,112 | 834 | 917 | 1,945 |
| 3,250 | 1,108 | 1,662 | 1,938 | 831 | 792 | 1,108 | 831 | 914 | 1,938 |
| 3,225 | 1,105 | 1,657 | 1,933 | 828 | 790 | 1,105 | 828 | 911 | 1,933 |
| 3,200 | 1,101 | 1,651 | 1,926 | 825 | 787 | 1,101 | 825 | 908 | 1,926 |
| 3,175 | 1,097 | 1,645 | 1,919 | 822 | 784 | 1,097 | 822 | 905 | 1,919 |
| 3,150 | 1,093 | 1,639 | 1,912 | 819 | 781 | 1,093 | 819 | 901 | 1,912 |
| 3,125 | 1,090 | 1,635 | 1,907 | 817 | 779 | 1,090 | 817 | 899 | 1,907 |
| 3,100 | 1,086 | 1,629 | 1,900 | 814 | 776 | 1,086 | 814 | 895 | 1,900 |
| 3,075 | 1,082 | 1,623 | 1,893 | 811 | 773 | 1,082 | 811 | 892 | 1,893 |
| 3,050 | 1,078 | 1,617 | 1,886 | 808 | 770 | 1,078 | 808 | 889 | 1,886 |
| 3,025 | 1,075 | 1,612 | 1,880 | 806 | 768 | 1,075 | 806 | 886 | 1,880 |
| 3,000 | 1,071 | 1,606 | 1,873 | 803 | 765 | 1,071 | 803 | 883 | 1,873 |
| 2,975 | 1,067 | 1,600 | 1,866 | 800 | 762 | 1,067 | 800 | 880 | 1,866 |
| 2,950 | 1,063 | 1,594 | 1,859 | 797 | 760 | 1,063 | 797 | 876 | 1,859 |
| 2,925 | 1,060 | 1,590 | 1,854 | 795 | 757 | 1,060 | 795 | 874 | 1,854 |
| 2,900 | 1,056 | 1,584 | 1,847 | 792 | 755 | 1,056 | 792 | 871 | 1,847 |
| 2,875 | 1,052 | 1,578 | 1,840 | 789 | 752 | 1,052 | 789 | 867 | 1,840 |
| 2,850 | 1,048 | 1,572 | 1,833 | 786 | 749 | 1,048 | 786 | 864 | 1,833 |
| 2,825 | 1,045 | 1,567 | 1,828 | 783 | 747 | 1,045 | 783 | 862 | 1,828 |
| 2,800 | 1,041 | 1,561 | 1,821 | 780 | 744 | 1,041 | 780 | 858 | 1,821 |
| 2,775 | 1,037 | 1,555 | 1,814 | 777 | 741 | 1,037 | 777 | 855 | 1,814 |
| 2,750 | 1,033 | 1,549 | 1,807 | 774 | 738 | 1,033 | 774 | 852 | 1,807 |
| 2,725 | 1,030 | 1,545 | 1,802 | 772 | 736 | 1,030 | 772 | 849 | 1,802 |
| 2,700 | 1,026 | 1,539 | 1,795 | 769 | 733 | 1,026 | 769 | 846 | 1,795 |
| 2,675 | 1,022 | 1,533 | 1,788 | 766 | 730 | 1,022 | 766 | 843 | 1,788 |
| 2,650 | 1,018 | 1,527 | 1,781 | 763 | 727 | 1,018 | 763 | 839 | 1,781 |
| 2,625 | 1,015 | 1,522 | 1,775 | 761 | 725 | 1,015 | 761 | 837 | 1,775 |
| 2,600 | 1,011 | 1,516 | 1,768 | 758 | 722 | 1,011 | 758 | 834 | 1,768 |
| 2,575 | 1,007 | 1,510 | 1,761 | 755 | 720 | 1,007 | 755 | 830 | 1,761 |
| 2,550 | 1,003 | 1,504 | 1,754 | 752 | 717 | 1,003 | 752 | 827 | 1,754 |
| 2,525 | 1,000 | 1,500 | 1,749 | 750 | 715 | 1,000 | 750 | 825 | 1,749 |
| 2,500 | 996 | 1,494 | 1,742 | 747 | 712 | 996 | 747 | 821 | 1,742 |
| 2,475 | 992 | 1,488 | 1,735 | 744 | 709 | 992 | 744 | 818 | 1,735 |
| 2,450 | 988 | 1,482 | 1,728 | 741 | 706 | 988 | 741 | 815 | 1,728 |
| 2,425 | 985 | 1,477 | 1,723 | 738 | 704 | 985 | 738 | 812 | 1,723 |
| 2,400 | 981 | 1,471 | 1,716 | 735 | 701 | 981 | 735 | 809 | 1,716 |
| 2,375 | 977 | 1,465 | 1,709 | 732 | 698 | 977 | 732 | 806 | 1,709 |
| 2,350 | 973 | 1,459 | 1,702 | 729 | 695 | 973 | 729 | 802 | 1,702 |
| 2,325 | 968 | 1,452 | 1,693 | 726 | 692 | 968 | 726 | 798 | 1,693 |
| 2,300 | 960 | 1,440 | 1,679 | 720 | 686 | 960 | 720 | 792 | 1,679 |
| 2,275 | 952 | 1,428 | 1,665 | 714 | 680 | 952 | 714 | 785 | 1,665 |
| 2,250 | 944 | 1,416 | 1,651 | 708 | 674 | 944 | 708 | 778 | 1,651 |
| 2,225 | 936 | 1,404 | 1,637 | 702 | 669 | 936 | 702 | 772 | 1,637 |
| 2,200 | 928 | 1,392 | 1,624 | 696 | 663 | 928 | 696 | 765 | 1,624 |
| 2,175 | 920 | 1,380 | 1,614 | 690 | 657 | 920 | 690 | 759 | 1,614 |
| 2,150 | 912 | 1,368 | 1,603 | 684 | 652 | 912 | 684 | 752 | 1,603 |
| 2,125 | 904 | 1,356 | 1,592 | 678 | 646 | 904 | 678 | 745 | 1,592 |
| 2,100 | 896 | 1,344 | 1,582 | 672 | 640 | 896 | 672 | 739 | 1,582 |
| 2,075 | 888 | 1,332 | 1,571 | 666 | 634 | 888 | 666 | 732 | 1,571 |
| 2,050 | 880 | 1,320 | 1,560 | 660 | 629 | 880 | 660 | 726 | 1,560 |
| 2,025 | 872 | 1,308 | 1,549 | 654 | 623 | 872 | 654 | 719 | 1,549 |

| Average Indexed Monthly Earnings | Worker's PIA | Surviving Spouse & 1 Child; or 2 Children | Surviving Spouse & 2 Children or 3 Children | One Child (No Mother) | Widow or Widower Age 60 | Widow or Widower Age 65 | Each of Two Parents | Sole Parent | Maximum Family Benefits |
|---|---|---|---|---|---|---|---|---|---|
| 2,000 | 864 | 1,296 | 1,539 | 648 | 617 | 864 | 648 | 712 | 1,539 |
| 1,975 | 856 | 1,284 | 1,528 | 642 | 612 | 856 | 642 | 706 | 1,528 |
| 1,950 | 848 | 1,272 | 1,517 | 636 | 606 | 848 | 636 | 699 | 1,517 |
| 1,925 | 840 | 1,260 | 1,507 | 630 | 600 | 840 | 630 | 693 | 1,507 |
| 1,900 | 832 | 1,248 | 1,496 | 624 | 594 | 832 | 624 | 686 | 1,496 |
| 1,875 | 824 | 1,236 | 1,485 | 618 | 589 | 824 | 618 | 679 | 1,485 |
| 1,850 | 816 | 1,224 | 1,474 | 612 | 583 | 816 | 612 | 673 | 1,474 |
| 1,825 | 808 | 1,212 | 1,464 | 606 | 577 | 808 | 606 | 666 | 1,464 |
| 1,800 | 800 | 1,200 | 1,453 | 600 | 572 | 800 | 600 | 660 | 1,453 |
| 1,775 | 792 | 1,188 | 1,442 | 594 | 566 | 792 | 594 | 653 | 1,442 |
| 1,750 | 784 | 1,176 | 1,431 | 588 | 560 | 784 | 588 | 646 | 1,431 |
| 1,725 | 776 | 1,164 | 1,421 | 582 | 554 | 776 | 582 | 640 | 1,421 |
| 1,700 | 768 | 1,152 | 1,410 | 576 | 549 | 768 | 576 | 633 | 1,410 |
| 1,675 | 760 | 1,140 | 1,399 | 570 | 543 | 760 | 570 | 627 | 1,399 |
| 1,650 | 752 | 1,128 | 1,389 | 564 | 537 | 752 | 564 | 620 | 1,389 |
| 1,625 | 744 | 1,116 | 1,378 | 558 | 531 | 744 | 558 | 613 | 1,378 |
| 1,600 | 736 | 1,104 | 1,367 | 552 | 526 | 736 | 552 | 607 | 1,367 |
| 1,575 | 728 | 1,092 | 1,356 | 546 | 520 | 728 | 546 | 600 | 1,356 |
| 1,550 | 720 | 1,080 | 1,346 | 540 | 514 | 720 | 540 | 594 | 1,346 |
| 1,525 | 712 | 1,068 | 1,332 | 534 | 509 | 712 | 534 | 587 | 1,332 |
| 1,500 | 704 | 1,056 | 1,310 | 528 | 503 | 704 | 528 | 580 | 1,310 |
| 1,475 | 696 | 1,044 | 1,289 | 522 | 497 | 696 | 522 | 574 | 1,289 |
| 1,450 | 688 | 1,032 | 1,267 | 516 | 491 | 688 | 516 | 567 | 1,267 |
| 1,425 | 680 | 1,020 | 1,245 | 510 | 486 | 680 | 510 | 561 | 1,245 |
| 1,400 | 672 | 1,008 | 1,223 | 504 | 480 | 672 | 504 | 554 | 1,223 |
| 1,375 | 664 | 996 | 1,202 | 498 | 474 | 664 | 498 | 547 | 1,202 |
| 1,350 | 656 | 984 | 1,180 | 492 | 469 | 656 | 492 | 541 | 1,180 |
| 1,325 | 648 | 972 | 1,158 | 486 | 463 | 648 | 486 | 534 | 1,158 |
| 1,300 | 640 | 960 | 1,136 | 480 | 457 | 640 | 480 | 528 | 1,136 |
| 1,275 | 632 | 948 | 1,115 | 474 | 451 | 632 | 474 | 521 | 1,115 |
| 1,250 | 624 | 936 | 1,093 | 468 | 446 | 624 | 468 | 514 | 1,093 |
| 1,225 | 616 | 924 | 1,071 | 462 | 440 | 616 | 462 | 508 | 1,071 |
| 1,200 | 608 | 912 | 1,049 | 456 | 434 | 608 | 456 | 501 | 1,049 |
| 1,175 | 600 | 900 | 1,028 | 450 | 429 | 600 | 450 | 495 | 1,028 |
| 1,150 | 592 | 888 | 1,006 | 444 | 423 | 592 | 444 | 488 | 1,006 |
| 1,125 | 584 | 876 | 984 | 438 | 417 | 584 | 438 | 481 | 984 |
| 1,100 | 576 | 864 | 962 | 432 | 411 | 576 | 432 | 475 | 962 |
| 1,075 | 568 | 852 | 941 | 426 | 406 | 568 | 426 | 468 | 941 |
| 1,050 | 560 | 840 | 919 | 420 | 400 | 560 | 420 | 462 | 919 |
| 1,025 | 552 | 828 | 897 | 414 | 394 | 552 | 414 | 455 | 897 |
| 1,000 | 544 | 816 | 875 | 408 | 388 | 544 | 408 | 448 | 875 |
| 975 | 536 | 804 | 854 | 402 | 383 | 536 | 402 | 442 | 854 |
| 950 | 528 | 792 | 832 | 396 | 377 | 528 | 396 | 435 | 832 |
| 925 | 520 | 780 | 810 | 390 | 371 | 520 | 390 | 429 | 810 |
| 900 | 512 | 768 | 788 | 384 | 366 | 512 | 384 | 422 | 788 |
| 875 | 504 | 756 | 766 | 378 | 360 | 504 | 378 | 415 | 766 |
| 850 | 496 | 744 | 745 | 372 | 354 | 496 | 372 | 409 | 745 |
| 825 | 488 | 732 | 732 | 366 | 348 | 488 | 366 | 402 | 732 |
| 800 | 480 | 720 | 720 | 360 | 343 | 480 | 360 | 396 | 720 |
| 775 | 472 | 708 | 708 | 354 | 337 | 472 | 354 | 389 | 708 |
| 750 | 464 | 696 | 696 | 348 | 331 | 464 | 348 | 382 | 696 |
| 725 | 456 | 684 | 684 | 342 | 326 | 456 | 342 | 376 | 684 |
| 700 | 448 | 672 | 672 | 336 | 320 | 448 | 336 | 369 | 672 |
| 675 | 440 | 660 | 660 | 330 | 314 | 440 | 330 | 363 | 660 |
| 650 | 432 | 648 | 648 | 324 | 308 | 432 | 324 | 356 | 648 |

## TABLE 11—DISABILITY BENEFITS

| Average Indexed Monthly Earnings | Disabled Worker | Disabled Worker Spouse and Children | One Child (No Spouse) | Spouse Age 62 |
|---|---|---|---|---|
| $4,625 | $1,314 | $1,971 | $657 | 492 |
| 4,600 | 1,311 | 1,966 | 655 | 491 |
| 4,575 | 1,307 | 1,960 | 653 | 489 |
| 4,550 | 1,303 | 1,954 | 651 | 488 |
| 4,525 | 1,299 | 1,948 | 649 | 486 |
| 4,500 | 1,296 | 1,944 | 648 | 486 |
| 4,475 | 1,292 | 1,938 | 646 | 484 |
| 4,450 | 1,288 | 1,932 | 644 | 483 |
| 4,425 | 1,284 | 1,926 | 642 | 481 |
| 4,400 | 1,281 | 1,921 | 640 | 480 |
| 4,375 | 1,277 | 1,915 | 638 | 478 |
| 4,350 | 1,273 | 1,909 | 636 | 477 |
| 4,325 | 1,269 | 1,903 | 634 | 475 |
| 4,300 | 1,266 | 1,899 | 633 | 474 |
| 4,275 | 1,262 | 1,893 | 631 | 473 |
| 4,250 | 1,258 | 1,887 | 629 | 471 |
| 4,225 | 1,254 | 1,881 | 627 | 470 |
| 4,200 | 1,251 | 1,876 | 625 | 468 |
| 4,175 | 1,247 | 1,870 | 623 | 467 |
| 4,150 | 1,243 | 1,864 | 621 | 465 |
| 4,125 | 1,239 | 1,858 | 619 | 464 |
| 4,100 | 1,236 | 1,854 | 618 | 463 |
| 4,075 | 1,232 | 1,848 | 616 | 462 |
| 4,050 | 1,228 | 1,842 | 614 | 460 |
| 4,025 | 1,224 | 1,836 | 612 | 459 |
| 4,000 | 1,221 | 1,831 | 610 | 457 |
| 3,975 | 1,217 | 1,825 | 608 | 456 |
| 3,950 | 1,213 | 1,819 | 606 | 454 |
| 3,925 | 1,209 | 1,813 | 604 | 453 |
| 3,900 | 1,206 | 1,809 | 603 | 452 |
| 3,875 | 1,202 | 1,803 | 601 | 450 |
| 3,850 | 1,198 | 1,797 | 599 | 449 |
| 3,825 | 1,194 | 1,791 | 597 | 447 |
| 3,800 | 1,191 | 1,786 | 595 | 446 |
| 3,775 | 1,187 | 1,780 | 593 | 444 |
| 3,750 | 1,183 | 1,774 | 591 | 443 |
| 3,725 | 1,179 | 1,768 | 589 | 441 |
| 3,700 | 1,176 | 1,764 | 588 | 441 |
| 3,675 | 1,172 | 1,758 | 586 | 439 |
| 3,650 | 1,168 | 1,752 | 584 | 438 |
| 3,625 | 1,165 | 1,747 | 582 | 436 |
| 3,600 | 1,161 | 1,741 | 580 | 435 |
| 3,575 | 1,157 | 1,735 | 578 | 433 |
| 3,550 | 1,153 | 1,729 | 576 | 432 |
| 3,525 | 1,150 | 1,725 | 575 | 431 |
| 3,500 | 1,146 | 1,719 | 573 | 429 |
| 3,475 | 1,142 | 1,713 | 571 | 428 |
| 3,450 | 1,138 | 1,707 | 569 | 426 |
| 3,425 | 1,135 | 1,702 | 567 | 425 |
| 3,400 | 1,131 | 1,696 | 565 | 423 |

| Average Indexed Monthly Earnings | Disabled Worker | Disabled Worker Spouse and Children | One Child (No Spouse) | Spouse Age 62 |
|---|---|---|---|---|
| 3,375 | 1,127 | 1,690 | 563 | 422 |
| 3,350 | 1,123 | 1,684 | 561 | 420 |
| 3,325 | 1,120 | 1,680 | 560 | 420 |
| 3,300 | 1,116 | 1,674 | 558 | 418 |
| 3,275 | 1,112 | 1,668 | 556 | 417 |
| 3,250 | 1,108 | 1,662 | 554 | 415 |
| 3,225 | 1,105 | 1,657 | 552 | 414 |
| 3,200 | 1,101 | 1,651 | 550 | 412 |
| 3,175 | 1,097 | 1,645 | 548 | 411 |
| 3,150 | 1,093 | 1,639 | 546 | 409 |
| 3,125 | 1,090 | 1,635 | 545 | 408 |
| 3,100 | 1,086 | 1,629 | 543 | 407 |
| 3,075 | 1,082 | 1,623 | 541 | 405 |
| 3,050 | 1,078 | 1,617 | 539 | 404 |
| 3,025 | 1,075 | 1,612 | 537 | 402 |
| 3,000 | 1,071 | 1,606 | 535 | 401 |
| 2,975 | 1,067 | 1,600 | 533 | 399 |
| 2,950 | 1,063 | 1,594 | 531 | 398 |
| 2,925 | 1,060 | 1,590 | 530 | 397 |
| 2,900 | 1,056 | 1,584 | 528 | 396 |
| 2,875 | 1,052 | 1,578 | 526 | 394 |
| 2,850 | 1,048 | 1,572 | 524 | 393 |
| 2,825 | 1,045 | 1,567 | 522 | 391 |
| 2,800 | 1,041 | 1,561 | 520 | 390 |
| 2,775 | 1,037 | 1,555 | 518 | 388 |
| 2,750 | 1,033 | 1,549 | 516 | 387 |
| 2,725 | 1,030 | 1,545 | 515 | 386 |
| 2,700 | 1,026 | 1,539 | 513 | 384 |
| 2,675 | 1,022 | 1,533 | 512 | 384 |
| 2,650 | 1,018 | 1,527 | 509 | 381 |
| 2,625 | 1,015 | 1,522 | 507 | 380 |
| 2,600 | 1,011 | 1,516 | 505 | 378 |
| 2,575 | 1,007 | 1,510 | 503 | 377 |
| 2,550 | 1,003 | 1,504 | 501 | 375 |
| 2,525 | 1,000 | 1,500 | 500 | 375 |
| 2,500 | 996 | 1,494 | 498 | 373 |
| 2,475 | 992 | 1,488 | 496 | 372 |
| 2,450 | 988 | 1,482 | 494 | 370 |
| 2,425 | 985 | 1,477 | 492 | 369 |
| 2,400 | 981 | 1,471 | 490 | 367 |
| 2,375 | 977 | 1,465 | 488 | 366 |
| 2,350 | 973 | 1,459 | 486 | 364 |
| 2,325 | 968 | 1,452 | 484 | 363 |
| 2,300 | 960 | 1,440 | 480 | 360 |
| 2,275 | 952 | 1,428 | 476 | 357 |
| 2,250 | 944 | 1,416 | 472 | 354 |
| 2,225 | 936 | 1,404 | 468 | 351 |
| 2,200 | 928 | 1,392 | 464 | 348 |
| 2,175 | 920 | 1,380 | 460 | 345 |
| 2,150 | 912 | 1,368 | 456 | 342 |
| 2,125 | 904 | 1,356 | 452 | 339 |
| 2,100 | 896 | 1,344 | 448 | 336 |
| 2,075 | 888 | 1,332 | 444 | 333 |
| 2,050 | 880 | 1,320 | 440 | 330 |
| 2,025 | 872 | 1,308 | 436 | 327 |

| Average Indexed Monthly Earnings | Disabled Worker | Disabled Worker Spouse and Children | One Child (No Spouse) | Spouse Age 62 |
|---|---|---|---|---|
| 2,000 | 864 | 1,296 | 432 | 324 |
| 1,975 | 856 | 1,284 | 428 | 321 |
| 1,950 | 848 | 1,272 | 424 | 318 |
| 1,925 | 840 | 1,260 | 420 | 315 |
| 1,900 | 832 | 1,248 | 416 | 312 |
| 1,875 | 824 | 1,236 | 412 | 309 |
| 1,850 | 816 | 1,224 | 408 | 306 |
| 1,825 | 808 | 1,212 | 404 | 303 |
| 1,800 | 800 | 1,200 | 400 | 300 |
| 1,775 | 792 | 1,188 | 396 | 297 |
| 1,750 | 784 | 1,176 | 392 | 294 |
| 1,725 | 776 | 1,164 | 388 | 291 |
| 1,700 | 768 | 1,152 | 384 | 288 |
| 1,675 | 760 | 1,140 | 380 | 285 |
| 1,650 | 752 | 1,128 | 376 | 282 |
| 1,625 | 744 | 1,116 | 372 | 279 |
| 1,600 | 736 | 1,104 | 368 | 276 |
| 1,575 | 728 | 1,092 | 364 | 273 |
| 1,550 | 720 | 1,080 | 360 | 270 |
| 1,525 | 712 | 1,068 | 356 | 267 |
| 1,500 | 704 | 1,056 | 352 | 264 |
| 1,475 | 696 | 1,044 | 348 | 261 |
| 1,450 | 688 | 1,032 | 344 | 258 |
| 1,425 | 680 | 1,020 | 340 | 255 |
| 1,400 | 672 | 1,008 | 336 | 252 |
| 1,375 | 664 | 996 | 332 | 249 |
| 1,350 | 656 | 984 | 328 | 246 |
| 1,325 | 648 | 972 | 324 | 243 |
| 1,300 | 640 | 960 | 320 | 240 |
| 1,275 | 632 | 948 | 316 | 237 |
| 1,250 | 624 | 936 | 312 | 234 |
| 1,225 | 616 | 924 | 308 | 231 |
| 1,200 | 608 | 912 | 304 | 228 |
| 1,175 | 600 | 900 | 300 | 225 |
| 1,150 | 592 | 888 | 296 | 222 |
| 1,125 | 584 | 876 | 292 | 219 |
| 1,100 | 576 | 864 | 288 | 216 |
| 1,075 | 568 | 852 | 284 | 213 |
| 1,050 | 560 | 840 | 280 | 210 |
| 1,025 | 552 | 828 | 276 | 207 |
| 1,000 | 544 | 816 | 272 | 204 |
| 975 | 536 | 804 | 268 | 201 |
| 950 | 528 | 792 | 264 | 198 |
| 925 | 520 | 780 | 260 | 195 |
| 900 | 512 | 768 | 256 | 192 |
| 875 | 504 | 756 | 252 | 189 |
| 850 | 496 | 744 | 248 | 186 |
| 825 | 488 | 732 | 244 | 183 |
| 800 | 480 | 720 | 240 | 180 |
| 775 | 472 | 708 | 236 | 177 |
| 750 | 464 | 696 | 232 | 174 |
| 725 | 456 | 684 | 228 | 171 |
| 700 | 448 | 672 | 224 | 168 |
| 675 | 440 | 660 | 220 | 165 |
| 650 | 432 | 648 | 216 | 162 |

## TABLE 12 — TABLE OF BENEFITS IN EFFECT IN DECEMBER 1979*
### (To be used for *first eligibility or death prior to 1979*)

| Average Monthly Earnings | Primary Insurance Amount | Maximum Family Benefits | Average Monthly Earnings | Primary Insurance Amount | Maximum Family Benefits |
|---|---|---|---|---|---|
| $1471—1475 | $695.40 | $1,216.90 | $1171—1175 ¹ | $627.50 | $1,098.00 |
| 1466—1470 | 694.30 | 1,215.10 | 1166—1170 | 626.20 | 1,095.80 |
| 1461—1465 | 693.30 | 1,213.20 | 1161—1165 | 624.90 | 1,093.40 |
| 1456—1460 | 692.20 | 1,211.40 | 1156—1160 | 623.60 | 1,091.10 |
| 1451—1455 | 691.10 | 1,209.50 | 1151—1155 | 622.20 | 1,088.80 |
| 1446—1450 | 690.10 | 1,207.70 | 1146—1150 | 621.10 | 1,086.70 |
| 1441—1445 | 689.00 | 1,205.70 | 1141—1145 | 619.80 | 1,084.40 |
| 1436—1440 | 687.90 | 1,203.90 | 1136—1140 | 618.40 | 1,082.20 |
| 1431—1435 | 686.90 | 1,202.00 | 1131—1135 | 617.10 | 1,079.70 |
| 1426—1430 | 685.80 | 1,200.20 | 1126—1130 | 615.80 | 1,077.60 |
| 1421—1425 | 684.70 | 1,198.30 | 1121—1125 | 614.60 | 1,075.30 |
| 1416—1420 | 683.70 | 1,196.50 | 1116—1120 | 613.20 | 1,073.10 |
| 1411—1415 | 682.60 | 1,194.60 | 1111—1115 | 612.00 | 1,070.70 |
| 1406—1410 | 681.50 | 1,192.70 | 1106—1110 | 610.60 | 1,068.50 |
| 1401—1405 | 680.50 | 1,190.80 | 1101—1105 | 609.20 | 1,066.10 |
| 1396—1400 | 679.40 | 1,189.00 | 1096—1100 | 608.20 | 1,064.00 |
| 1391—1395 | 678.30 | 1,187.10 | 1091—1095 | 606.80 | 1,061.70 |
| 1386—1390 | 677.30 | 1,185.30 | 1086—1090 | 605.40 | 1,059.40 |
| 1381—1385 | 676.20 | 1,183.40 | 1081—1085 | 604.20 | 1,057.10 |
| 1376—1380 | 675.20 | 1,181.60 | 1076—1080 | 602.80 | 1,054.90 |
| 1371—1375 | 674.10 | 1,179.60 | 1071—1075 | 601.60 | 1,052.60 |
| 1366—1370 | 672.90 | 1,177.70 | 1066—1070 | 600.30 | 1,050.50 |
| 1361—1365 | 671.90 | 1,175.60 | 1061—1065 | 599.00 | 1,048.00 |
| 1356—1360 | 670.70 | 1,173.70 | 1056—1060 | 597.60 | 1,045.90 |
| 1351—1355 | 669.60 | 1,171.70 | 1051—1055 | 596.20 | 1,043.40 |
| 1346—1360 | 668.40 | 1,169.70 | 1046—1050 | 595.20 | 1,041.30 |
| 1341—1345 | 667.40 | 1,167.70 | 1041—1045 | 593.80 | 1,039.10 |
| 1336—1340 | 666.20 | 1,165.80 | 1036—1040 | 592.40 | 1,036.70 |
| 1331—1335 | 665.00 | 1,163.80 | 1031—1035 | 591.20 | 1,034.50 |
| 1326—1330 | 664.00 | 1,161.90 | 1026—1030 | 589.80 | 1,032.20 |
| 1321—1325 | 662.80 | 1,159.80 | 1021—1025 | 588.60 | 1,029.90 |
| 1316—1320 | 661.70 | 1,157.90 | 1016—1020 | 587.40 | 1,027.80 |
| 1311—1315 | 660.60 | 1,155.90 | 1011—1015 | 586.00 | 1,025.30 |
| 1306—1310 | 659.40 | 1,154.00 | 1006—1010 | 584.60 | 1,023.20 |
| 1301—1305 | 658.30 | 1,152.00 | 1001—1005 | 583.50 | 1,020.70 |
| 1296—1300 | 657.20 | 1,150.00 | 996—1000 | 582.20 | 1,018.60 |
| 1291—1295 | 656.10 | 1,148.00 | 991—995 | 580.70 | 1,016.20 |
| 1286—1290 | 654.90 | 1,146.10 | 986—990 | 579.20 | 1,013.60 |
| 1281—1285 | 653.70 | 1,144.10 | 981—985 | 577.90 | 1,011.10 |
| 1276—1280 | 652.70 | 1,142.20 | 976—980 | 576.40 | 1,008.50 |
| 1271—1275 | 651.50 | 1,140.00 | 971—975 | 574.90 | 1,006.20 |
| 1266—1270 | 650.30 | 1,138.00 | 966—970 | 573.40 | 1,003.60 |
| 1261—1265 | 649.20 | 1,135.90 | 961—965 | 572.30 | 1,001.00 |
| 1256—1260 | 647.90 | 1,133.80 | 956—960 | 570.80 | 998.60 |
| 1251—1255 | 646.70 | 1,131.60 | 951—955 | 569.30 | 996.10 |
| 1246—1250 | 645.50 | 1,129.60 | 946—950 | 567.70 | 993.50 |
| 1241—1245 | 644.40 | 1,127.50 | 941—945 | 566.30 | 991.00 |
| 1236—1240 | 643.10 | 1,125.40 | 936—940 | 564.90 | 988.50 |
| 1231—1235 | 641.90 | 1,123.10 | 931—935 | 563.40 | 985.90 |
| 1226—1230 | 640.80 | 1,121.20 | 926—930 | 561.90 | 983.40 |
| 1221—1225 | 639.50 | 1,119.00 | 921—925 | 560.60 | 981.00 |
| 1216—1220 | 638.30 | 1,117.00 | 916—920 | 559.30 | 978.30 |
| 1211—1215 | 637.10 | 1,114.90 | 911—915 | 557.80 | 976.00 |
| 1206—1210 | 636.00 | 1,112.90 | 906—910 | 556.30 | 973.50 |
| 1201—1205 | 634.70 | 1,110.60 | 901—905 | 554.90 | 970.90 |
| 1196—1200 | 633.50 | 1,108.60 | 896—900 | 553.40 | 968.30 |
| 1191—1195 | 632.30 | 1,106.50 | 891—895 | 551.90 | 966.00 |
| 1186—1190 | 531.20 | 1,104.30 | 886—890 | 550.40 | 963.20 |
| 1181—1185 | 629.90 | 1,102.20 | 881—885 | 549.10 | 960.80 |
| 1176—1180 | 628.70 | 1,100.20 | 876—880 | 547.60 | 958.20 |

## TABLE 12 — TABLE OF BENEFITS IN EFFECT IN DECEMBER 1979*
### (Continued)

| Average Monthly Earnings | Primary Insurance Amount | Maximum Family Benefits | Average Monthly Earnings | Primary Insurance Amount | Maximum Family Benefits |
|---|---|---|---|---|---|
| $871—875 | $546.30 | $955.70 | $599—602 | $446.00 | $788.90 |
| 866—870 | 544.80 | 953.20 | 596—598 | 443.80 | 785.60 |
| 861—865 | 543.40 | 950.70 | 592—595 | 441.60 | 783.50 |
| 856—860 | 541.90 | 948.10 | 589—591 | 439.50 | 780.50 |
| 851—855 | 540.50 | 945.70 | 585—588 | 436.90 | 778.20 |
| 846—850 | 538.90 | 943.00 | 582—584 | 435.00 | 775.20 |
| 841—845 | 537.60 | 940.80 | 578—581 | 432.70 | 772.80 |
| 836—840 | 536.10 | 938.10 | 575—577 | 430.70 | 769.90 |
| 831—835 | 534.70 | 935.70 | 571—574 | 428.50 | 767.60 |
| 826—830 | 533.30 | 933.10 | 568—570 | 426.50 | 764.50 |
| 821—825 | 531.90 | 930.60 | 564—567 | 424.10 | 762.30 |
| 816—820 | 530.40 | 928.00 | 561—563 | 421.90 | 759.30 |
| 811—815 | 529.00 | 925.60 | 557—560 | 419.60 | 756.90 |
| 806—810 | 527.50 | 923.00 | 554—556 | 417.60 | 753.90 |
| 801—805 | 526.20 | 920.50 | 549—553 | 415.30 | 751.60 |
| 796—800 | 524.60 | 918.00 | 544—548 | 412.80 | 747.80 |
| 791—795 | 523.10 | 915.40 | 539—543 | 410.20 | 744.10 |
| 786—790 | 521.70 | 912.90 | 535—538 | 407.70 | 740.20 |
| 781—785 | 520.40 | 910.40 | 530—534 | 405.60 | 737.10 |
| 776—780 | 518.90 | 907.90 | 525—529 | 402.70 | 733.40 |
| 771—775 | 517.40 | 905.40 | 521—524 | 400.30 | 729.50 |
| 766—770 | 516.00 | 903.00 | 516—520 | 398.00 | 726.70 |
| 761—765 | 514.70 | 900.40 | 511—515 | 395.30 | 722.80 |
| 756—760 | 513.20 | 897.80 | 507—510 | 392.90 | 719.00 |
| 751—755 | 511.70 | 895.40 | 502—506 | 390.50 | 715.80 |
| 751—755 | 511.70 | 895.40 | 497—501 | 388.20 | 712.10 |
| 746—750 | 510.10 | 892.70 | 493—496 | 385.50 | 708.40 |
| 741—745 | 508.50 | 889.90 | 488—492 | 383.10 | 705.40 |
| 736—740 | 506.90 | 886.70 | 483—487 | 380.70 | 701.60 |
| 731—735 | 505.10 | 883.80 | 479—482 | 378.00 | 697.70 |
| 726—730 | 503.40 | 880.70 | 474—478 | 375.60 | 694.60 |
| 721—725 | 501.70 | 877.60 | 469—473 | 373.50 | 690.80 |
| 716—720 | 500.00 | 874.60 | 465—468 | 370.60 | 687.10 |
| 711—715 | 498.20 | 871.50 | 460—464 | 368.30 | 683.80 |
| 706—710 | 496.40 | 868.60 | 455—459 | 365.90 | 680.10 |
| 701—705 | 494.70 | 865.60 | 451—454 | 363.50 | 676.30 |
| 696—700 | 492.90 | 862.60 | 446—450 | 360.80 | 673.40 |
| 691—695 | 491.20 | 859.60 | 441—445 | 358.40 | 669.70 |
| 686—690 | 489.70 | 856.40 | 437—440 | 356.20 | 665.70 |
| 681—685 | 487.80 | 853.50 | 432—436 | 353.20 | 662.70 |
| 676—680 | 486.10 | 850.50 | 427—431 | 351.10 | 655.10 |
| 671—675 | 484.40 | 847.40 | 422—426 | 348.70 | 647.50 |
| 666—670 | 482.60 | 844.50 | 418—421 | 346.00 | 639.90 |
| 661—665 | 480.90 | 841.50 | 413—417 | 343.50 | 633.80 |
| 657—660 | 479.20 | 838.40 | 408—412 | 341.10 | 626.30 |
| 653—656 | 477.80 | 836.10 | 404—407 | 338.90 | 618.60 |
| 649—652 | 476.50 | 833.70 | 399—403 | 336.00 | 612.70 |
| 645—648 | 474.40 | 830.10 | 394—398 | 333.40 | 605.10 |
| 642—644 | 472.10 | 826.10 | 390—393 | 330.50 | 597.40 |
| 638—641 | 470.10 | 822.40 | 385—389 | 328.00 | 591.30 |
| 635—637 | 467.80 | 818.50 | 380—384 | 325.60 | 583.90 |
| 631—634 | 465.60 | 814.70 | 376—379 | 322.90 | 576.30 |
| 628—630 | 463.40 | 810.70 | 371—375 | 320.20 | 569.90 |
| 624—627 | 461.20 | 807.90 | 366—370 | 317.30 | 562.50 |
| 621—623 | 459.10 | 804.80 | 362—365 | 314.90 | 554.90 |
| 617—620 | 456.80 | 802.50 | 357—361 | 312.40 | 548.80 |
| 613—616 | 454.70 | 799.50 | 352—356 | 309.40 | 541.20 |
| 610—612 | 452.60 | 796.50 | 348—351 | 307.10 | 533.60 |
| 606—609 | 450.30 | 794.00 | 343—347 | 304.20 | 527.50 |
| 603—605 | 448.10 | 791.10 | 338—342 | 301.40 | 519.90 |

### TABLE 12 — TABLE OF BENEFITS IN EFFECT IN DECEMBER 1979*
#### (Continued)

| Average Monthly Earnings | Primary Insurance Amount | Maximum Family Benefits | Average Monthly Earnings | Primary Insurance Amount | Maximum Family Benefits |
|---|---|---|---|---|---|
| $334—337 | $299.30 | $512.50 | $90—90 | $141.40 | $212.10 |
| 329—333 | 296.20 | 506.20 | 88—89 | 138.60 | 207.90 |
| 324—328 | 293.80 | 498.70 | 86—87 | 136.50 | 204.80 |
| 320—323 | 291.00 | 491.10 | 84—85 | 134.00 | 201.00 |
| 315—319 | 288.30 | 485.10 | 82—83 | 131.20 | 196.80 |
| 310—314 | 286.00 | 477.40 | 81—81 | 128.90 | 193.50 |
| 306—309 | 283.10 | 469.80 | 79—80 | 126.60 | 189.90 |
| 301—305 | 280.70 | 463.80 | 77—78 | 123.70 | 185.60 |
| 296—300 | 278.10 | 456.10 | 76—76 | 121.80 | 182 70 |
| 292—295 | 275.10 | 448.50 | 75—75 | 120.20 | 180.30 |
| 287—291 | 272.90 | 442.60 | 74—74 | 118.60 | 177.90 |
| 282—286 | 270.00 | 434 90 | 73—73 | 117.00 | 175.50 |
| 278—281 | 267.40 | 427.20 | 72—72 | 115.40 | 173.10 |
| 273—277 | 264.90 | 421.20 | 71—71 | 113.80 | 170.70 |
| 268—272 | 262.10 | 413.70 | 70—70 | 112.20 | 168.30 |
| 264—267 | 259.60 | 406.00 | 69—69 | 110.60 | 165.90 |
| 259—263 | 256.50 | 400.00 | 68—68 | 109.00 | 163.50 |
| 254—258 | 254.30 | 392.50 | 67—67 | 107.40 | 161.10 |
| 250—253 | 251.80 | 384.90 | 66—66 | 105.80 | 158.70 |
| 245—249 | 248.70 | 378.80 | 65—65 | 104.20 | 156.30 |
| 240—244 | 246.30 | 371.10 | 64—64 | 102.60 | 153.90 |
| 236—239 | 244.00 | 366.10 | 63—63 | 101.00 | 151.50 |
| 231—235 | 241.10 | 361.70 | 62—62 | 99.40 | 149.10 |
| 226—230 | 238.50 | 357.80 | 61—61 | 97.80 | 146.70 |
| 222—225 | 235.60 | 353.40 | 60—60 | 96.20 | 144.30 |
| 217—221 | 233.00 | 349.50 | 59—59 | 94.60 | 141.90 |
| 212—216 | 230.10 | 345.20 | 58—58 | 93.00 | 139.50 |
| 208—211 | 228.00 | 342.00 | 57—57 | 91.40 | 137.10 |
| 203—207 | 225.30 | 338.00 | 56—56 | 89.80 | 134.70 |
| 198—202 | 222.40 | 333.60 | 55—55 | 88.20 | 132.30 |
| 194—197 | 219.90 | 329.90 | 54—54 | 86.60 | 129.90 |
| 189—193 | 217.20 | 326.00 | 53—53 | 85.00 | 127.50 |
| 184—188 | 214.40 | 321.70 | 52—52 | 83.40 | 125.10 |
| 179—183 | 211.90 | 318.00 | 51—51 | 81.80 | 122.70 |
| 175—178 | 209.10 | 313.70 | 50—50 | 80.20 | 120.30 |
| 170—174 | 206.70 | 310.10 | 49—49 | 78.60 | 117.90 |
| 165—169 | 203.90 | 305.90 | 48—48 | 77.00 | 115.50 |
| 161—164 | 201.30 | 302.00 | 47—47 | 75.40 | 113.10 |
| 156—160 | 198.70 | 298 10 | 46—46 | 73.80 | 110.70 |
| 151—155 | 195.90 | 293.90 | 45—45 | 72.20 | 108.30 |
| 147—150 | 193.60 | 290 40 | 44—44 | 70.60 | 105.90 |
| 142—146 | 190.80 | 286 20 | 43—43 | 69.00 | 103.50 |
| 137—141 | 188.00 | 282 10 | 42—42 | 67 40 | 101.10 |
| 133—136 | 185.50 | 278.30 | 41—41 | 65.80 | 98.70 |
| 128—132 | 183.00 | 274.60 | 40—40 | 64 20 | 96.30 |
| 123—127 | 180.40 | 270.60 | 39—39 | 62.60 | 93.90 |
| 119—122 | 177.60 | 266.50 | 38—38 | 60.90 | 91.40 |
| 114—118 | 174.90 | 262.40 | 37—37 | 59.30 | 89.00 |
| 110—113 | 172.50 | 258.80 | 36—36 | 57.70 | 86.60 |
| 108—109 | 169.80 | 254.80 | 35—35 | 56.10 | 84.20 |
| 107—107 | 167.30 | 251.00 | 34—34 | 54.50 | 81.80 |
| 105—106 | 164.60 | 246.90 | 33—33 | 52.90 | 79.40 |
| 103—104 | 161.60 | 242.40 | 32—32 | 51.30 | 77.00 |
| 102—102 | 158.90 | 238.50 | 31—31 | 49.70 | 74.60 |
| 100—101 | 156.70 | 235.10 | 30—30 | 48.10 | 72.20 |
| 98—99 | 153.70 | 230.60 | 29—29 | 46 50 | 69.80 |
| 97—97 | 151.30 | 227.00 | 28—28 | 44 90 | 67 40 |
| 95—96 | 148.50 | 222.80 | 27—27 | 43 30 | 65 00 |
| 93—94 | 146.20 | 219.30 | 26—26 | 41 70 | 62 60 |
| 91—92 | 143.80 | 215.70 | 25—25 | 40.10 | 60 20 |

### TABLE 12 — TABLE OF BENEFITS IN EFFECT IN DECEMBER 1979*
### (Continued)

| Average Monthly Earnings | Primary Insurance Amount | Maximum Family Benefits | Average Monthly Earnings | Primary Insurance Amount | Maximum Family Benefits |
|---|---|---|---|---|---|
| $24—24 | $38.50 | $57.80 | $ 9—9 | $14.50 | $ 21.80 |
| 23—23 | 36.90 | 55.40 | 8—8 | 12.90 | 19.40 |
| 22—22 | 35.30 | 53.00 | 7—7 | 11.30 | 17.00 |
| 21—21 | 33.70 | 50.60 | 6—6 | 9.70 | 14.60 |
| 20—20 | 32.10 | 48.20 | 5—5 | 8.10 | 12.20 |
| 19—19 | 30.50 | 45.80 | 4—4 | 6.50 | 9.80 |
| 18—18 | 28.90 | 43.40 | 3—3 | 4.90 | 7.40 |
| 17—17 | 27.30 | 41.00 | 2—2 | 3.30 | 5.00 |
| 16—16 | 25.70 | 38.60 | 0—1 | 1.70 | 2.60 |
| 15—15 | 24.10 | 36.20 | | | |
| 14—14 | 22.50 | 33.80 | | | |
| 13—13 | 20.90 | 31.40 | | | |
| 12—12 | 19.30 | 29.00 | | | |
| 11—11 | 17 70 | 26.60 | | | |
| 10—10 | 16 10 | 24.20 | | | |

* Figures do not include automatic cost-of-living benefit increases beginning in year of first eligibility. Benefits increased 5.9% in 1977, 6.5% in 1978, 9.9% in 1979, 14.3% in 1980, 11.2% in 1981, 7.4% in 1982, 3.5% in 1984, 3.5% in 1985, 3.1% in 1986, 1.3% in 1987, 4.2% in 1988, 4.0% in 1989, 4.7% in 1990, 5.4% in 1991, and 3.7% in 1992.

# FEDERAL EMPLOYEE TABLES

## TABLE 1—GENERAL PAY SCHEDULE FOR FEDERAL GOVERNMENT WORKERS EFFECTIVE IN JANUARY 1992

| Step | 1 | 2 | 3 | 4 | 5 | 6 | 7 | 8 | 9 | 10 |
|------|------|------|------|------|------|------|------|------|------|------|
| GS-1 | $11,478 | $11,861 | $12,242 | $12,263 | $13,006 | $13,230 | $13,606 | $13,986 | $14,003 | $14,356 |
| 2 | 12,905 | 13,212 | 13,640 | 14,003 | 14,157 | 14,573 | 14,989 | 15,405 | 15,821 | 16,237 |
| 3 | 14,082 | 14,551 | 15,020 | 15,489 | 15,958 | 16,427 | 16,896 | 17,365 | 17,834 | 18,303 |
| 4 | 15,808 | 16,335 | 16,862 | 17,389 | 17,916 | 18,443 | 18,970 | 19,497 | 20,024 | 20,551 |
| 5 | 17,686 | 18,276 | 18,866 | 19,456 | 20,046 | 20,636 | 21,226 | 21,816 | 22,406 | 22,996 |
| 6 | 19,713 | 20,370 | 21,027 | 21,684 | 22,341 | 22,998 | 23,655 | 24,312 | 24,969 | 25,626 |
| 7 | 21,906 | 22,636 | 23,366 | 24,096 | 24,826 | 25,556 | 26,286 | 27,016 | 27,746 | 28,476 |
| 8 | 24,262 | 25,071 | 25,880 | 26,689 | 27,498 | 28,307 | 29,116 | 29,925 | 30,734 | 31,543 |
| 9 | 26,798 | 27,691 | 28,584 | 29,477 | 30,370 | 31,263 | 32,156 | 33,049 | 33,942 | 34,835 |
| 10 | 29,511 | 30,495 | 31,479 | 32,463 | 33,447 | 34,431 | 35,415 | 36,399 | 36,383 | 38,367 |
| 11 | 32,423 | 33,504 | 34,485 | 35,666 | 36,747 | 37,828 | 38,909 | 39,990 | 41,071 | 42,152 |
| 12 | 38,861 | 40,156 | 41,451 | 42,746 | 44,041 | 45,336 | 46,631 | 47,926 | 49,221 | 50,516 |
| 13 | 46,210 | 47,750 | 49,290 | 50,830 | 52,370 | 53,910 | 55,450 | 56,990 | 58,530 | 60,070 |
| 14 | 54,607 | 56,427 | 58,247 | 60,067 | 61,887 | 63,707 | 65,527 | 67,347 | 69,167 | 70,987 |
| 15 | 64,233 | 66,374 | 68,515 | 70,656 | 72,797 | 74,938 | 77,079 | 79,220 | 81,361 | 83,502 |

## TABLE 2—BASIC MONTHLY RETIREMENT ANNUITY FOR CSRS EMPLOYEES

| High-3 Annual Salary | 5 | 10 | 15 | Years of Service 20 | 25 | 30 | 35 | 40 |
|---|---|---|---|---|---|---|---|---|
| $15,000 | $ 94 | $ 203 | $ 328 | $ 453 | $ 578 | $ 703 | $ 828 | $ 953 |
| 16,000 | 100 | 217 | 350 | 483 | 617 | 750 | 883 | 1,017 |
| 17,000 | 106 | 230 | 372 | 514 | 655 | 797 | 939 | 1,080 |
| 18,000 | 113 | 244 | 394 | 544 | 694 | 844 | 994 | 1,144 |
| 19,000 | 119 | 257 | 415 | 574 | 732 | 891 | 1,049 | 1,207 |
| 20,000 | 125 | 270 | 438 | 604 | 771 | 938 | 1,104 | 1,271 |
| 21,000 | 131 | 284 | 459 | 634 | 809 | 984 | 1,159 | 1,334 |
| 22,000 | 138 | 298 | 481 | 665 | 848 | 1,031 | 1,215 | 1,398 |
| 23,000 | 144 | 311 | 503 | 695 | 886 | 1,078 | 1,270 | 1,461 |
| 24,000 | 150 | 325 | 525 | 725 | 925 | 1,125 | 1,325 | 1,525 |
| 25,000 | 156 | 339 | 547 | 755 | 964 | 1,172 | 1,380 | 1,589 |
| 26,000 | 163 | 352 | 574 | 785 | 1,002 | 1,219 | 1,435 | 1,652 |
| 27,000 | 169 | 366 | 591 | 816 | 1,041 | 1,266 | 1,491 | 1,716 |
| 28,000 | 175 | 379 | 613 | 846 | 1,079 | 1,313 | 1,546 | 1,779 |
| 29,000 | 181 | 393 | 634 | 876 | 1,118 | 1,359 | 1,601 | 1,843 |
| 30,000 | 188 | 406 | 656 | 906 | 1,156 | 1,406 | 1,656 | 1,906 |
| 31,000 | 194 | 420 | 678 | 936 | 1,195 | 1,453 | 1,711 | 1,970 |
| 32,000 | 200 | 433 | 700 | 967 | 1,233 | 1,500 | 1,767 | 2,033 |
| 33,000 | 206 | 447 | 722 | 997 | 1,272 | 1,547 | 1,822 | 2,097 |
| 34,000 | 213 | 460 | 744 | 1,027 | 1,310 | 1,594 | 1,877 | 2,160 |
| 35,000 | 219 | 474 | 766 | 1,057 | 1,349 | 1,641 | 1,932 | 2,224 |
| 36,000 | 225 | 488 | 788 | 1,088 | 1,388 | 1,688 | 1,988 | 2,288 |
| 37,000 | 231 | 501 | 809 | 1,118 | 1,426 | 1,734 | 2,043 | 2,351 |
| 38,000 | 238 | 515 | 831 | 1,148 | 1,465 | 1,781 | 2,098 | 2,415 |
| 39,000 | 244 | 528 | 853 | 1,178 | 1,503 | 1,828 | 2,153 | 2,478 |
| 40,000 | 250 | 542 | 875 | 1,208 | 1,542 | 1,875 | 2,208 | 2,542 |
| 41,000 | 256 | 555 | 897 | 1,239 | 1,580 | 1,922 | 2,264 | 2,605 |
| 42,000 | 263 | 569 | 919 | 1,269 | 1,619 | 1,969 | 2,319 | 2,669 |
| 43,000 | 269 | 582 | 941 | 1,299 | 1,657 | 2,016 | 2,374 | 2,732 |
| 44,000 | 275 | 596 | 963 | 1,329 | 1,699 | 2,063 | 2,429 | 2,796 |
| 45,000 | 281 | 609 | 984 | 1,359 | 1,734 | 2,109 | 2,484 | 2,859 |
| 46,000 | 288 | 623 | 1,006 | 1,390 | 1,773 | 2,156 | 2,540 | 2,923 |
| 47,000 | 294 | 636 | 1,028 | 1,420 | 1,811 | 2,203 | 2,595 | 3,986 |
| 48,000 | 300 | 650 | 1,050 | 1,450 | 1,850 | 2,250 | 2,650 | 3,050 |
| 49,000 | 306 | 663 | 1,071 | 1,479 | 1,888 | 2,296 | 2,704 | 3,113 |
| 50,000 | 312 | 676 | 1,092 | 1,509 | 1,926 | 2,342 | 2,759 | 3,163 |
| 51,000 | 318 | 689 | 1,114 | 1,539 | 1,964 | 2,389 | 2,814 | 3,239 |
| 52,000 | 325 | 704 | 1,137 | 1,570 | 2,004 | 2,437 | 2,870 | 3,304 |
| 53,000 | 331 | 717 | 1,158 | 1,600 | 2,042 | 2,483 | 2,925 | 3,367 |
| 54,000 | 337 | 730 | 1,180 | 1,630 | 2,080 | 2,530 | 2,980 | 3,430 |
| 55,000 | 343 | 744 | 1,202 | 1,660 | 2,119 | 2,577 | 3,035 | 3,494 |
| 56,000 | 350 | 758 | 1,224 | 1,691 | 2,158 | 2,624 | 3,091 | 3,558 |
| 57,000 | 356 | 771 | 1,246 | 1,721 | 2,196 | 2,671 | 3,146 | 3,621 |
| 58,000 | 362 | 784 | 1,267 | 1,750 | 2,234 | 2,717 | 3,200 | 3,684 |
| 59,000 | 368 | 798 | 1,289 | 1,781 | 2,273 | 2,764 | 3,256 | 3,748 |
| 60,000 | 375 | 812 | 1,312 | 1,812 | 2,312 | 2,812 | 3,312 | 3,812 |
| 61,000 | 381 | 825 | 1,333 | 1,841 | 2,350 | 2,858 | 3,366 | 3,875 |
| 62,000 | 387 | 839 | 1,355 | 1,872 | 2,389 | 2,905 | 3,422 | 3,939 |
| 63,000 | 393 | 852 | 1,377 | 1,902 | 2,427 | 2,952 | 3,477 | 4,002 |
| 64,000 | 400 | 866 | 1,399 | 1,932 | 2,441 | 2,999 | 3,532 | 4,066 |
| 65,000 | 406 | 880 | 1,422 | 1,964 | 2,505 | 3,047 | 3,589 | 4,130 |
| 66,000 | 413 | 894 | 1,444 | 1,994 | 2,544 | 3,094 | 3,644 | 4,194 |
| 68,000 | 425 | 921 | 1,488 | 2,054 | 2,621 | 3,188 | 3,754 | 4,321 |
| 70,000 | 438 | 948 | 1,531 | 2,115 | 2,698 | 3,281 | 3,865 | 4,448 |
| 72,000 | 450 | 975 | 1,575 | 2,175 | 2,775 | 3,375 | 3,975 | 4,575 |
| 74,000 | 463 | 1,002 | 1,619 | 2,235 | 2,852 | 3,469 | 4,085 | 4,702 |

# TABLE 3—BASIC MONTHLY RETIREMENT ANNUITY
## FOR FERS EMPLOYEES

| High Annual Salary | 5 | 10 | 15 | Years of Service 20 | 25 | 30 | 35 | 40 |
|---|---|---|---|---|---|---|---|---|
| $15,000 | $ 63 | $ 125 | $ 188 | $ 250 | $ 313 | $ 375 | $ 438 | $ 500 |
| 16,000 | 67 | 133 | 200 | 267 | 333 | 400 | 467 | 533 |
| 17,000 | 71 | 142 | 213 | 283 | 354 | 425 | 496 | 567 |
| 18,000 | 75 | 150 | 225 | 300 | 375 | 450 | 525 | 600 |
| 19,000 | 79 | 158 | 238 | 317 | 396 | 475 | 554 | 633 |
| 20,000 | 83 | 167 | 250 | 333 | 417 | 500 | 583 | 667 |
| 22,000 | 92 | 183 | 275 | 367 | 458 | 550 | 642 | 733 |
| 24,000 | 100 | 200 | 300 | 400 | 500 | 600 | 700 | 800 |
| 26,000 | 108 | 217 | 325 | 433 | 542 | 650 | 758 | 867 |
| 28,000 | 117 | 233 | 350 | 467 | 583 | 700 | 817 | 933 |
| 30,000 | 125 | 250 | 375 | 500 | 625 | 750 | 875 | 1,000 |
| 32,000 | 133 | 267 | 400 | 533 | 667 | 800 | 933 | 1,067 |
| 34,000 | 142 | 283 | 425 | 567 | 708 | 850 | 992 | 1,133 |
| 36,000 | 150 | 300 | 450 | 600 | 750 | 900 | 1,050 | 1,200 |
| 38,000 | 158 | 317 | 475 | 633 | 792 | 950 | 1,108 | 1,267 |
| 40,000 | 167 | 333 | 500 | 667 | 833 | 1,000 | 1,167 | 1,333 |
| 42,000 | 175 | 350 | 525 | 700 | 875 | 1,050 | 1,225 | 1,400 |
| 44,000 | 183 | 367 | 550 | 733 | 917 | 1,100 | 1,283 | 1,467 |
| 46,000 | 192 | 383 | 575 | 767 | 958 | 1,150 | 1,342 | 1,533 |
| 48,000 | 200 | 400 | 600 | 800 | 1,000 | 1,200 | 1,400 | 1,600 |
| 50,000 | 208 | 417 | 625 | 833 | 1,042 | 1,250 | 1,458 | 1,667 |
| 53,000 | 221 | 442 | 663 | 883 | 1,104 | 1,325 | 1,546 | 1,767 |
| 55,000 | 229 | 458 | 688 | 917 | 1,146 | 1,375 | 1,604 | 1,833 |
| 57,000 | 238 | 475 | 713 | 950 | 1,188 | 1,425 | 1,663 | 1,900 |
| 60,000 | 250 | 500 | 750 | 1,000 | 1,250 | 1,500 | 1,750 | 2,000 |
| 65,000 | 271 | 542 | 813 | 1,083 | 1,354 | 1,625 | 1,896 | 2,167 |
| 66,000 | 275 | 550 | 825 | 1,100 | 1,375 | 1,650 | 1,925 | 2,200 |
| 68,000 | 283 | 567 | 850 | 1,133 | 1,417 | 1,700 | 1,983 | 2,267 |
| 70,000 | 292 | 583 | 875 | 1,167 | 1,458 | 1,750 | 2,042 | 2,333 |
| 72,000 | 300 | 600 | 900 | 1,200 | 1,500 | 1,800 | 2,100 | 2,400 |
| 74,000 | 308 | 617 | 925 | 1,233 | 1,542 | 1,850 | 2,158 | 2,467 |

# SERVICEMEN AND VETERANS TABLES

# TABLE 1—COMPARATIVE RANKS

## *Comparative Officer Ranks*

| GRADE | ARMY | AIR FORCE | MARINE CORPS | NAVY |
|---|---|---|---|---|

### COMMISSIONED OFFICERS

| GRADE | ARMY | AIR FORCE | MARINE CORPS | NAVY |
|---|---|---|---|---|
| O-10 | General | General | General | Fleet Admiral |
| O-9 | Lieutenant General | Lieutenant General | Lieutenant General | Vice Admiral |
| O-8 | Major General | Major General | Major General | Rear Admiral (Upper Half) |
| O-7 | Brigadier General | Brigadier General | Brigadier General | Rear Admiral (Lower Half) |
| | | | | Commodore |
| O-6 | Colonel | Colonel | Colonel | Captain |
| O-5 | Lieutenant Colonel | Lieutenant Colonel | Lieutenant Colonel | Commander |
| O-4 | Major | Major | Major | Lieutenant Commander |
| O-3 | Captain | Captain | Captain | Lieutenant |
| O-2 | First Lieutenant | First Lieutenant | First Lieutenant | Lieutenant Junior Grade |
| O-1 | Second Lieutenant | Second Lieutenant | Second Lieutenant | Ensign |

### WARRANT OFFICERS

| GRADE | ARMY | AIR FORCE | MARINE CORPS |
|---|---|---|---|
| W-4 | Chief Warrant | Chief Warrant | Com. Warrant over 20 years' service |
| W-3 | Chief Warrant | Chief Warrant | Com. Warrant over 10 years' service |
| W-2 | Chief Warrant | Chief Warrant | Com. Warrant less than 10 years' service |
| W-1 | Warrant Officer, Jr. Grade | Warrant Officer, Jr. Grade | Warrant Officer |

## *Comparative Ranks —— Enlisted Personnel*

| GRADE | ARMY | AIR FORCE | MARINE CORPS | NAVY |
|---|---|---|---|---|
| E-9 | Sergeant Major | Chief Master Sergeant | Sgt. Major & M/Gy. Sgt. | Master Chief Petty Officer |
| E-8 | Master Sergeant | Senior Master Sergeant | 1st Sgt. & Master Sgt. | Senior Chief Petty Officer |
| E-7 | Sergeant First Class | Master Sergeant | Gunnery Sergeant | Chief Petty Officer |
| E-6 | Staff Sergeant | Technical Sergeant | Staff Sergeant | Petty Officer, First Class |
| E-5 | Sergeant | Staff Sergeant | Sergeant | Petty Officer, Second Class |
| E-4 | Corporal | Airman, First Class | Corporal | Petty Officer, Third Class |
| E-3 | Private First Class | Airman, Second Class | Lance Corporal | Seaman |
| E-2 | Private | Airman, Third Class | Private, First Class | Seaman Apprentice |
| E-1 | Private (Recruit) | Airman, Basic | Private | Seaman Recruit |

## TABLE 2—BASIC MONTHLY PAY RATES‡
### (eff. January 1, 1992)
### 2 or Less Years through Over 10 Years

| Pay Grade | 2 or Less | Over 2 | Over 3 | Over 4 | Over 6 | Over 8 | Over 10 |
|---|---|---|---|---|---|---|---|
| **COMMISSIONED OFFICERS** | | | | | | | |
| O-10 | 6,417.60 | 6,643.50 | 6,643.50 | 6,643.50 | 6,643.50 | 6,898.20 | 6,898.20 |
| O-9 | 5,687.70 | 5,836.50 | 5,961.00 | 5,961.00 | 5,961.00 | 6,112.50 | 6,112.50 |
| O-8 | 5,151.60 | 5,306.10 | 5,431.80 | 5,431.80 | 5,431.80 | 5,836.50 | 5,836.50 |
| O-7 | 4,280.40 | 4,571.40 | 4,571.40 | 4,571.40 | 4,776.60 | 4,776.60 | 5,053.50 |
| O-6 | 3,172.80 | 3,485.70 | 3,714.30 | 3,714.30 | 3,714.30 | 3,714.30 | 3,714.30 |
| O-5 | 2,537.40 | 2,979.30 | 3,185.40 | 3,185.40 | 3,185.40 | 3,185.40 | 3,281.70 |
| O-4 | 2,138.70 | 2,604.60 | 2,778.30 | 2,778.30 | 2,829.90 | 2,954.70 | 3,156.30 |
| O-3 | 1,987.50 | 2,222.40 | 2,375.70 | 2,628.60 | 2,754.30 | 2,853.00 | 3,007.50 |
| O-2 | 1,733.10 | 1,892.70 | 2,274.30 | 2,350.50 | 2,399.40 | 2,399.40 | 2,399.40 |
| O-1 | 1,504.80 | 1,566.30 | 1,892.70 | 1,892.70 | 1,892.70 | 1,892.70 | 1,892.70 |
| **COMMISSIONED OFFICERS** (over 4 years' service as enlisted member) | | | | | | | |
| O-3E | | | | 2,628.60 | 2,754.30 | 2,853.00 | 3,007.50 |
| O-2E | | | | 2,350.50 | 2,399.40 | 2,475.60 | 2,604.60 |
| O-1E | | | | 1,892.70 | 2,022.30 | 2,096.70 | 2,172.60 |
| **WARRANT OFFICERS** | | | | | | | |
| W-5 | | | | | | | |
| W-4 | 2,025.00 | 2,172.60 | 2,172.60 | 2,222.40 | 2,323.20 | 2,425.80 | 2,527.50 |
| W-3 | 1,840.50 | 1,996.50 | 1,996.50 | 2,022.30 | 2,045.70 | 2,195.40 | 2,323.20 |
| W-2 | 1,611.90 | 1,743.90 | 1,743.90 | 1,794.90 | 1,892.70 | 1,996.50 | 2,072.10 |
| W-1 | 1,342.80 | 1,539.90 | 1,539.90 | 1,668.30 | 1,743.90 | 1,818.90 | 1,892.70 |
| **ENLISTED PERSONNEL** | | | | | | | |
| E-9 | | | | | | | 2,355.90 |
| E-8 | | | | | | 1,975.50 | 2,031.90 |
| E-7 | 1,379.10 | 1,488.90 | 1,544.10 | 1,598.10 | 1,652.40 | 1,705.20 | 1,759.80 |
| E-6 | 1,186.60 | 1,293.30 | 1,347.30 | 1,404.60 | 1,457.10 | 1,509.60 | 1,565.10 |
| E-5 | 1,041.30 | 1,133.40 | 1,188.60 | 1,240.20 | 1,321.80 | 1,375.50 | 1,430.10 |
| E-4 | 971.10 | 1,025.70 | 1,086.00 | 1,170.00 | 1,216.20 | 1,216.20 | 1,216.20 |
| E-3 | 915.00 | 965.40 | 1,003.80 | 1,043.40 | 1,043.40 | 1,043.40 | 1,043.40 |
| E-2 | 880.50 | 880.50 | 880.50 | 880.50 | 880.50 | 880.50 | 880.50 |
| E-1** | 785.70 | 785.70 | 785.70 | 785.70 | 785.70 | 785.70 | 785.70 |
| E-1*** | 726.60 | — | — | — | — | — | — |

## TABLE 2—BASIC MONTHLY PAY RATES‡ (continued)
### (eff. January 1, 1992)
### Over 12 Years through Over 26 Years

| Pay Grade | Over 12 | Over 14 | Over 16 | Over 18 | Over 20 | Over 22 | Over 26 |
|---|---|---|---|---|---|---|---|
| **COMMISSIONED OFFICERS** | | | | | | | |
| O-10 | 7,280.40 | 7,280.40 | 7,801.20 | 7,801.20 | 8,323.50 | 8,323.50 | 8,733.30 |
| O-9 | 6,366.90 | 6,366.90 | 6,898.20 | 6,898.20 | 7,280.40 | 7,280.40 | 7,801.20 |
| O-8 | 6,112.50 | 6,112.50 | 6,366.90 | 6,643.50 | 6,898.20 | 7,068.30 | 7,068.30 |
| O-7 | 5,053.50 | 5,306.10 | 5,836.50 | 6,238.20 | 6,238.20 | 6,238.20 | 6,238.20 |
| O-6 | 3,714.30 | 3,840.30 | 4,447.50 | 4,674.60 | 4,776.60 | 5,053.50 | 5,480.70 |
| O-5 | 3,458.40 | 3,690.30 | 3,966.60 | 4,193.70 | 4,320.90 | 4,471.80 | 4,471.80 |
| O-4 | 3,333.60 | 3,485.70 | 3,638.70 | 3,739.20 | 3,739.20 | 3,739.20 | 3,739.20 |
| O-3 | 3,156.30 | 3,233.70 | 3,223.70 | 3,233.70 | 3,233.70 | 3,233.70 | 3,233.70 |
| O-2 | 2,399.40 | 2,399.40 | 2,399.40 | 2,399.40 | 2,399.40 | 2,399.40 | 2,399.40 |
| O-1 | 1,892.70 | 1,892.70 | 1,892.70 | 1,892.70 | 1,892.70 | 1,892.70 | 1,892.70 |
| **COMMISSIONED OFFICERS** (over 4 years' service as enlisted member) | | | | | | | |
| O-3E | 3,156.30 | 3,281.70 | 3,281.70 | 3,281.70 | 3,281.70 | 3,281.70 | 3,281.70 |
| O-2E | 2,704.60 | 2,778.30 | 2,778.30 | 2,778.30 | 2,778.30 | 2,778.30 | 2,778.30 |
| O-1E | 2,248.20 | 2,350.50 | 2,350.50 | 2,350.50 | 2,350.50 | 2,350.50 | 2,350.50 |
| **WARRANT OFFICERS** | | | | | | | |
| W-5 | | | | | 3,455.90 | 3,587.10 | 3,846.30 |
| W-4 | 2,704.20 | 2,829.90 | 2,929.20 | 3,007.50 | 3,104.70 | 3,208.50 | 3,458.40 |
| W-3 | 2,399.40 | 2,475.60 | 2,549.40 | 2,628.60 | 2,730.90 | 2,829.90 | 2,929.20 |
| W-2 | 2,148.30 | 2,222.40 | 2,300.40 | 2,375.70 | 2,450.70 | 2,549.40 | 2,549.40 |
| W-1 | 1,971.00 | 2,045.70 | 2,121.90 | 2,195.40 | 2,274.30 | 2,274.30 | 2,274.30 |
| **ENLISTED PERSONNEL** | | | | | | | |
| E-9 | 2,408.70 | 2,463.30 | 2,519.70 | 2,576.10 | 2,626.20 | 2,763.90 | 3,032.70 |
| E-8 | 2,085.60 | 2,139.60 | 2,196.30 | 2,246.70 | 2,301.90 | 2,436.90 | 2,708.40 |
| E-7 | 1,814.70 | 1,896.90 | 1,950.60 | 2,004.90 | 2,031.00 | 2,167.20 | 2,436.90 |
| E-6 | 1,645.80 | 1,697.40 | 1,752.30 | 1,779.00 | 1,779.00 | 1,779.00 | 1,779.00 |
| E-5 | 1,482.60 | 1,509.60 | 1,509.60 | 1,509.60 | 1,509.60 | 1,509.60 | 1,509.60 |
| E-4 | 1,216.20 | 1,216.20 | 1,216.20 | 1,216.20 | 1,216.20 | 1,216.20 | 1,216.20 |
| E-3 | 1,043.40 | 1,043.40 | 1,043.40 | 1,043.40 | 1,043.40 | 1,043.40 | 1,043.40 |
| E-2 | 880.50 | 880.50 | 880.50 | 880.50 | 880.50 | 880.50 | 880.50 |
| E-1** | 785.70 | 785.70 | 785.70 | 785.70 | 785.70 | 785.70 | 785.70 |
| E-1*** | — | — | — | — | — | — | — |

See Table 1 for rank corresponding with pay rate. Rates are rounded to nearest dollar.
*    Basic pay is limited to $8,733.30 by level V of the Executive Schedule.
**   Applies to personnel who have served 4 months or more on active duty.
*** Applies to personnel who have served less than 4 months on active duty.

# TABLE 3—CSRS MILITARY MONTHLY RETIREMENT PAY*
## Effective January 1, 1992

## RETIREES WHO ENTERED SERVICE BEFORE
## SEPTEMBER 8, 1980

| Pay Grade** Over: | 50.00% 20 Yrs | 52.50% 21 Yrs | 55.00% 22 Yrs | 57.50% 23 Yrs | 60.00% 24 Yrs | 62.50% 25 Yrs | 65.00% 26 Yrs | 67.50% 27 Yrs | 70.00% 28 Yrs | 72.50% 29 Yrs | 75.00% 30 Yrs |
|---|---|---|---|---|---|---|---|---|---|---|---|
| O-10 | 4,161.00 | 4,369.00 | 4,577.00 | 4,786.00 | 4,994.00 | 5,202.00 | 5,676.00 | 5,894.00 | 6,113.00 | 6,331.00 | 6,549.00 |
| O-9 | 3,640.00 | 3,822.00 | 4,004.00 | 4,186.00 | 4,368.00 | 4,550.00 | 5,070.00 | 5,265.00 | 5,460.00 | 5,655.00 | 5,850.00 |
| O-8 | 3,449.00 | 3,621.00 | 3,887.00 | 4,064.00 | 4,240.00 | 4,417.00 | 4,594.00 | 4,771.00 | 4,947.00 | 5,124.00 | 5,301.00 |
| O-7 | 3,119.00 | 3,275.00 | 3,275.00 | 3,586.00 | 3,742.00 | 3,898.00 | 4,054.00 | 4,210.00 | 4,366.00 | 4,522.00 | 4,678.00 |
| O-6 | 2,388.00 | 2,507.00 | 2,779.00 | 2,905.00 | 3,032.00 | 3,158.00 | 3,562.00 | 3,699.00 | 3,836.00 | 3,973.00 | 4,110.00 |
| O-5 | 2,160.00 | 2,268.00 | 2,459.00 | 2,571.00 | 2,683.00 | 2,794.00 | 2,906.00 | 3,018.00 | 3,130.00 | 3,242.00 | 3,353.00 |
| O-4 | 1,869.00 | 1,963.00 | 2,056.00 | 2,150.00 | 2,243.00 | 2,337.00 | 2,430.00 | 2,523.00 | 2,617.00 | 2,710.00 | 2,804.00 |
| O-3 | 1,616.00 | 1,697.00 | 1,778.00 | 1,859.00 | 1,940.00 | 2,021.00 | 2,101.00 | 2,182.00 | 2,263.00 | 2,344.00 | 2,425.00 |
| O-2 | 1,199.00 | 1,259.00 | 1,319.00 | 1,379.00 | 1,439.00 | 1,499.00 | 1,559.00 | 1,619.00 | 1,679.00 | 1,739.00 | 1,799.00 |
| O-1 | 946.00 | 993.00 | 1,040.00 | 1,088.00 | 1,135.00 | 1,182.00 | 1,230.00 | 1,277.00 | 1,324.00 | 1,372.00 | 1,419.00 |
| W-4 | 1,552.00 | 1,629.00 | 1,764.00 | 1,844.00 | 1,925.00 | 2,005.00 | 2,247.00 | 2,334.00 | 2,420.00 | 2,507.00 | 2,593.00 |
| W-3 | 1,365.00 | 1,433.00 | 1,556.00 | 1,627.00 | 1,697.00 | 1,768.00 | 1,903.00 | 1,977.00 | 2,050.00 | 2,123.00 | 2,196.00 |
| W-2 | 1,225.00 | 1,286.00 | 1,402.00 | 1,465.00 | 1,529.00 | 1,593.00 | 1,657.00 | 1,720.00 | 1,784.00 | 1,848.00 | 1,912.00 |
| W-1 | 1,137.00 | 1,194.00 | 1,250.00 | 1,307.00 | 1,364.00 | 1,421.00 | 1,478.00 | 1,535.00 | 1,592.00 | 1,648.00 | 1,705.00 |
| E-9 | 1,313.00 | 1,378.00 | 1,520.00 | 1,589.00 | 1,658.00 | 1,727.00 | 1,971.00 | 2,047.00 | 2,122.00 | 2,198.00 | 2,274.00 |
| E-8 | 1,150.00 | 1,208.00 | 1,340.00 | 1,401.00 | 1,462.00 | 1,523.00 | 1,760.00 | 1,828.00 | 1,895.00 | 1,963.00 | 2.031.00 |
| E-7 | 1,015.00 | 1,066.00 | 1,191.00 | 1,246.00 | 1,300.00 | 1,354.00 | 1,583.00 | 1,644.00 | 1,705.00 | 1,766.00 | 1,827.00 |
| E-6 | 889.00 | 933.00 | 978.00 | 1,022.00 | 1,067.00 | 1,111.00 | 1,156.00 | 1,200.00 | 1,245.00 | 1,289.00 | 1,334.00 |
| E-5 | 754.00 | 792.00 | 830.00 | 868.00 | 905.00 | 943.00 | 981.00 | 1,018.00 | 1,056.00 | 1,094.00 | 1,132.00 |

*Does not apply to reservists; rounded out to nearest dollar. Participation in the Survivor Benefit Plan reduces these amounts.
**See Table 1 for rank corresponding with pay grade.

## TABLE 4 — RATES OF DEPENDENCY AND INDEMNITY COMPENSATION—SURVIVING SPOUSE AND CHILDREN

### 38 USC §411
### Effective December 1, 1991

| Pay Grade* | Surviving Spouse** Only | Surviving Spouse** and 1 Child | Surviving Spouse** and 2 Children | Extra Per Child |
|---|---|---|---|---|
| **COMMISSIONED OFFICERS** | | | | |
| O-10 | 1,580.00*** | 1,651.00 | 1,722.00 | 71.00 |
| O-9 | 1,440.00 | 1,511.00 | 1,582.00 | 71.00 |
| O-8 | 1,343.00 | 1,414.00 | 1,485.00 | 71.00 |
| O-7 | 1,225.00 | 1,296.00 | 1,367.00 | 71.00 |
| O-6 | 1,134.00 | 1,205.00 | 1,276.00 | 71.00 |
| O-5 | 1,005.00 | 1,076.00 | 1,147.00 | 71.00 |
| O-4 | 912.00 | 983.00 | 1,054.00 | 71.00 |
| O-3 | 862.00 | 933.00 | 1,004.00 | 71.00 |
| O-2 | 805.00 | 876.00 | 947.00 | 71.00 |
| O-1 | 780.00 | 851.00 | 922.00 | 71.00 |
| **WARRANT OFFICERS** | | | | |
| W-4 | 884.00 | 955.00 | 1,026.00 | 71.00 |
| W-3 | 835.00 | 906.00 | 977.00 | 71.00 |
| W-2 | 811.00 | 882.00 | 953.00 | 71.00 |
| W-1 | 780.00 | 851.00 | 922.00 | 71.00 |
| **ENLISTED PERSONNEL** | | | | |
| E-9 | 841.00**** | 912.00 | 983.00 | 71.00 |
| E-8 | 805.00 | 876.00 | 947.00 | 71.00 |
| E-7 | 762.00 | 833.00 | 904.00 | 71.00 |
| E-6 | 727.00 | 798.00 | 869.00 | 71.00 |
| E-5 | 711.00 | 782.00 | 853.00 | 71.00 |
| E-4 | 693.00 | 764.00 | 835.00 | 71.00 |
| E-3 | 652.00 | 723.00 | 794.00 | 71.00 |
| E-2 | 635.00 | 717.00 | 788.00 | 71.00 |
| E-1 | 616.00 | 687.00 | 758.00 | 71.00 |

* See Table 1, for rank corresponding to pay grade.
** Monthly rate for the surviving spouse is increased by $185 if he or she is a patient in a nursing home or is virtually helpless or blind.
*** If the veteran served as Chairman or Vice-Chairman of the Joint Chiefs of Staff or Chief of Staff to one of the services, the surviving spouse's rate shall be $1,893.
**** The payment to a surviving spouse alone if the veteran was Sergeant Major of the Army, senior enlisted advisor of the Navy, Chief Master Sergeant of the Air Force, or Sergeant Major of the Marine Corps, or Master Chief Petty Officer of the Coast Guard is $907.

## TABLE 5 — RATES OF DEPENDENCY AND INDEMNITY
## COMPENSATION — PARENTS
### Effective December 1, 1991

| Annual Income Amount | 1 Parent Only (1) | Each of 2 Parents Not Living Together (1) | Each of 2 Parents Living Together or Remarried Parent Living with Spouse (2) |
|---|---|---|---|
| $ 800 | $349 | $250 | $235 |
| 900 | 341 | 244 | 235 |
| 1000 | 333 | 237 | 235 |
| 1100 | 325 | 230 | 232 |
| 1200 | 317 | 222 | 229 |
| 1300 | 309 | 214 | 226 |
| 1400 | 301 | 206 | 223 |
| 1500 | 293 | 198 | 220 |
| 1600 | 285 | 190 | 216 |
| 1700 | 277 | 182 | 212 |
| 1800 | 269 | 174 | 208 |
| 1900 | 261 | 166 | 204 |
| 2000 | 253 | 158 | 199 |
| 2100 | 245 | 150 | 194 |
| 2200 | 237 | 142 | 189 |
| 2300 | 229 | 134 | 184 |
| 2400 | 221 | 126 | 179 |
| 2500 | 213 | 118 | 173 |
| 2600 | 205 | 110 | 167 |
| 2700 | 197 | 102 | 161 |
| 2800 | 189 | 94 | 155 |
| 2900 | 181 | 86 | 149 |
| 3000 | 173 | 78 | 142 |
| 3100 | 165 | 70 | 135 |
| 3200 | 157 | 62 | 128 |
| 3300 | 149 | 54 | 120 |
| 3400 | 141 | 46 | 112 |
| 3500 | 133 | 38 | 104 |
| 3600 | 125 | 30 | 96 |
| 3700 | 117 | 22 | 88 |
| 3800 | 109 | 14 | 80 |
| 3900 | 101 | 6 | 72 |
| 4000 | 93 | 5 | 64 |
| 4100 | 85 | 5 | 56 |
| 4200 | 77 | 5 | 48 |
| 4300 | 69 | 5 | 40 |
| 4400 | 61 | 5 | 32 |
| 4500 | 53 | 5 | 24 |
| 4600 | 45 | 5 | 16 |
| 4700 | 37 | 5 | 8 |
| 4800 | 29 | 5 | 5 |
| 4900 | 21 | 5 | 5 |
| 5000 | 13 | 5 | 5 |
| 5100-8414 | 5 | 5 | 5 |
| 8414-11,313 | 0 | 0 | 5 |
| over 11,313 | 0 | 0 | 0 |

(1) Payment based on total annual income.
(2) Payment based on total combined annual income.

## Beat Inflation.  Lock in price savings through automatic renewal.

Starting with the 1993 edition, have the *Social Security Manual* automatically sent to you each year and get billed at the previous year's price.  Simply fill out the first order form below.

If you need extra copies for other people in your office, or if you would like to distribute copies of the *1992 Social Security Manual* to your key clients and/or prospects, use the bottom order card below.  You can also order from our complete line of Social Security and Medicare publications by calling our  800 number listed below.

| | | |
|---|---|---|
| Single copy......$12.50 | 50 copies, ea.... $8.50 | To order by phone, call TOLL FREE |
| 5 copies, ea........11.00 | 100 copies, ea......8.00 | **1-800-543-0874** |
| 10 copies, ea......10.25 | 250 copies, ea......7.50 | and ask for Operator 4Y |
| 25 copies, ea........9.25 | 500 copies, ea......6.75 | or, FAX order card 513-721-0874 |

*Shipping, handling and sales tax are extra.  Prices effective through 12/31/92*

---

AUTOMATIC RENEWAL

2-4Y

The National Underwriter Co.
Customer Service Department 2-4Y
505 Gest Street
Cincinnati, OH 45203-1716

Please enter my automatic standing offer for the new edition of the *Social Security Manual* each year at the previous year's price.  I understand I will receive notice each year prior to publication, asking for verification of my order, the quantity and correct mailing address. (YOU MAY CANCEL THIS ORDER AT TIME OF VERIFICATION IF SO DESIRED).

_____Copies of *1993 Social Security Manual* (#286)

| | |
|---|---|
| *Name* | *Title* |
| *Company* | |
| *Street Address* | |
| *City* | *State*  *Zip* |
| (          ) | |
| *Business Phone* | |

---

**NATIONAL UNDERWRITER**

FOR ADDITIONAL COPIES

2-4Y

The National Underwriter Co.
Customer Service Department 2-4Y
505 Gest Street
Cincinnati, OH 45203-1716

Please send me: (indicate quantities)

_____Copies of *1992 Social Security Manual* (#286)

| | |
|---|---|
| *Name* | *Title* |
| *Company* | |
| *Street Address* | |
| *City* | *State*  *Zip* |
| (          ) | |
| *Business Phone* | |

# BUSINESS REPLY MAIL
FIRST CLASS MAIL          PERMIT NO. 68          CINCINNATI, OH

POSTAGE WILL BE PAID BY ADDRESSEE

THE   NATIONAL   UNDERWRITER   CO
DEPARTMENT   2-4Y
505   GEST   ST
CINCINNATI   OH   45203-9928

NO POSTAGE
NECESSARY
IF MAILED
IN THE
UNITED STATES

# BUSINESS REPLY MAIL
FIRST CLASS MAIL          PERMIT NO. 68          CINCINNATI, OH

POSTAGE WILL BE PAID BY ADDRESSEE

THE   NATIONAL   UNDERWRITER   CO
DEPARTMENT   2-4Y
505   GEST   ST
CINCINNATI   OH   45203-9928